I Can See Clearly Now

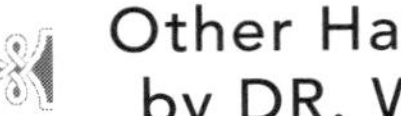 Other Hay House Products by DR. WAYNE W. DYER 

BOOKS

Being in Balance
Change Your Thoughts—Change Your Life
Everyday Wisdom
Everyday Wisdom for Success
Excuses Begone!
Getting in the Gap (book-with-CD)
Good-bye, Bumps! (children's book with Saje Dyer)
I Am (children's book with Kristina Tracy)
Incredible You! (children's book with Kristina Tracy)
Inspiration
The Invisible Force
It's Not What You've Got! (children's book with Kristina Tracy)
Living the Wisdom of the Tao
My Greatest Teacher (with Lynn Lauber)
No Excuses! (children's book with Kristina Tracy)
The Power of Intention
The Power of Intention gift edition
A Promise Is a Promise
The Shift
Staying on the Path
10 Secrets for Success and Inner Peace
Unstoppable Me! (children's book with Kristina Tracy)
Your Ultimate Calling
Wishes Fulfilled

AUDIO/CD PROGRAMS

Advancing Your Spirit (with Marianne Williamson)
Applying the 10 Secrets for Success and Inner Peace
The Caroline Myss & Wayne Dyer Seminar
Change Your Thoughts—Change Your Life (unabridged audio book)
Change Your Thoughts Meditation
Divine Love
Dr. Wayne W. Dyer Unplugged (interviews with Lisa Garr)
Everyday Wisdom (audio book)
Excuses Begone! (available as an audio book and a lecture)
How to Get What You Really, Really, Really, Really Want
I AM Wishes Fulfilled Meditation (with James Twyman)
I Can See Clearly Now (unabridged audio book)
The Importance of Being Extraordinary (with Eckhart Tolle)
Inspiration (abridged 4-CD set)
Inspirational Thoughts

Making the Shift (6-CD set)
Making Your Thoughts Work for You (with Byron Katie)
Meditations for Manifesting
101 Ways to Transform Your Life (audio book)
The Power of Intention (abridged 4-CD set)
A Promise Is a Promise (audio book)
Secrets of Manifesting
The Secrets of the Power of Intention (6-CD set)
10 Secrets for Success and Inner Peace
There Is a Spiritual Solution to Every Problem
The Wayne Dyer Audio Collection/CD Collection
Wishes Fulfilled (unabridged audio book)

DVDs

Change Your Thoughts—Change Your Life
Excuses Begone!
Experiencing the Miraculous
I Can See Clearly Now
The Importance of Being Extraordinary (with Eckhart Tolle)
Inspiration
Modern Wisdom from the Ancient World
My Greatest Teacher (a film with bonus material featuring Wayne)
The Power of Intention
The Shift, the movie (available as a 1-DVD program and an expanded 2-DVD set)
10 Secrets for Success and Inner Peace
There's a Spiritual Solution to Every Problem
Wishes Fulfilled

MISCELLANEOUS

Change Your Thoughts—Change Your Life Perpetual Flip Calendar
Everyday Wisdom Perpetual Flip Calendar
Inner Peace Cards
Inspiration Perpetual Flip Calendar
The Power of Intention Cards
The Power of Intention Perpetual Flip Calendar
The Shift Box Set (includes *The Shift* DVD and *The Shift* tradepaper book)
10 Secrets for Success and Inner Peace Cards
10 Secrets for Success and Inner Peace gift products: *Notecards, Candle*, and *Journal*

All of the above are available at your local bookstore, or may be ordered by visiting: Hay House USA: www.hayhouse.com; Hay House Australia: www.hayhouse.com.au; Hay House UK: www.hayhouse.co.uk; Hay House South Africa: www.hayhouse.co.za; Hay House India: www.hayhouse.co.in

I Can See Clearly Now

DR. WAYNE W. DYER

HAY HOUSE, INC.
Carlsbad, California • New York City
London • Sydney • Johannesburg
Vancouver • Hong Kong • New Delhi

Published and distributed in the United States by: Hay House, Inc.: www.hayhouse.com® • ***Published and distributed in Australia by:*** Hay House Australia Pty. Ltd.: www.hayhouse.com.au • ***Published and distributed in the United Kingdom by:*** Hay House UK, Ltd.: www.hayhouse.co.uk • ***Published and distributed in the Republic of South Africa by:*** Hay House SA (Pty), Ltd.: www.hayhouse.co.za • ***Distributed in Canada by:*** Raincoast Books: www.raincoast.com • ***Published in India by:*** Hay House Publishers India: www.hayhouse.co.in

Wayne Dyer's editor: Joanna Pyle
Cover design: Julie Davison • *Interior design:* Tricia Breidenthal

Quotes from Elisabeth Kübler-Ross have been reprinted by permission of the EKR Family Limited Partnership.

Library of Congress Cataloging-in-Publication Data

Dyer, Wayne W.
I can see clearly now / Dr. Wayne W. Dyer. -- 1st edition.
pages cm
ISBN 978-1-4019-4403-2 (hardback)
1. Dyer, Wayne W. 2. Motivational speakers--United States--Biography. 3. Counselors--United States--Biography. 4. Motivation (Psychology) I. Title.
BF503.D94 2014
158.3092--dc23
[B]

2013022893

Hardcover ISBN: 978-1-4019-4403-2

17 16 15 14 4 3 2 1
1st edition, February 2014

Printed in the United States of America

For all the way-showers that
I have written about here—
The diamonds and the stones—
With awe and profound gratitude.

And to my eight children—all diamonds,
Tracy, Shane, Stephanie, Skye, Sommer,
Serena, Sands, and Saje—
You are the lights of my life.

"If we stop for a moment, it is possible to perceive a pattern in our lives; the motivators that have influenced us become more obvious. We are able to see life unfolding <u>from both ends at once</u>, coming into the present moment. But until we have got to a certain point of realization, this is not possible, because everything is still seen as a series of apparent causes and effects."

— RESHAD FEILD

1

It's Christmastime 1941, a few weeks after the bombing of Pearl Harbor. America has been drawn into war; two of my mother's brothers are serving in the military, one in Europe and the other in the Pacific. My father is no longer in the picture. His persistent carousing with other women, excessive drinking, and regular encounters as a lawbreaker, which have landed him in jail on several occasions, have finally made living with him impossible for my mother. He has simply walked away from his fatherly responsibilities, never to be heard from again. My mother is alone with three children under the age of five to feed. She's taking her three boys to her mother's house to be watched while she goes to work for the day.

My two older brothers and I are waiting with our mother for the bus to arrive on Jefferson Avenue on the east side of Detroit. We're dressed in our snowsuits, mittens, galoshes, and earmuffs, standing at the bus stop next to what appears to us to be a huge mountain of freshly plowed snow. The road is littered with salt to melt the continually falling snow, and it is one big nasty mess. A truck drives past the four of us, spraying us so hard with slush that we're knocked off of our feet. We land safely but soaked on the gigantic pile of snow.

My mother breaks down—she's dressed for work and covered with dirty, salty slush. She is exasperated. Her life is obviously out of control with the departure of her former husband, and she's doing her best to make ends meet. The lingering Depression, along with a world war, contributes to her overall situation. Work is difficult to come by, and my mother must rely upon the meager help that comes from her family. They too are overburdened by the long-term economic downturn. It is a difficult period under the best of circumstances, due to shortages of all manner of goods, and the fog of war itself.

My two brothers are very upset, too. Five-year-old Jim attempts to console our mother; three-year-old David is crying uncontrollably. Me? I am having the time of my life. This is like a nice surprise party with a big castle of snow that we're all lying on top of. We can have fun! I don't quite understand why everyone is so angry and frustrated.

And then these words came out of my mouth: "It's okay, Mommy. Don't cry. We can all just stay here and play in the snow."

I'm the baby who seldom cries; the toddler who tries to make everyone laugh and feel good, regardless of what's going on. I'm the kid who makes silly faces to change the environment from sad to glad. I am that little boy who'd be sure *There must be a pony here somewhere* if the sandbox was full of manure. I don't know how to be filled with sadness. My demeanor seems to be naturally inclined to look for the bright side and pay little heed to things that make everyone else dreary.

According to my mother, I'm the most independent and inquisitive little boy she and her family have ever encountered. Apparently I arrived with this happy disposition intact. I am so happy to be here in this world. At 19 months of age I am almost the same size as Dave, who is 18 months older. I try to get my brother to laugh and feel safe, because he seems to be afraid, sick, and most of the time, sad, but he seldom even smiles. I find the world so exciting, and I love wandering and exploring.

As I grow up, nothing seems to disturb or distress me. I look around and all I see brings me to a state of awe and wonder. I want everyone to be happy. I want all of the despair in my family to just disappear. I am sure we don't *have* to be miserable just because our father is such a shit. I want to see my mother have joy in her soul rather than all of this distress. I want my oldest brother, Jim, to stop worrying so much about Mother and his two younger brothers. If I can make them happy and have some fun, maybe all of this other stuff will just go away.

I just can't comprehend why everyone seems so dour. There are so many things to be excited about. I can play for hours with a spoon or an empty cardboard box. I love to go outside and gaze at the flowers, the butterflies, or the stray cat that keeps coming to our yard. I am in a kind of blissful state of appreciation and bewilderment almost all of the time. I also have a very strong mind of my own. I won't let anyone tell me what I can or cannot do—I insist upon discovering my boundaries on my own. When I am told *no,* I simply smile and then proceed to do what my inner self instructs me to do—regardless of what any big people might say about it.

I seem to be totally in a world of my own—one that's joyful, full of exciting, unlimited potentialities and discoveries that I can make on my own. No matter how hard anyone tries to make me be gloomy, they can never succeed because I came here from a Divine light, and there is nothing anyone can do to put out that light. This is who I am —a piece of God who hasn't forgotten that God is love. As am I.

I Can See Clearly Now

I can't count the number of times that my mother told me that sloshy snow-pile story. It was her favorite recollection of me just before she was forced to place David and me in a series of foster homes and orphanages; while my oldest brother, Jim, went to live with our grandmother for the better part of the next decade.

As I look back at the earliest days of my life in this incarnation, I can see clearly that the old maxim *There are no accidents in this universe* is a truism that applies right from the moment of our creation, and way before that as well. In an infinite universe there's truly no beginning or ending. It is only our form that is born and dies—that which occupies our form is changeless and therefore birthless and deathless.

As the father of eight children, I'm quite convinced that each individual arrives here with their own unique personality. We are intended here from an invisible field of infinite potentiality. That which has no form, has no boundaries—it's the *I* that's in the ever-changing body. All of the accomplishments that fill my personal résumé began taking shape at the moment of my conception, throughout my nine months of embryonic existence, and as I took my first birth breath on arrival. I look back at that little 19-month-old tyke lying on a snowbank, and not one cell that comprised that little boy is still here on planet Earth. Yet the *I* that was in that body is the same infinite *I* that recalls it all some 70 years later.

Even before I could read or write I needed a personality that would be congruous with the *music* I came here to play. I can see clearly now that as a child I needed to feel that I could reach out to others and help them feel better about themselves and their circumstances. I somehow knew that *attitude is everything* in life—even as a baby, so that the attitude my mother described to me that characterized my infancy was in some mysterious way connected to the dharma that I was to fulfill throughout this lifetime.

Lying on top of that snowbank with the rest of my family, seeing them in a deep state of distress, and instantly deciding to try to make things a bit more bearable by making them laugh or inviting them to have fun instead of being sad, is—on a spiritual level—the same as writing books about breaking free of the trap of negative thinking and enjoying life to the fullest. The form is adult with a bigger and older body, but the same infinite *I* is communicating through a brand-new set of eyes and ears.

I've watched all eight of my children blossom into their own awakenings. They all showed up here at birth with their own unique personalities, perhaps from a series of previous lives—the mysterious possibilities are endless. But I know for certain that the one Divine mind that is responsible for all of creation has a hand in this engaging mystery. Same parents, same environment, same culture, and yet eight unique individuals, all of whom arrived with their own distinct character traits. I think Khalil Gibran stated it perfectly in *The Prophet:* "Your children are not your children. They are the sons and daughters of Life's longing for itself. They come through you but not from you, and though they are with you yet they belong not to you."

We all have a mission of some kind to fulfill at the moment we make the shift from *nowhere* to *now here,* from Spirit to form. I've long realized how important it is to allow my own children to live out their inner dictates, realizing that that's precisely what I've done for my entire life, based on the stories that my mother told me of my life as a baby and then as a toddler. She was never surprised that my life unfolded as it did, because of what she observed in my infancy. Each of my children had their blueprint from God as well. My job has been to guide, then step aside, and let whatever is inside them that is their own uniqueness, steer the course of their lives.

I know that I came here to fulfill a purpose that I decided upon before undertaking that journey from invisible to solid—from Spirit to hardening into a physical reality. Beginning with the three unhappy people with me in that slushy predicament, I was actually doing the early research and practice for living a life in which I could help influence millions of people. While I was in that snowbank, I was intuitively trying to get everyone to see that we had a choice about how we looked at the situation. The *I* inside the kid wanted the others to know it's not really so bad—*we can turn this whole thing around by laughing rather than being upset.*

The greatest service that can be offered to children who show personality traits or inclinations that might not be understood by the adults around them is to allow them to express their own unique humanity. I was blessed to be able to live much of the first decade of my life in an environment where parental and other adult meddling in my life was kept to a minimum. I know that I came into the world with what I call "big dharma"—with a blueprint to teach self-reliance and a positive loving approach to large numbers of people all over the globe. I am ever so grateful for the circumstances of my life that allowed me to be pretty much left alone and to develop as I was so intended in this incarnation.

Just as everything we need for our physical development is handled by a Divine, mysterious, invisible force while we develop for nine months in utero, so too is all that we need handled by the same Source for all other aspects of our being. We come from a state of perfect well-being—Divine love—and our creator needs no assistance in taking care of this unfoldment. It is only when we interfere with this celestial programming that we get off the path of God-realization.

I can see clearly today this entire universe is on purpose. I see now that our earliest personality traits and predilections are expressed because they represent our highest selves. At these early ages we are still very much connected to our Source, because we haven't yet had the chance to **e**dge **G**od **o**ut and assume the mantle of the false self, which is the ego.

2

It's spring of 1948—David is nine years old, and I'm about to turn eight. I'm screaming at the nearby customs officials who are inspecting cars entering Canada in Sombra, Ontario: "My brother is drowning—my brother is drowning! You have to do something right now—right this minute!"

It's our first time swimming in the St. Clair River this year. Last August there was a sandbar about 50 yards away from the customs dock where we swim during our summer visits. (The cottage where we stay in Sombra is owned by my mother's boyfriend and my future stepfather, Bill Drury.) During the winter, the rapid currents in the river swept the sandbar away, and David is now caught in the fast currents, unable to stand. As I watch in horror, his head goes under, and his hand is barely visible above the water's surface. This is my brother, my best friend, and my one companion through our many excursions into foster homes since we were both toddlers. He is disappearing below the surface, and for a split second I am immobilized by shock.

At this point I run into the customs shack, where Bill Laing, a friendly faced customs inspector who knows us, hears me and instantly runs to a moored boat, starts the engine, and heads toward the last spot where my brother was seen. As the boat nears the spot that I am pointing to, Dave's little hand appears one last time right above the surface. Bill and his assistant are able to pull my brother into the boat, turn him over, and push the water out of his lungs and mouth. I watch his skin color come back from its grayish non-color—Dave is going to be all right. I am so grateful that the people in the customs shack listened to my panicky screams for help. I'm amazed how quickly they got that boat started and rescued my brother.

That evening when we tell our mother about the close call, Dave is still in a state of shock. The next day, he refuses to go back into the water—and this continues for the foreseeable future.

My brother's reaction to the near-death experience is one of the most mysterious things I have ever encountered. Dave not only avoids swimming, he breaks out in severe hives if anyone tries to persuade him to go back into the water. I watch my brother carefully, as we are always together, and I notice that even when he is caught outside in a sudden rain, each drop of water that touches his skin leaves a hive mark. Dave is so severely traumatized by this incident that this condition will last for most of the rest of his life. In adulthood, raindrops continue to leave nasty reminders on his skin of his flirtation with the Grim Reaper in the St. Clair River when he was a nine-year-old boy.

Fast-forward almost three decades. David is in the Army, stationed at Ft. Riley, Kansas. I am on a trip with my nine-year-old daughter, Tracy, to publicize my book *Your Erroneous Zones.* We're in St. Louis and then Kansas City, so I decide to make a trip to Junction City, Kansas, to visit my brother, whom I haven't seen in many years. Dave has been stationed overseas and has done two tours of duty during the Vietnam War; he's received the Bronze Star for his extraordinary service and bravery under fire.

Here is how Dave describes what happened during our visit, in his book titled *From Darkness to Light.* It brings home to me the significance of his brush with death back in 1948:

> In 1976 I was stationed at Fort Riley, Kansas, and lived in Junction City. Wayne was in town promoting his best-selling book, *Your Erroneous Zones*. He and his daughter Tracy were staying at the Travelodge down the street from me and invited me over for a swim in the pool.

Wayne told me to focus my thoughts on anything other than hives as we entered the pool. He kept talking to me, and I didn't have a chance to think about anything other than what he was saying. In fact, he was speaking so softly that I couldn't make out what he was saying, so I had to keep moving closer and closer to him.

Wayne purposely had drawn my attention to him. Before I knew it, I had been in the water for half an hour. When I got out of the pool and dried off, I couldn't find a single hive on my body. For the first time in 27 years, I didn't experience a breakout of hives when I went swimming. Immediately I went back into the water for another half hour with the same results. Since then I've enjoyed swimming and have never experienced an outbreak of hives again.

I Can See Clearly Now

As I stood on that dock watching my brother being swept away in those fast currents, I felt the presence of something that I am unable to express adequately here, or anyplace else in my entire lifetime. That presence is here right now in this moment as I write about one of the most significant events of my life. It is a feeling of not being alone, and a force that propels one into action instantaneously. On that late spring day it was not Dave's time to exit this lifetime, and I was the appointed one to ensure that his dharma continued.

That scene is so real to me even now—every detail of it has been emblazoned on my inner screen. I learned in those few moments when I was propelled into action that I could make people listen to me, and that I actually held the power of life over death within me. To delay would be to invite disaster. To stand there and cry was not an option. To let fear overwhelm me was not for me to consider. I felt a life force pushing me away from the scene I was watching unfold before me, sweeping me into that customs shack, insisting that I scream at the top of my lungs at Bill Laing.

I cannot say what this mysterious force is, but I do know it to be something that has been there for me on many occasions in my life. It is something invisible that I can feel and that I talk about in my lectures and in many of the 41 books I've written. It is a powerful knowing, like an angelic invisible guide that I trust. The experience with my brother's brush with death was the first time I absolutely knew that it was much more than an eight-year-old boy springing into action on that river dock in Sombra, Ontario. It is a comforting presence that I feel more and more frequently in my life now, and that I absolutely never ignore.

From a clearer perspective now as I look back at that event in 1948, and then at what happened in 1976 at Ft. Riley, I can see the connection, as well as how it ties in with the course that my life has taken. Little did I know at the time that my brother's near drowning and his body's extreme reaction would be an opportunity for me to put into practice what I intuitively knew as the mind-body connection and its incredibly amazing capacity for healing. At the time of my visit with Dave, I was just at the beginning of my exploration into the power of the mind and its ability to perform healing miracles.

The quarter of a century in which hives appeared on Dave's skin whenever he was in a situation of having to go in, or even near, the water, was overcome in one episode of putting his mind on healing rather than the fearsome thought of catastrophe. From a clearer perspective, I can now see how my presence on that dock that resulted in my brother's rescue was instrumental in giving me the information and the confidence to become a teacher and practitioner of mind-body healing. That childhood experience helped guide us both, leading us to explore and realize the power we possess to accomplish anything that we place our attention on with love rather than fear as our anchor.

In some incomprehensible way everything is connected. My brother's near drowning gave me an opportunity many years later to help heal him of the traumatic reaction that caused him to have serious skin outbreaks, as well as launch me into a career of teaching self-empowerment.

The year is 1950, and I am in fourth grade at Arthur Elementary School in Detroit. This is my very first time attending school while living with my reunited family.

Each day at precisely 2:45 P.M., if the entire class has behaved reasonably well—meaning there's no talking out of turn—our teacher, Mrs. Engels, reads *The Secret Garden* to us. I am enthralled listening to her, particularly by the way she makes all of the characters come alive.

In the classroom I'm in my assigned seat, going through the motions of memorizing my multiplication tables, reviewing the week's spelling words, looking at maps for our geography lesson, practicing cursive handwriting, and all of the other tedious details of my fourth-grade school day. But secretly I'm eagerly anticipating listening to *The Secret Garden* at 2:45, so I sit at my desk and gaze at the clock on the wall. (As I sit here at my desk some 62 years later, I can see the words *Seth Thomas* in my imagination on the face of that clock in the classroom.)

I seem to be the only kid in the class who is obsessed with the story unfolding each afternoon, and I notice that many of my classmates seem oblivious to the fact that if they don't behave, the story won't be forthcoming. I am ten years old and have already become aware that I don't see the world the way the other children around me do. I have discovered that people will listen to me if I speak with conviction. I have also learned that I enjoy spending most of my time in my own inner world, exploring ideas that my contemporaries never even seem to consider.

Here in Mrs. Engels's fourth-grade classroom, I realize how much power I have to make things happen that are important to me. Each day I voluntarily assume the role of "Enforcer" of the silence that Mrs. Engels so cherishes. If the class gets even slightly unruly, I leave my seat and remind the offenders that they're jeopardizing our *Secret Garden* time, and that I won't stand for this disruptive behavior. They listen and they calm down, not because they want to hear the story but because I take a position of authority.

This is an illuminating experience for the ten-year-old me. I realize it's happened before in the foster homes where I had lived, and now here again in a brand-new school. When I speak with confidence and kindness, I'm listened to. Anyone misbehaving in a way that prevents Mrs. Engels from reading to us is brought to order by me without threats or unkindness. Oh, how I love just closing my eyes and listening to the magic that is, for me, my own secret garden.

The story, written by Frances Hodgson Burnett in 1911, is about ten-year-old orphaned Mary Lennox, who is sent from India to live in England after her parents both die in a cholera epidemic. She arrives in England a dour, hurt, negative young girl who feels that her parents didn't want her. The story describes her discovery of a whole new world that changes her outlook on her life. Here I am, a ten-year-old boy, just having spent the majority of my life with similar feelings of being unwanted, now listening to a story that speaks to another way of looking at life. The idea of there being a secret place either in the world or in one's mind fascinates me.

I listen mesmerized by conversations that Mary and her sickly friend, Colin, have with the flowers and a bird called robin redbreast. Robins fly around me, too, building their nests and chirping away while I walk home from school at the end of each day. I engage in conversations with these new avian friends all the way home, living in my own imaginary secret garden, where sickness and weakness disappear and where a positive attitude is the antidote to all suffering.

I feel the exquisite power of the words read by Mrs. Engels and create my own secret garden to escape into a world where all things are possible. Here I talk to the animals and the flowers and feel the presence of real magic in my life.

Coming to this new home to live with my family isn't nearly as comfortable as living in someone else's home. Bill, my new stepfather, drinks a lot and when he does is argumentative and mean. But I manage to stay somewhat oblivious to his ranting, largely because of my awareness that in my imagination I can create a secret space much like Mary Lennox's garden in England. In this space no one is allowed entry without my permission. I am fascinated by this idea that life is not restricted to what I see and hear with my senses. I discover that I can be here in this world in my body, and I can also get outside of the limitations of my physical self and live within my own private world.

In *The Secret Garden* I hear Mrs. Engels speak about healing people of serious illness and think to myself, *If Mary can do that, so can I.* If Mary and Dickon and Colin and all of her secret-garden companions can talk to the animals and listen to the trees, then so can I.

My imagination soars. I envision myself as a magician who can do anything he puts his mind to. I see guidance for me in all of nature. I learn how to go within and clear my inner world of everything that interferes with the bliss of my inner peace. I make a decision that Bill can never get to me with his craziness, or his obsessive tirades over issues that exist only in his own impaired mind. I have a secret garden of my own, which I realize I've retreated to often in the previous years of living in foster homes.

Here in this new environment, living in an undersized home with three people who are essentially strangers, one of whom spends his days and nights drinking beer, I am given a gift that is immensely beneficial. The gift is *awareness* of my secret garden—the place within me that has no restrictions, no obstacles, and where I can create for myself a way of living that is immune to any and all influences that might bring me down.

Throughout the years to come, living in an environment of verbal and alcoholic abuse that is the norm, I have secure within my imagination a refuge that I treasure, and I'm anxious to tell others about it.

Mrs. Engels reading *The Secret Garden* for 30 minutes at the end of each school day is quite likely not memorable for the other kids in that fourth-grade classroom. For me it was a benefaction that sparked a fire within me for which I am always grateful. It was the beginning of an awareness that I have something inside of me that trumps what goes on outside of me—my own secret garden where all things are possible.

I Can See Clearly Now

Even after six decades have passed, I often look back to that classroom with Mrs. Engels and think about how Divine providence was working on my behalf. Somehow I was guided into her classroom by a force that was conspiring to set a fire within me that would propel me to write and speak about the ideas presented in that novel written over a century ago now. Before beginning to write *I Can See Clearly Now,* I decided to peruse *The Secret Garden* again, to remind myself of what had ignited such a provocative interest in my young self. The following passage, which the author writes about ten-year-old Mary Lennox, truly piqued my attention: "She was a great believer in magic. Secretly she quite believed that Dickon worked magic, of course good magic, on everything near him and that was why people liked him so much and wild creatures knew he was their friend."

The excitement that this idea germinated in me back in 1950 was to become the impetus for a body of work encompassing my entire adult life. At the time I was unaware I'd spend a lifetime examining and exploring this idea of there being a solitary chamber within all of us that when nurtured and tested, gives us a power to live our lives at extraordinary levels. In a universe that has no accidents—a universe that is Divinely orchestrated—it seems clear to me that Mrs. Engels, my prescient fourth-grade teacher, was in my life to awaken a passion within me for going way beyond the ordinary. This experience opened my life to a passion for greatness, for achieving miracles, and for believing that there are no limits to what one can accomplish if one tunes in to the powers of the invisible world that is our birthright.

As a ten-year-old boy I was introduced to two ideas that were guideposts for the journey that was to become my destiny. The first is that people will respond for the benefit of all concerned if you speak to them with confidence and in a nonjudgmental manner. The second guidepost is that there's a secret garden where miracles and magic abound, and it's available to anyone who makes the choice to visit there.

Of course I didn't realize at the time that those hours sitting and listening to *The Secret Garden* were in reality my grooming for a life's work. Those were purely thrilling moments for me. When the bell rang and class was dismissed, all the way home I traipsed through my own secret garden. It was a passion that was ignited then, and I still feel almost giddy when I contemplate what all of us are capable of experiencing when we allow ourselves to reach our own full potential.

Years later as I read *Candide,* Voltaire's best-known work, I was reminded of Mrs. Engels's class. After traveling the world and seeing the worst of humankind, the title character wryly explains at the end of this satirical tale that the violence and plunder of kings could not compare with the productive and peaceful lives of those who minded their own business and *cultivated their own garden.*

Every time I read this passage from Voltaire I see the ten-year-old boy I was, contemplating his own secret garden and—unbeknownst to him—setting the stage for a lifetime of encouraging others to eschew the ordinary life and truly tend to their own garden.

4

I'm in a new school, Marquette Elementary, my fifth school in as many years, listening to Mrs. Cooper tell us—her fifth-grade students —that she's quite hurt and upset by the way we are behaving. She goes so far as to say that we're the worst class she's ever taught.

Sitting in the back of the classroom I find myself amused by her angry response. These thoughts swirl through my head as I watch a grown woman lose control of herself: *How could she allow the misconduct of a group of children to be the source of her discomfort? She's the teacher, she's the boss, she's supposedly in charge of this room, and she is allowing everyone else's behavior to get the best of her. How could she possibly give her power away to a group of small children who are only being unruly because this class is so boring?* I recognize that our teacher is attempting to make all of us behave through the tactic of trying to make us feel guilty. And I realize that I am not at all like the other kids in the way that I think.

In my mind I return to Mrs. Scarf's home at 231 Townhall Road in Mt. Clemens, Michigan—a foster home where I was living less than two years before. Many children arrived and left during the time my brother David and I were living there, and I remember a young girl named Martha hysterically crying after being dropped off by two adults. I overheard Mrs. Scarf tell her husband, "Go find Wayne; he'll be able to make her calm down."

I came into the room and took Martha by the hand, telling her what a great place this was and how much she was going to enjoy living here. I found Dave and we took her on a tour of the chicken coop, the cherry and peach trees, and the garden. Then I took her over to my favorite bush, where lilacs were blooming and lilies of the valley were growing close to the ground. I gave her the two flowers and asked her to smell them and to think happy thoughts—and right before my eyes, Martha was transformed into a cheerful, excited playmate.

Now in the classroom with Mrs. Cooper, I think about what it felt like to miss my mother so much in those years and how I had to look after my older brother, who was frequently bullied by some cruel children because he was small for his age as a result of a serious anemic disorder. I remember that through all of those years I simply used my thoughts to turn sad events into blessings—and here's a grown woman all bent out of shape over a little bit of disruptive noise, not knowing how to be happy by imagining herself sniffing the tantalizingly scrumptious fragrance of a lilac or a lily of the valley. *And she wants me to feel guilty over her own inability to find joy in every moment?!*

I have a knowing within myself that none of the other kids seem to have. It is so perfectly obvious to me that no one has the ability to make me feel bad or cajole me into feeling guilty over *their* powerlessness. I am so aware that I am different. I know I can choose how I am going to feel at any moment. I rest my head on my desk, aware that I can choose peace rather than what Mrs. Cooper chooses for herself.

The class is dismissed and we all head out to the playground after lunch. Sue is terribly upset because of the things that the teacher said to the class and is crying with her friends Janice and Luann. It seems that she feels singled out as one of the instigators of the incident that set Mrs. Cooper off.

I begin to talk to Sue, with an understanding in my heart that I have the ability within me to make her see this situation for what it is, rather than what she imagines it to be. "Why are you so upset?" I ask her. "Can't you see that she is only trying to make you feel guilty?"

"Because she was looking right at me and saying how bad I was and that I made her feel bad."

"Why do you suppose she was doing this?"

"To get us to behave."

"Do you need her to feel bad in order for you to behave?" I ask.

"No, I just don't like it that she is mad at me and thinks I'm bad."

"What difference does it make what she thinks of you?"

"It makes me feel bad if someone is mad at me."

"Isn't her being mad *her* problem?" I want to know.

"Not if it's my fault she feels bad."

"What if she told you that you were a tree—would you be a tree and would you feel bad because she thought that?"

"Of course not," Sue responds.

I spend the recess period getting Sue to realize that Mrs. Cooper is attempting to control and manipulate her by playing on her weakness. I want to help my fellow student realize that no one can make her feel bad without her giving them permission to do so.

As we walk back into the classroom Sue has a bit of a smile on her face, but in my heart I know that she has a long way to go to learn how to be independent of the need for approval. I also know that I have something within myself that gives me a freedom that the other children don't have. I know that how I feel is something I can choose in any circumstance, and that no one can take that away from me, unless I allow them to do so. I also know I can help others feel better by simply talking common sense to them.

I Can See Clearly Now

Looking back at that experience in the fifth grade I now realize that I seemed to be wired together in a way that was unlike my peers. That day on the playground with Janice, Luann, and Sue has always been stamped on my mind. It was only one of many similar occurrences in which I was almost able to step back from what was taking place and watch myself behaving in ways that I had never seen demonstrated by any adults, let alone by 11-year-old contemporaries.

At the time, it just seemed like the thing to do. It made perfect sense to me to not let external things bother me or impede me from my own sense of well-being.

From this vantage point it is so obvious to me that I was actually in a kind of training camp for becoming an active teacher of higher spiritual and commonsense principles. I know that this universe has a creative Source of energy supporting it that is literally the matrix of all matter. Nothing occurs by happenstance anywhere, because this universal mind is perpetually on call, going about its miraculous ways in a myriad of infinite possibilities. Those inner thoughts of mine that were prompting me to rely upon my own mind and to help my classmates get past their ordinary ways of looking at things were a part and parcel of this universal Source's plan for me. Those early experiences are still so vivid in my mind today.

This was my training ground, and those were my baby steps toward a lifetime of teaching self-reliance. As I look back at my earliest days here on earth, I can see that spending the better part of my first decade in a series of foster homes was all a part of God's infallible plan for me. If I was to spend my adult life teaching, lecturing, and writing on self-reliance, then I obviously needed to learn to rely upon myself and thus be in a position to never be dissuaded from this awareness. What better training ground for teaching self-reliance than an early childhood that required a sense of independence and a need for self-sufficiency?

At the time, of course, I wasn't aware of all of the future implications that these early experiences were to offer me. Now, from a position of being able to see much more clearly, I know that every single encounter, every challenge, and every situation are all spectacular threads in the tapestry that represents and defines my life, and I am deeply grateful for all of it.

5

It's a new school year at Marquette Elementary, where I am beginning grade seven. On the first day of school classmate after classmate approaches me, telling me that we have two new transfer students in our class, and we should shun them. I'm perplexed as they inform me that these new kids are somehow different and therefore undeserving of my companionship. Rather than judging these new classmates, I'm intrigued by what is so threatening about them.

One of the new kids is a boy named Guy, a transfer student from a local Catholic school, Our Lady Queen of Peace. Apparently the fact that he's from a Catholic school, and has been in some kind of trouble at that school and was kicked out, is sufficient reason to boycott Guy from any possibility of joining in our seventh-grade camaraderie. I hear most of my friends speak ill of this boy. They have no knowledge of him whatsoever other than a few rumors being bandied about—origin unknown.

I'm very much aware that I wield enormous influence on my classmates. My willingness to speak up fearlessly endears me to them. Thus, I know that if I shun these new students, they'll indeed stay outsiders, but if I embrace them, the others will fall in line and welcome rather than ostracize them. This is a power I've had in every school situation I have been in for the previous seven years.

The other new student that year is a girl who lives right down the street from me. Her name is Rhoda and I have yet to speak with her. My classmates keep coming up to me and whispering, as if they were giving me forbidden and tainted information about this new girl at our school, "Don't talk to Rhoda; she's a Jew." This is a word I haven't heard before, so I ask, "What's a Jew? What does it mean? What does she have that makes her so undesirable?" Not one of my classmates has an answer. They only know they've been told something about Jews somewhere by somebody, and that means they can't be friends with them. They're all willing to shun this new girl because of a label that's somehow made her an outcast.

Rhoda lives a half block from me on Moross Road on the east side of Detroit. That same evening I decide to find out what all the fuss is about. I knock on the door and Rhoda's mother greets me; in fact, she's one of my customers on my paper route, where I deliver *The Detroit News* every afternoon on my bicycle. I discover that Rhoda is just like the rest of us, but that she practices a different set of religious beliefs.

Having been exposed to a variety of religious experiences in the foster homes I lived in, being Protestant, Catholic, Jewish, or anything else means absolutely nothing to me. I have already formed an opinion that the so-called religious teachings that I've been exposed to simply make no sense. So, I've just ignored the Sunday-school message of fear and judgment and paid no attention to any of it. I see no need for all of this craziness in my life, and long ago decided not to participate in it because every time I was required to go to church I ended up feeling worse for the experience—and I want, more than anything, to feel good.

Rhoda's family couldn't have been any nicer, and right then and there, I decide that Rhoda is going to be my friend and welcomed into our seventh-grade class.

With my acceptance of both Rhoda and Guy, their transition into a new school setting is made smooth and both of these kids are accepted as a part of our classroom. The use of the word *Jew* as a pejorative label is halted almost immediately. I am befuddled by the willingness of so many of my friends to judge someone on the basis of what their parents had told them about a word that they didn't even understand. Rather than thinking for themselves, they use their minds to reflect what others tell them to think.

I am so lucky—I don't have any older people around me to tell me who to hate or reject or judge.

I Can See Clearly Now

These two experiences with Guy and Rhoda stand out conspicuously as I look back at my early life and now realize that I was being prepared for an adult life of teaching compassion and tolerance, even though I was unaware of any such destiny at the time. I didn't feel special or more enlightened than anyone else—in fact, I was just one of the 30 or so students in the class—it just seemed like the thing to do at the time.

I can now see quite clearly that I was being guided to behave in these ways as a young boy. Divine guidance was obviously directing the play that was only in Act One at the time. I cannot say why I assumed this kind of a role in the early stages of my life, other than to speculate that a higher power was at work during these formative years. While many of my friends and acquaintances were quite willing to use epithets of hate, I was innately offended by that language and would bristle inside when I heard it. I did not choose to make a big scene when such conduct surfaced. I knew inside, just like when I dealt with the bully who was threatening my brother, that fighting was a waste of time and would accomplish nothing. I heard different voices in my head—inner proclamations that encouraged me to be an example of what I knew to be right.

This theme of compassion and kindness toward others has been with me since I was a little boy. Perhaps it was a leftover from a previous life. Perhaps it grew from feelings of early abandonment, wherein I wanted to give love because of the love I felt was not coming to me.

But from this vantage point I see it as the hand of Divine providence on my shoulder guiding me to behave in compassionate ways early on, in order that I might write and speak about the importance of extending love to all as a part of a lifetime mission.

However that spark of motivation was placed in me back then, I want to express my deep and heartfelt appreciation for it. It has not only brightened up my life immeasurably, but has been a source of comfort and healing for millions of people throughout the world.

6

"When I'm on *The Tonight Show* talking to Steve Allen, I'll be much more interesting than the people who were on last night!"

I'm having a conversation with my mother and two brothers early in the morning before she catches her bus for work and we head out to school. I am 14 years old in 1954—watching Steve Allen almost every night. I'm lost in fascination as I watch the show, and I see myself right there in the studio talking to Steve and kibitzing with his cast of nutty characters. I don't *think* I'll be a guest—I *know* it.

We have a small black-and-white Admiral television set, the first TV in the neighborhood. On the roof of our small duplex at 20217 Moross Road is an antenna that brings in reception—depending on how the winds blow. To me this is the absolute height of luxury, and I become addicted to my late-night entertainment long after the rest of the house is asleep. I sit up close to this strange new contraption and keep the sound down as low as possible, because my mother has her alarm set for 5 A.M. and I don't want to disturb her . . . or have her discover that I am wide awake while she thinks I'm sound asleep.

These nights watching Steve Allen on *The Tonight Show* are more than mere entertainment to me. In my imagination I merge myself with the entire show. Somehow I can see myself not only in the present, as a boy sitting in my living room watching electronic transmissions, but I see myself in the future as well. I have such an incredible feeling of being connected to what I will be doing in the future that on some occasions I look at the tiny screen and see myself sitting on the set and talking to Steve as an adult.

I cannot shake this image—ever. I speak about it to very few people, but somehow I am able to merge the present with the future, and these inner pictures become my own private world. Probably this seems crazy to most others, but it's *very real* to me. I see myself using this little television screen as a means for reaching and teaching people, not just in my city or my country, but also in the entire world.

When I share these images with my family and friends they largely scoff at my naïveté, so I begin to practice keeping these inner pictures just that: inner only. And the knowing never leaves me, night after night, as I watch Steve Allen on *The Tonight Show.*

I Can See Clearly Now

Fast-forward to 1976. I had published my first book for the public, titled *Your Erroneous Zones.* I was embarking on a national tour, largely at my own expense, visiting city after city doing as many media interviews as I could arrange. Being that I was an unknown personality, every request that was made for me to do a national television spot was firmly rejected. And so I decided that the other way to reach everyone in America was to go to them directly.

I packed my books up, and with my nine-year-old daughter, Tracy, spent many months on the road. I did every interview that my personal friend and publicist, Donna Gould, was able to arrange. Finally, in August I received a call from a man who worked as a talent coordinator for *The Tonight Show Starring Johnny Carson.* His name was Howard Papush, and he had just read *Your Erroneous Zones* and wanted to know if I'd be willing to come in for a preinterview for a possible appearance on *The Tonight Show.* I of course immediately accepted and arrived in Burbank, California, at the NBC studios. Here

Howard and I spoke for several hours and ultimately became close friends.

A couple of days later I received a call from Howard informing me that I was scheduled to appear the following Monday evening on *The Tonight Show* with guest host Shecky Greene, a comedian who frequently performed on the Strip in Las Vegas. This would be my first opportunity to speak to the people of America about the message I wanted to share with the world in *Your Erroneous Zones.* I was ecstatic—thrilled beyond anything I might write here today. I was scheduled to be the last guest, in what in those days was called the "author's spot," in the final 15 minutes of the 90-minute show, and I would be airing at 12:45 A.M.

The evening that the show was being taped, as I was ushered to my dressing room I passed a bank of pay phones—and there, completing a call, was none other than Mr. Steve Allen, who was scheduled to be the first guest. I introduced myself to Steve and walked to my dressing room in a cloud of amazement. *I am going to appear on national television with the man I have so admired since I was a 14-year-old boy!*

The show finished being taped at around 6 P.M., and my segment with Shecky Greene went extremely well. Shecky was engaging, funny, and managed to get me to relax and sound coherent and interesting.

I headed out to LAX in a state of pure delirium. As I was about to get on the plane I heard my name broadcast over the PA system, telling me that I had an urgent call. I found a phone, and it was Howard calling to give me some bad news. For the first time in the history of *The Tonight Show* it had been preempted because at the Republican National Convention in Kansas City, the vice-presidential nominee, Bob Dole, went beyond his allotted time and NBC didn't cut away—so my one and only national television appearance had been wiped away. I went from blissed to pissed in an instant!

The next day, Tuesday, Howard called me in Detroit to tell me that Johnny Carson would like to have me on the show the following night, Wednesday. It turns out that in the Tuesday-morning meeting

Johnny was told about this new guest who was fabulous the night before, even though the show wasn't aired.

I received a plane ticket back to Los Angeles, to appear with Johnny on Wednesday night. However, because the show ran long with Johnny talking with Orson Welles and Robert Blake, there was very little time left for me. So Johnny said to me on the air, "I'm sorry we ran long tonight. Would you be willing to stay over and do the show again on Friday, and we'll give you more time than you had tonight?" I said yes and appeared again with Johnny on Friday night—then on the following Monday night, they aired the show that had preempted the week before with Shecky Greene!

I suddenly went from zero national TV appearances to three *Tonight Show* spots in five days. This marked the beginning of a string of 37 *Tonight Show* appearances over the next two years, as well as regular spots on *The Merv Griffin Show; The Mike Douglas Show; The Phil Donahue Show;* Dinah Shore's syndicated talk show, *Dinah!; The John Davidson Show;* the *Today* show; *Good Morning America;* and so on.

As I walked past that phone bank and saw that I was about to be making an appearance with Steve Allen on *The Tonight Show* I had an immediate and almost overpowering sensation within me that I had actually created my own future by having such a strong knowing back when I was 14 years of age. In fact, I am quite certain that time itself is much more of an illusion than we are capable of understanding with our body-mind.

Perhaps my *knowing* back in 1954 was one possibility of a future event being present at what I now think of as the past. But if time is an illusion and oneness is what truly defines our experience, then the idea of past and future must also be an illusion. And if this seems wacky and undecipherable to you, at it often does to me, then just consider your dream state. Here you can fly; your long-dead grandparents are alive; and you are able to be a young child, an older person, or any age you desire if you place your attention on it. Consider that for one-third of your life, you are in a nontime dimension and everything is possible, and the only way you know for certain that you were dreaming is to awaken and look back at it.

From a more awakened perspective in my life today, I look back at my 14-year-old self who had an inner knowing, which became an intention that connected to the all-knowing, all-creating Divine mind and allowed me to become what I was placing my awareness on, just like I do in my dream state. This is how powerful I believe our thoughts and intentions are, throughout our lives.

I see now, from a clearer perspective, that every moment of our existence holds an infinite number of possibilities. The strongest knowing within us about what we are going to do or become is actually being lived out right then and there, even though we haven't yet experienced it in our everyday reality. A thought that persists is a thought that is aligned with the Divine mind, and becomes a reality in what we call the future, but is actually a part of the oneness that is just that: one. No division; just one experience, which is now.

Remember—everything that happened to you in the past actually happened in the now, and likewise for the future. Everything you will ever experience will also happen now. Yes, now is all there is, and when I saw and felt myself on *The Tonight Show* with Steve Allen in 1954, it was a now experience just waiting to show up. It had to. There was no possibility of it not showing up, since I had such a knowing about it.

What I know from this vantage point is that whenever I have that absolute knowing within me that something is going to transpire, I sense that I have guidance available from ascended masters, who are working with me and steering the ship of my life in the direction that's been my own personal dharma from the moment I incarnated into this lifetime. With this awareness I'm convinced that I have been in some kind of ascended-master training course from the very beginning, and that these *knowings* that were so persuasive to me as a young boy were actually a part of that training regimen. Past—present—future in a timeless dimension are simply all occurring at the same time, even if our time-based dimension sees it otherwise.

Today I know that I have spiritual guidance with me, directing me on a path of living and teaching God-realization. I have no reason to doubt that this same angelic assistance was with me back in 1954 when I saw myself in the future.

There seems to have been a fundamental truth at work back in 1976 that has guided me throughout my entire life. As I look back on what was taking place as I was self-promoting *Your Erroneous Zones,* I never once felt any frustration because I couldn't garner any appearances on national television. I simply decided to go to as many cities as possible and take on whatever local offerings I could generate, and I would leave the rest up to whatever higher powers were directing my efforts. And as I followed my own inner callings, all the while having the time of my life, out of that consciousness came three appearances on the most prestigious national TV show within five days, and a launch into national prominence for the rest of my professional lifetime. I wasn't chasing success—I was pursuing my own inner vision.

This is all wrapped up in a quote that I have cited many times, which was written back in the 19th century by one of the most influential spiritual masters ever to grace my path. His name is Henry David Thoreau, and his words have always rung sharply in my consciousness: "If one advances confidently in the direction of his dreams, and endeavors to live the life which he has imagined, he will meet with a success unexpected in common hours."

I can see clearly now that this wisdom was operating overtime in my life. It sure was unexpected and beyond anything I had even dared to contemplate. I was advancing confidently in the direction of my own personal dream and living the life I had imagined for myself —and loving every minute of it. I let success chase me, which it has been doing ever since. The one thing I am certain of is that I can control what goes into my imagination, and I simply have allowed any success I've enjoyed to come to me.

At the point when three *Tonight Show* appearances in five days showed up, I had already resigned from a full-time position as a professor at a major university in order to go into the world on my own and speak to whoever would listen. Truly the words of Thoreau resonated with me as I followed my dream and allowed the universe to handle the details.

7

I'm bicycling round and round the block, trying to avoid walking into the chaos in my house. Life at home in my 15th year is filled with confusion, and growing worse by the day.

My mother works as a secretary for the Chrysler Corporation and is hard put to make enough money to support her three boys, since her husband has no interest in doing much of anything other than drinking and making violent outbursts. She has finally decided that enough is enough and filed papers for divorce from Bill Drury—she's going to bring some long-desired peace and tranquility to our home, and also change her last name back to the same name as my own.

My stepfather's drinking is getting way out of hand, erupting into the common verbal onslaught used by most drunks: aggressive, loud, fast, angry ranting. He picks on me for anything he can find to be upset with me about—anything at all. So now I'm riding my bike waiting for him to get into his black 1954 Chevrolet and drive off to the bar. My high school guidance counselor's words are fresh in my mind as I pedal around the block: "I want your mother to come into school and talk with the principal. Until then, you are suspended."

Mr. Cutter is punishing me because I refused to fill out student personnel forms in the proper fashion. When I came to the line that asked for the names of my parents, I was confused about what to insert in that space. Should I write in the name of my stepfather, or my own father whom I've never seen? And how do I explain my mother's impending name change? I felt violated—I didn't want to put anything in these forms that would make my mother look bad, and I disliked being asked for personal information about my family. So I wrote in big letters across the form: THAT'S MY BUSINESS. As a result, Mr. Cutter suspended me and demanded that my mother lose a day's work and take three buses to have a conference with the principal, Mr. Irwin Wolf.

For three days I cannot participate in any school activities; instead, I get to sit on a bench in the principal's office. At least there's an interesting book on the parolees' bench, placed there presumably in the hope of changing the wayward malcontents who are sentenced to sit in this spot.

I'm readmitted to school after my mother explains to the principal and Mr. Cutter that I'm trying to protect her, and promises that I'll contain my antipathy for filling out forms and treat the registration process each semester with respect. Nothing is said to me about what prompts my anger toward school regulations. Buried deep is the pain of living with "outrageous fortune" in the form of alcoholism, along with the prospect of another imminent family breakup and the fear I have of being sent back to foster care and losing daily contact with my mother once again.

It's a few months later, and my tenth-grade biology teacher has informed me that I must make a scrapbook of the various leaves in the neighborhood and turn it in before the end of the semester. I won't get a passing grade and will have to retake biology if I don't comply.

I am 15 years of age and not taking school very seriously. The most important thing to me at this time in my life is my job, which is pretty much a full-time thing. I work as an assistant manager/cashier/produce manager/butcher/whatever else is needed at Stahl's market, a small independent store that caters to the local population. I give a portion of my earnings to my mother, as do my two brothers, who are also working very hard at their jobs and floundering when it comes to being stellar students.

One of the girls in my biology class, Mary Jo Mercurio, has offered to do the leaf collection for me, just so I don't have to go through the ignominy of failing biology for no sensible reason. I refuse—it's become a moral issue with me. I am not a troublemaker in any sense of the word. But there is something inside me that reacts strongly, almost violently, to the idea of doing frivolous busywork tasks, and doing them because everyone else simply goes along and never questions the authority figures.

I'm very frustrated with my biology teacher's intransigence on this matter of gathering and pasting leaves into a scrapbook simply because everyone has *always* done it. I plead with him—but to no avail. He maintains his stance of: *Do the leaf collection or fail the course, even though you have high grades on all your schoolwork and have demonstrated that you know the difference between leaves produced by oak, elm, and evergreen trees.*

My frustration gets the best of me, and I speak out forcefully, "This is just so stupid. I have a full-time job, and I don't have the time to do such a silly assignment. I'm not going to do it."

Back I go to the principal's office, to sit on delinquents' row. I must once again have my mother leave work and come to a second appointment with Mr. Wolf, so she can hear why my insolence cannot and will not be tolerated.

As I sit there, I see the same book that caught my eye a few months before. The book is a paperback edition of *Walden,* by Henry David Thoreau. The last time I was here I just thumbed through the pages—now, as I sit on the long bench awaiting my appointment with justice for my failure to be just like everybody else, I decide to read the entire thing.

I love this man's writing! I become totally engrossed in Thoreau's stream-of-consciousness style as he describes how it felt to live in the wilderness and learn about life by listening and being content in nature. My refusal to participate in what seems to me to be foolish conformity for sake of conformity is strengthened by reading *Walden* while awaiting disciplinary action. Admittedly, I'm slightly skeptical about the stance I'm taking, because following through with it means attending summer school and retaking biology.

I come to school every day and head for the varnished bench in the principal's office, where I continue reading Thoreau's account of his time living in the Massachusetts wilderness. I also dream of living peacefully in nature and having no silly rules imposed upon me. I am lost in his words and all that he learns from the mysterious forces of nature. I decide that this man, writing one hundred or so years ago, is my hero. I learn that he went to jail rather than pay taxes to a government that allowed slavery and participated in the horrors of the Mexican-American War. He is a rebel, urging against foolish laws and immoral behavior toward others.

I am so grateful for whoever left this treasure and for all of the wisdom pouring forth from this man, who thinks like I do—something I have never encountered previously in my life.

When I finish reading *Walden,* I find an essay in the back of the book titled "Civil Disobedience." I have one more day left to sit on the bench in the principal's office, so I commit to reading this essay. I am beyond excited—I am flabbergasted! This man is writing directly to my heart. The entire essay is written around the central idea that every person has both a right and an obligation to follow their conscience—especially when burdensome and foolish rules are forced upon them by government authority.

I feel as if I've found a literary soul mate—a man I can respect. Thoreau lived out his ideas and was even willing to be jailed rather than pay a poll tax in his hometown of Concord, Massachusetts. I make a decision that one day I will visit Concord and immerse myself in the same world that produces people who have such a revolutionary way of thinking.

I'm assuming that the school officials, who supplied this book to me to read while in limbo, wanted me to apply the principles I was reading. I am excited to share Thoreau's ideas with Mr. Wolf in tomorrow's scheduled conference with my mother. I feel I'm not so weird sitting here for the second time awaiting my punishment for the crime of believing in myself, and being willing to stand up for what I believe. I feel good about this advice regarding the importance of obeying my own conscience and practicing civil disobedience.

My mother arrives, obviously annoyed at having to take time off work for another meeting at the school. By this time I've lived with her for five years, so she has a pretty good idea that her son Wayne is not like most other kids when it comes to obeying silly rules and being told how to live his life. She trusts in my ability to make my own decisions, largely because that's what I've done ever since I was a very little boy.

In this second visit with Mr. Wolf I show him what I've been reading the past week while awaiting my fate: "Must the citizen ever for a moment, or in the least degree, resign his conscience to the legislator? Why has every man a conscience then? I think that we should be men first, and subjects afterward. . . . The only obligation which I have a right to assume is to do at any time what I think right."

My mother, bless her heart, backs up the position I've taken, just as she did a few months before when she explained why I'd taken the extreme position of refusing to fill out a myriad of forms that might make her look bad.

I will be attending summer school, but I am unbowed—I am so deeply grateful for the days I was suspended from school, reading the words of a man who is to become one of the most influential people in my life. I look forward to taking biology again in just a few weeks.

I Can See Clearly Now

The events described above are the two most significant things that happened to me during my entire four years of high school. I look back at the inner rage I felt over having to fill out forms and reveal family discord that I preferred to keep private, and can now see the wealth of benefits I received. That experience singularly helped me become a better parent to my eight children whenever they ran afoul of any school regulations. I could think back to my encounters with rules and regulations that didn't seem to make much sense to me, and have empathy for my children's frustrations. I understood as a very young boy that to blindly follow rules just because they're rules is to lose control over your whole life.

I can now see that my early encounters as an adolescent in high school with those who attempted to get me to conform were placed before me so that I might write and speak about a higher form of consciousness. Much later in life, I began to live as a man who respects the wisdom of the Tao Te Ching, written by Lao-tzu in the 5th century B.C. I discovered the higher form of consciousness revealed in the Tao. This philosophy declares that when the greatness of the Tao (God) is present, action arises from one's heart; and when the greatness of the Tao is not present, action arises from the rules—a sure sign that virtue is absent.

My early entanglements with having to live by a set of rules, which often seemed so unnecessary, were the fodder that allowed me to write and speak on the importance of self-reliance. Had I been a young person who simply fell into line and did what he was told without questioning authority or the reason for the rules in the first place, I'd have a very different-looking résumé today. Within me there's something I call my *I am* presence, which is my connection to my Source of being—the Tao, Divine mind, God, Allah, Krishna, Christ consciousness, it doesn't matter the name. This *I am* presence is something that speaks very loudly to me, and it always has. It never lets me down, although there are times when listening to its inner pleadings forces me to face once again what appear to be the slings and arrows of outrageous fortune, but are really the great lessons I incarnated to learn.

The *I am* presence within me is exceedingly persuasive, and it was already this way when I was a young boy. I just couldn't be one of the herd, and when I saw herdlike behavior I railed against it in a much more ego-involved way than I do today. I was a bit too loud back then—drawing some unwanted attention to myself to be sure! I can see clearly today that the inner provocations that I experienced in high school were my earlier callings to teach others not to be voluntarily victimized by groupthink mentality.

The summer I took biology for the second time turned out to be another memorable experience of my high school years. My new teacher, a woman in her 30s named Olive Fletcher, was one of the best teachers I ever had—anywhere. She took the time to get to know me as a young man who had all this potential but was filled to the brim with confusion and heartache. She took me bowling—I was bowled over! Here was a teacher who *cared* and wanted to spend time talking *with* me, rather than *at* me. Mrs. Fletcher got me to look within and to treasure what I found there. Had I gone along with my original biology teacher and thrown together a leaf collection, I might never have had the opportunity to know a compassionate, caring teacher who modeled for me the kind of practices I'd adopt when I became a teacher myself.

The grandest irony of this story is that 16 years later, I had just completed my doctoral studies and was given a position as a guest professor. I was teaching a course in the College of Education that was a requirement for graduate students who were practicing teachers and would like to become school administrators. There on my roster sheet was a familiar name. The same man who gave me a failing grade in biology was enrolled in the course that I was teaching! There are no accidents. I enjoyed imagining that I'd send him to Australia to complete *his* leaf collection—a course requirement. In reality I never mentioned the incident from high school, and I don't think he even remembered it.

I am ever so grateful for whatever Divine intervention was so moved as to place a copy of Thoreau's *Walden* in the principal's office when I was just 15 years of age. I can't explain why this man's words rang so true for me in my earliest years in high school, but it was the beginning of a lifelong love affair with this 19th-century American philosopher who only published two books in his lifetime.

Over the years, I've made many visits to the homes of both Ralph Waldo Emerson and Henry David Thoreau in Concord, Massachusetts. In fact, I was so moved at the Thoreau Lyceum on one visit that I persuaded the curator of the museum, which once was Thoreau's study and home, to allow me to lie down on his bed and sit at the desk where he wrote the essay on civil disobedience that so moved me as a teenager.

From my perspective here today, I can see quite clearly that Emerson and Thoreau have been angelic lookouts for me through most of my adult life—their words like beacons of light in a cloudy world. I first became aware of their messages of transformation and higher awareness when I was a young boy sitting in the principal's office, but I knew then that something magical was being ushered into my life.

I had chills inside me as I entered that conference with my mother and Mr. Wolf, because I had an ally—an ally that the school officials endorsed! Why else would they leave that book there so conspicuously for me to read at a time that clearly cried out for some kind of civil disobedience? I felt the presence of Thoreau with me then, and he's here with me now as I relate to you how powerful the early transcendentalists were in my teenage life—and still are today.

It seems clear to me today that this giant of independent thought was there with me as I was forming memes of self-reliance during my adolescence. He was there with me when I went to his home, lay in his bed, sat at his desk, and meditated in his personal lair; and he was there with me as I recorded a PBS special in his hometown. He's with me now as I write, reminding me that we are never alone and that we can call in the spiritual essence of any teacher who has ever breathed a breath on this planet, and fulfill our own destiny with their assistance.

I see clearly that my teenage resistance became the basis for the unstoppable energy I feel within me and that it was my way of saying *Yes!* to a calling to become an international teacher on self-reliance and higher awareness. The great Tao (God) works in mysterious ways, and who's to say that Thoreau himself didn't intervene in my adolescent life and put me on a path that I continue to travel. . . .

8

I'm speaking to Mrs. Olive Fletcher, my former biology teacher, who gave me an *A* in the same course I'd previously failed due to an irresistible force meeting an immovable object and my having to give in. I tell her, "I'm going to write my own novel this year. I know I can write, and I have an idea for a book that I want to try out."

I'm fascinated by the idea of extraordinary consciousness. In my mind it's a level of awareness that allows for instantaneous manifestation, telepathic communication, self-healing, and extraordinary powers to communicate with angelic beings. I envision a fictional character who possesses these otherworldly qualities. He's achieved Divine God-realization and has a job as a paleontologist on an archeological dig. I name my book *The Anomalous Compatriot,* and every evening I sneak off to a quiet spot and let my fantasies pour forth. My handwritten tome grows, and I secretly stash it away in big brown paper bags in the small attic of our home. I love these subdued, hidden-away moments where I escape into the fictional characterizations I create.

I love reading and am always in the middle of a new book. Most of my friends detest reading and never consider writing as something they might do as an occupation. Plainly, to their way of thinking, writing is for nerds and sissies.

In English class each student has a manila folder for book reports on their reading during the semester. The more reports, the more a student is thought of as a burgeoning scholar. When I'm short of cash I write and sell book reports at 25 cents apiece to supplement my income. If the grade received is lower than a *B,* I don't ask for payment. I work as a writer now and thus feel confident that I have writing ability —I've tested that out in the real world of profit and loss!

I write on any subject and often think of my writing as automatic writing. My hand moves across the page, but it isn't actually me doing the writing. It's a kind of connection with an invisible part of me that occurs when I sit down with purple pen in hand and allow the words to form on the paper beneath my moving fingers. I feel most at home when I have a writing assignment. I love essay tests, knowing that my writing abilities will help me to overcome lapses I may have on the material I am writing about.

My writing is like having a friend with me at all times. I love my space where I escape each day to bring my characters to life, though the story is becoming less important—it's just the opportunity to sit in a sacred space with a blank piece of paper staring back at me that I so enjoy. When I take the time to write on my novel, I think to myself, *Writing is not something that I do. It is what I am.* I like the feel of it and saying and remembering, *I am writing.* What brings me the greatest sense of accomplishment is feeling aligned with what I am on the planet for in the first place. That's what writing is to me.

I Can See Clearly Now

I still retreat frequently to my writing space, as I have done for well over 45 years, and I feel safe and closest to my Source of being when I'm surrounded by personal photos and memorabilia in what I refer to as my *sacred writing space.*

I was aware even in my teenage years that writing would play a big role in my life. I came alive inside as I read Thoreau and Emerson in high school, and I had such a feeling of completeness and of doing what I was sent to do while writing my novel, as well as a collection of personal essays with topics like, "Avoiding Groupthink," "All Things Are Possible," and "How to Really Know God, and Live Forever." This was a hobby as a young man that I happily added to a scheduled full-time job and a full-time high school curriculum.

I knew as I wrote book-report summaries for my friends for payment that I had something special going on. When I wrote essays on subjects that refused to quiet down in my thoughts, the feedback I received was a variation on, "You should really consider writing." I often heard that I had a way of putting things on paper that made sense.

As I went on to the Navy and then to college, I most enjoyed that my writing gave me a kind of confirmation that I didn't need anything outside of myself in order to make a living. I loved knowing that I carried whatever tools I needed to ultimately become completely self-sufficient. I wanted to not have to go to a workplace and be told what to do and how to think—I wanted to listen to my inner voices and write what I thought about in my own way, and know that I could earn a living without all of the onerous requirements that seemed to come with being an employee.

I was *already* an employee, many weeks working well over 40 hours, and I didn't feel free. But when I wrote and people paid me, or when I finished a chapter in my book and realized that I could sell my novel and anything else I wrote, I felt as if I had been invited to sit on God's lap and just say what I wanted to say and be paid for it as my bonus! I can see now that I was destined to have no bosses, no judges, no employers, no rules, only my own inner callings.

I look back on my early writing times and the inner awareness that spoke loudly to me of the freedom I would one day know. By following my instincts and my good feelings that always arose when I took pen in hand and declared myself to be a writer—even if no one else yet shared in the same opinion—I was following my soul's calling. It was enough for me to claim it and declare myself to be an expert on what I felt so passionate about.

9

"I hate you so much. How could you simply walk away from your children and never make a phone call to see if we are okay? I want to smash your face in I am so angry at you!"

At nighttime my anger and pain erupt in dreams of me screaming at my father. I awaken almost every morning in a cold sweat after these nightly encounters. I dream that I'm in a state of rage when I see him, and I demand answers. This man I've never seen in waking life remains distant and disinterested, unbothered by anything I might be saying to him in my dream state.

Even though I have no memory of this man, and I know the stories about his mistreatment of my mother and my grandparents, I'm perplexed by his continued indifference toward the three children that he left some 15 years ago. I've heard stories of his stealing jewelry from my grandmother, spending time in prison for theft, and refusing to work to support his family—along with his constant womanizing, drinking, and sexual violence. Most egregiously, he simply walked out of our lives, never making a phone call to see how his three children might be doing or making good on the paltry sum of money he was supposed to provide for child support. No, Melvin Lyle Dyer simply disappeared and never once looked back.

I'm now living with my brothers and our mother, as Bill Drury has finally departed the roost. Jim and Dave are not interested in finding and confronting our father, but I am. My nightly dreams reveal a young man deeply conflicted by his father's abandonment. I try to get my mother to describe him, but she refuses—except to say that he was an absolute asshole, a fast-talking con man, stealing money wherever he went, and refusing to take on the responsibilities of fatherhood. She recalls one job he had: selling brooms and brushes door-to-door for an agency for the blind. When he neglected to turn in the money he collected, he was fired.

Although my mother has nothing positive to say about this man who's my father, I want to know him. My indignation and rage insist that I confront him and ask to hear his side of the story. I think about him every day, imagining that I'll accidentally run into him and have a long conversation about what motivated him to leave a beautiful woman and three little boys under the age of five. I want to know if he even knew me or had any feelings of love for this little boy who is fast growing into manhood.

I attempt to locate him so that we can talk. I make phone calls to relatives of his and pick up a few clues as to his whereabouts (someplace in the Deep South), but I never make contact. I have this fantasy that I am going to finally meet this man who so mysteriously walked out of my life, and that we are going to resolve these internal issues I have concerning being abandoned.

I ask questions incessantly, and I can see that my mother is very threatened by my inquisitiveness about my father. My brothers don't ask and simply don't want to know anymore. Maybe my oldest brother, Jim, remembers some of our father's abusive actions toward our mother and us and that explains his disinterest. Perhaps he simply wants to put it all behind him.

My mother has so much obvious hatred toward him that my questions are usually met with, "He was no good, and you are better off not knowing him." I stop pursuing my curiosity about him with her, but my soul longs to know more: to talk to him, to hear his viewpoints and explanations, to maybe even find out that he really did love me even though he chose to stay away. I often think that maybe he made a noble choice to stay away, knowing in his heart that his presence in my life would not be in my own best interest, and that his departure was a selfless rather than a selfish choice.

At any rate, the absence of a father in my life is huge for me as a teenager. I am curious; I want desperately to find him. And the bitterness I feel grows into a furor that manifests in the frenzied dreams of violence I express toward him in my slumber. I make a vow to myself that, even though everyone in my immediate family feels that I should just drop the matter and be grateful that this loser of a man is out of my life, I am going to chase him down and one day talk to him man-to-man to get the answers I desire. I am not satisfied to just "let it go," as those around me are urging. I want to meet him. I want to hear it from him directly. I want him to know that I exist and, yes, I so very much want him to love me.

On Valentine's Day 1956, our telephone rings on our party line at TUxedo 1-5942. An aunt I've never met or even heard of is calling. Her name is Audrey, and I learn that she is my father's half-sister. She tells me that my grandmother Norah Mabel Wilhelm died that morning, and that my two brothers and I have been asked to be pallbearers at this woman's funeral. I didn't know my father's mother had been alive, I've never even heard her name mentioned, but I instantly say yes.

My decision is not based on my desire to pay tribute to a grandmother I never knew—my heart is racing at the prospect of finally being able to meet my father. Surely he'll be there at the funeral of his own mother, and won't be able to hide from me any longer.

I am a few weeks shy of turning 16 and have my learner's permit, which allows me to drive if accompanied by an older licensed driver. Jim, also a pallbearer designee, agrees to let me drive his car over to the west side of Detroit to a home filled with strangers. I am here for one reason and one reason only: I want to see this man who is my father. But he isn't there. There is a funeral service at a church, but no Melvin Lyle Dyer. Then we make a short trip to a cemetery, where I help carry the coffin of a woman who is my grandmother, the mother of my father, though a stranger to me. No Melvin Lyle Dyer at the cemetery.

We all return to the west-side home, the residence of my deceased grandmother. I'm bursting with excitement, certain that my long-absent father will surface. As we reenter this home for a buffet dinner, a truck pulls up to the house and delivers a few paltry flowers with a note. We are all informed that Lyle is down south in Alabama or Mississippi and unable to be at this final commemoration of his mother's life.

I am crestfallen. Once again my father comes up missing. An assortment of cousins and aunts that I didn't know I was related to make excuses for Lyle. He's afraid to show up, I'm told—probably because he's afraid that my mother will have him thrown back in jail for over a decade of unpaid court-ordered child-support payments.

I wonder what I'm doing here at this memorial service, and I urge my brothers to leave. Yet before we can get away, a cousin named Dorothy says that my father had several wives after he left my mother, including a young girl he picked up hitchhiking in a place called Bloomingrose, West Virginia; and before that a woman named Juanita, a nurse who now lives in Sandusky, Ohio. I take note, say good-bye to these unknown relatives, and realize for the umpteenth time that this man has no interest in getting to know me or my brothers. Even his own mother's funeral is not enough of a lure to have him make an appearance in my life.

I am now more determined than ever that I am going to have that face-to-face meeting with my father, and I have a fairly good idea about where he might be living. I remain uncertain why I'm so obsessed with finding this man who obviously wants nothing to do with me or my brothers—but I am full of resolve.

After I turn 16, I purchase a 1950 Plymouth with $200 I've saved. I make plans to drive down to Boone County, West Virginia, and pay a surprise visit to my father and the young hitchhiker I'd heard he'd married. As summer-vacation time arrives, my boss at Stahl's market, where I have been working for three years, asks me to work full-time all summer as assistant manager, which includes closing up the store and handling the day's receipts. This opportunity, coupled with the expense of owning and insuring a car, and my desire to be with my new girlfriend, lead me to postpone my trip. I decide instead to look for the ex-wife named Juanita in Sandusky, Ohio.

I drive three hours to Sandusky and meet my father's ex-wife, who works in a local hospital and speaks firmly and without any hesitation. "Your father was a bad man," she says bluntly. "Everything your mom told you about him is true, and even more. He refused to work and support our marriage; he was always in trouble with the law; he had no sense of right and wrong; he drank excessively and was mean and vicious when he was drunk, which was frequent. I recommend that you abandon your desire to meet him. He's a phony, and you are way better off without him in your life."

Juanita Dyer spends the entire day with me, and the most disappointing part of it is her direct response to my question, "Did he ever say anything to you about his three boys that he had deserted, and did he ever mention his youngest son, Wayne?" She looks at me with the caring eyes of a woman who works as a nurse in a hospital, seeing tragedies day in and day out. "No," she responds. "I didn't even know that he had any children, even though we were married for several years."

Such heartbreak . . . I have a father who doesn't even mention his own children to his wife? What kind of a man is this? Doesn't he love anybody? How could I be so dramatically different in every way from the man who is my biological father? *My* heart is full of love for so many people in my life: my mother, brothers, friends, and especially the downtrodden—and even my father. I leave Sandusky determined to squelch my interest in finding or understanding Melvin Lyle Dyer.

I return to Detroit and pour myself into my life as a local grocery-store assistant manager, earning a good living and helping my mother out financially. I have run into a myriad of obstacles attempting to locate this man who's on the run, who leaves heartbreak wherever he temporarily settles—but the yearning to know him never subsides. The bad dreams continue for years.

Twenty years will pass before I'm able to recognize him as my greatest teacher.

I Can See Clearly Now

As much as I wanted my father to show up and love me when I was a young boy, I now value his absence as one of the greatest gifts I've been granted. His waywardness and abandonment of me was truly part of my coming here to teach self-reliance, which is the one great theme of my life. I have been doing precisely this since I was a child, and it has dominated my entire life's work.

It's so clear that there are no mistakes in this universe. The stars are all in alignment. The sun is the exact distance from Earth, to the millimeter, to create and sustain life. There is a precision to this universe, whether looking through a telescope or a microscope, that defies intellectual comprehension. It is all perfect down to the tiniest subatomic particle and outward to the most distant celestial body. Included within this precision is all that comes our way as well, even though an understanding of the *why* is frequently not apparent.

I needed to be in a position of relying upon myself if I was to fulfill my own purpose and live out my dharma to be a spiritual teacher of self-reliance. My years spent in foster homes provided me with the opportunity to learn this firsthand. I had to rely upon myself—there was no one there to do it for me.

My relationship to my father was to be the single most significant relationship of my life. My wanting him to show up for me on my timetable, when I thought I needed him so desperately, was my own ego at work. Everything shows up in Divine time. We get what we need on the schedule of a force much larger than ourselves. This invisible force moves the pieces around in its own way, in its own time, to harmonize with the perfect precision that defines every cubic inch of space and time.

It might seem far-fetched to some, but I believe that my life without the benefit of a father was perfect in every way. From this vantage point I see that my books, lectures, films, and recordings came about because my father was absent from my life. My ego wanted him, but my spirit knew that I had a far greater purpose to fulfill.

Those years that I spent in agony over why and how a man could be so insensitive, so cruel, so distant, always ended up leaving me no other option other than to go within and resolve the issues for myself, or to turn to a new kind of Divine love practiced only by great spiritual masters and God himself—a love awash in forgiveness. Everything I needed to remain on course in my life was being provided—though the child I was couldn't know it at the time.

Today, from the perspective of looking back over my life, I can see that everything was absolutely perfect. Without my knowing it I was in some kind of training right from the get-go. Perhaps my father agreed to come into this world from the world of Spirit and live his own life in such a way that it would require his youngest son to learn how to live a life of self-reliance as a toddler, a teenager, and then a young adult.

Being given the opportunity to send love and forgiveness to my father for all of his perverse, mercurial behavior perhaps was a training stage for helping millions of people transform their own lives with a vision aligned with a God-realized perspective. I feel my father's presence frequently, and whenever I sense him near, it is like a soft mist of infinite love rather than the storms of fierce rage and angst that previously typified my thoughts of this man.

Yes, he was my greatest teacher. I know with certainty God works in mysterious ways—but not in accidental ways. Indeed, it is, and always has been, perfect in every way. I am so grateful.

10

In 1958 the possibility of being drafted into the Army and serving as a foot soldier is one of the most appalling scenarios I can imagine for myself. Being a factory worker in one of the automotive companies in Detroit, which many 18-year-olds from my neighborhood have done after completing high school, also has very low appeal for me. So I've opted to sign up for the Navy, as my oldest brother, Jim, did two years ago. Here I am two weeks later in Great Lakes, Illinois, feeling sick to my stomach as I wonder, *What have I done to myself?*

In my bunk bed early in the morning, I take stock of my new life. Last night I counted hundreds of cockroaches crawling over clothing, bedding, and sleeping bodies—had I chosen to, I could have counted to infinity. The place is overrun with this vermin who live in the cracks until the lights go out, and then come out in swarms, feasting on crumbs and living out their nocturnal destinies. I gag at the thought of them slithering over my face, but the cockroaches are a minor problem.

I've lived in many places and learned early in my life to not judge my circumstances. I have no allergies, no foods I won't eat, and no aversions to bodily functions. It's not that I'm having difficulty adjusting to living in close quarters with hundreds of men in the cramped quarters of the barracks of Company 417 here at the Naval Station Great Lakes. The cockroaches and smelly bathroom aromas are nothing compared to what's expected of me as a full-time active-duty member of the armed forces, where the rules rule.

The rules are that I am not to ever think for myself. I am to obey any order given to me by any superior and never question that order. Disobedience has serious consequences, including being put in confinement. There's a chain of command operating at all times, and I am to accept my role as the lowest of the low—doing what I'm told to do, and what everyone else is told to do as well. There is no individuality here. I am to simply say, "Yes, sir!" and obey.

I am told what time to go to sleep, when to awaken, what and when to eat, and what to wear, which is the same as what everyone else is wearing. My hair is all cut off, my shoes must be spit shined, and my face must be clean shaven and inspected several times a day by a superior who barks into my face that I'm a puny runt—to which I am to respond, "Yes, sir!" or incur his feigned wrath and be given some kind of absurd punishment.

Although I don't at the present time think in these terms, I believe on some level that this can't possibly be the place for someone who has incarnated into this earthly domain to teach self-reliance.

There is no escaping this military mind-set. I am being taught that there is no self, and that I will rely upon my superiors and their rules for any identification that I might require. I will wear the same uniform for the next four years, and I will either conform or go AWOL, the penalty for which is a long term in the brig and an undesirable discharge. I choose to accept this fate, knowing that I am something much more than a body—and whatever they decide to do to my body, I have the option of being in a state of peace within. I can live with the rules.

I make the choice to be obedient, and I can even acknowledge the need for this arrangement in an organization designed to engage in warfare. Doing what you're told without thinking or asking questions is necessary when destroying an enemy is the overall objective. I decide that I'll comply with the rules on the outside, but I will never accede on the inside. I will do these four years honorably, but within myself I will have no enemies. I will remain constant, convinced that I am a man of peace, treasuring and respecting everyone's individuality.

I am at peace with this new regimented way of living, trusting in my ability to be self-reliant and still function within the military establishment. I abhor the silly regulations and inspections, and I know myself well enough to be certain that I'll ultimately figure out a way to avoid them without anyone knowing what I am up to. My inner world is secure, and I will make a fun game of getting around the insanity of this way of life.

I am generally perplexed by what I see in my fellow young sailors. Whenever given a few moments of leisure, I notice that these grown men are happily perusing comic books—*Superman, Captain Marvel, Batman and Robin, Archie.* Most of them have reading levels and interests quite different from mine, yet these are the people I live with day and night.

On our first liberty, we have the opportunity to spend a weekend in Chicago, with a deadline to be back at the base by 10:00 P.M. Sunday. Wearing my uniform, I go into the city by train and spend my time walking around. I talk to many of the merchants who are anxious to reap a profit from these newly released young men having their first taste of freedom in two months.

The city teems with tattoo parlors, bars, prostitutes, and cheap souvenirs, which I see my colleagues exuberantly partaking of with their new freedom. I return to the base at Great Lakes early, and the barracks begin to fill up with several hundred severely inebriated sailors. Three out of four of my fellow sailors have had their bodies inked with large permanent tattoos, and all are swearing and hurling racial slurs in their states of out-of-control drunkenness and vomiting. *Does anyone read books?* I wonder. *Are these really to be my friends and comrades for the next four years of my life?*

I know it's impossible for me to permanently deface my body with symbols of the U.S. Navy, or anything else. I have long despised drunken behavior, and now I am surrounded by it. I have been writing my own novel, and now I am encased in a world where comic books, profanity, and prejudice abound. I despise violence of any kind, and now I am being prepared to be an instrument of killing, to wear a gun on guard duty, to take pride in exterminating assigned enemies. I become much more introspective and solitary.

What the hell am I doing here? I ask myself over and over. *This isn't what I'm here in the world to do. I see the reason for the existence of a military, but this is not my role. I am a fish out of water. I want to be a person who works toward creating a world where guns and battleships and hatreds and enemies are extinct.*

I'm perplexed because I made this choice so willingly. It seemed like precisely the right thing to do when I graduated from high school. I had no idea that this military lifestyle was designed to stifle all forms of independent thinking.

I think back to all of the times I was in conflict with authority figures who were persistently pushing me into a groupthink mentality. I think of a quote by E. E. Cummings that I memorized in high school English class: "To be nobody-but-yourself—in a world which is doing its best, night and day, to make you everybody else—means to fight the hardest battle which any human being can fight; and never stop fighting." And here I am, trapped in an organization I freely joined that's organized around the principle of making everyone just like everyone else.

I Can See Clearly Now

During my adjustment period of becoming accustomed to the stringent requirements of military life, I felt as if I had made the biggest mistake of my life in signing on for a four-year tour of active duty. From this vantage point of viewing it from a distance, it is all unclouded and crystal clear to me. While making the decision to join the armed forces at the age of 18, I can remember feeling that I was in some mysterious way being guided by an invisible hand. I knew beforehand that this type of regimented lifestyle was going to be anathema to me, largely because I had always championed the right to freely make my own choices without anyone telling me how to live and what to do. Yet there I was, talking to a Navy recruiter in downtown Detroit and signing an agreement to enlist in a few short weeks. It was as if I absolutely had to go through with this crazy impulse even though I also knew that it was going to be a monumental conflict for me.

What I know for sure is that in order to understand something *intellectually,* one must study it, analyze it, cogitate on it, examine what others have said about it, review formulas about it, and ultimately come to a conclusion and take an exam on it—getting a passing grade after all of this cerebral maneuvering. But in order to come to know and understand something *spiritually,* one must experience it—there is no other way.

I could write in endless detail about what an avocado tastes like, comparing its flavor to other foods and ultimately offering you a written discourse on this topic. Yet the only way you can know the sensation of eating an avocado is to experience it. As you eat it you become one with it, and you *know,* beyond any possibility of conveying the experience of it to anyone else. I knew that I disliked being told how to live my life. I knew that I rebelled against authority dictating to me, but in order to really have this brought home to me spiritually —where it would make a huge impact on me and send me in the direction of teaching self-reliance and self-actualization as a lifetime assignment—I had to experience it firsthand.

I have often cited the idea that the storms of our lives, the low points, the difficult times, are things to be grateful for. My brother David lived through over 50 years of alcoholism, a compulsive addiction to nicotine, merciless shyness and self-doubt, and an atheistic view of life. And then when he was 68, a diagnosis of Parkinson's disease that he was told was incurable and would lead to a life as an invalid turned everything around.

My brother decided to quit drinking and smoking, he began writing every day, he lost his timid personality traits, and began to speak in public before large audiences. He found God and volunteered to serve others who were less fortunate, and he published his book. He attributes all of these turnarounds in his life to his diagnosis of Parkinson's —his greatest teacher.

I can see clearly now that in order for me to get firmly on the path that I signed up for in this incarnation, I had to experience and truly know what it was that I didn't like. Those years in the military where I was expected to fit in and become just like everyone else offered me a firsthand opportunity to experience what I disliked so adamantly, and then to seek out and live from a perspective of knowing what I had to do, when that regimented time was over for me. I am so grateful for those early experiences.

My intense dislike for all things authoritarian propelled me to be just as fervent in living and teaching what I love and believe in. From this perspective, I know that gratitude needs to be expressed for all of it, even the stuff that seemed so insufferable at the time. There was a reason for my being pushed in that direction, and every day I'm grateful. In the present day, with my diagnosis of leukemia, I'm able to welcome it and know that it will bring me to a higher place—just as my military experiences did more than 50 years ago.

11

Boot camp behind me, I'm in Bainbridge, Maryland, attending school for six months to become a radioman and cryptographer. School is arduous, with daily classes from early morning until late in the evening, and requires nightly study. Mornings are spent learning Morse code, converting the dash-dot sounds into letters, and we have exams every other day. My classes also include study in the areas of communications, electronics, physics, learning to operate the latest equipment, encoding and decoding, and mastering typing. My subconscious mind is learning how to respond automatically when I hear the sounds in my headphones.

I am totally committed to pursuing this six-month academic adventure with excellence, and I'm reminded that when I choose to apply myself I can literally master any discipline. Back in high school, when I loved a subject I invariably received a grade of *A.* When I was uninterested, I'd simply withdraw, unattached to whether I got a passing or failing grade. Here in radioman school I am one determined young sailor; I strive to not only pass the course, but to do so with distinction. At graduation, I am at the top of my class.

My best friend at Bainbridge is a 19-year-old young man named Ray Dudley from Chicago. We study together, we bond like brothers, and basically we become inseparable. When we leave the base to go to Baltimore or Washington, D.C., for a weekend, we frequently do so together.

Ray and I are returning to the base after a weekend in D.C. It's 10 P.M. on a Sunday night and we are due back on base at Bainbridge before midnight. We decide to stop in the little town of Havre de Grace, Maryland, and have a dish of fried rice, as we haven't eaten all day. It is an inexpensive meal for two hungry sailors in the uniform of the United States Navy before the ten-mile cab ride to the base.

I'm startled when I hear, "Sorry, boys, we can't serve you in this restaurant." I ask the waitress why that is—the restaurant is open until midnight, and there are lots of returning servicemen eating. She looks sheepishly at me and simply shrugs her shoulders and points at my best friend, a U.S. Navy serviceman serving his country as a member of the armed forces . . . and then it hits me squarely in the face, as if someone just punched me with a vicious blow. Ray is an African American, and in this little town in Maryland they don't serve people who do not have white skin.

I ask to speak to a manager, but no one of higher authority appears. The waitress doesn't want to have an unpleasant scene, but I am outraged and embarrassed for my friend. Ray has lived with this kind of prejudice all of his life and motions to me to leave quietly to avoid any possibility of a serious conflict.

I have never experienced the horror of racial prejudice like this. I am perplexed, deeply saddened, and so hurt for my friend. But more than this, I am outraged at the insanity of refusing to serve another human being who is wearing the uniform of the armed forces of his country, and willing to go to war and die so that the opportunity to live and breathe freely is preserved for everyone—even the owners of restaurants, and the waitresses who work there.

I apologize to Ray as we head back to our barracks at the Bainbridge Naval Base. I vow to myself to never, ever prejudge anyone on the basis of their appearance. I am shaken to my core. I am changed forever. I will dedicate my life to ridding the world of such moronic thinking. Every day for the remainder of my time at Bainbridge, I am obsessed with what I, as one man, can do to eradicate this kind of simpleminded behavior. It is my life's mission. I am committed to being a man who judges no one.

I Can See Clearly Now

That Sunday night in Havre de Grace still stands out as one of the most influential evenings of my life, even though it was more than 50 years ago. That moment of looking into my friend Ray's eyes and seeing the pain that prejudice can cause inspired me to make a commitment to abolish prejudgment from my own way of being, and to incorporate this love for all of humanity as a cornerstone of my life's work.

From that night on, I became fully aware of my own propensity for labeling people on the basis of any external factors, and I began to traverse a path wherein I was able to see the unfolding of Spirit in every person I encountered. In many respects, that experience as a 19-year-old sailor was Divinely orchestrated. I had to be there as a witness and an unwilling participant in order to have the horror of this kind of behavior brought home to me.

That hapless waitress was only reacting due to inbred conditioning that had been imposed upon her by cultural circumstances when she was a child. She saw mistreatment of people with dark skin and accepted it as the thing to do. She was also an employee who was just "doing what I'm told to do—it's my job." This mentality has been the driving force behind endless heinous acts over the centuries. In order to replace these habits with behavior that is compassionate rather than prejudiced, people must examine how their subconscious minds have been programmed and then begin to change these habitual ways of being.

Back in 1959 I began to do precisely that. I had heard plenty of nigger/spic/kike/dago/Polack talk as I was growing up in the 1940s and '50s, and though I have no memory of ever using such language in my lifetime, I know that I witnessed it regularly and it didn't arouse any sense of outrage within me. My experience with Ray Dudley turned me around. I began a slow transformation of expressing my disdain for such language without making a scene. I began to read books that dealt with the subject of prejudice and hatred, and I railed against policies of the Navy wherein segregation was an established norm. As I look back on two of the most consequential themes of my writing and of my adult development, they both harken back to that painful night in Maryland.

The first of these themes is teaching people how to have a mind of their own, independent of what they have been taught to believe. If I know it is wrong and not in harmony with the Divine love espoused by our most revered spiritual masters, then regardless of what I have been taught, I must think for myself and come always from a place of love. If we are told that God is love, then we shouldn't just say it in our place of worship during a ceremonial weekly religious service. We must live it.

The second theme involves the subconscious mind wherein adult habits are ingrained. I wrote of my time in radio school learning Morse code. I practiced and practiced until it went from a conscious-mind activity to a permanent place in my subconscious habitual mind. I haven't used Morse code in over half a century—and every bit of the programming continues to be present in my being. I can still spell out any word or sentence instantaneously in my mind using the dots and dashes that were placed there several decades ago.

Similarly, we all have other ideas that we call *memes,* which drive our behavior today. Even though they may not serve us, they are still there operating, just like my unconscious tapping out of the Morse code today. That waitress in the restaurant in Havre de Grace in 1959 was acting out both of the themes. She was doing what she was told to do, even though her body language was saying, *I don't really feel this way—I'm just doing my job;* and she was also acting out of a host of memes that she had never taken the opportunity to correct and then eradicate completely from her subconscious mind.

I can still see that waitress and my young African-American friend Ray Dudley in my mind as I write these words. I believe they were both sent into my life that Sunday night to help me to not only see the light but to teach from a more illumined perspective.

12

It's the middle of winter in 1959; I have been temporarily assigned to a brief tour of duty at Naval Air Station Patuxent River by Lexington Park, Maryland. I decide to put on my uniform and hitchhike home to Detroit to visit my mother, and especially my girlfriend, Linda, who is matriculating at the University of Michigan in Ann Arbor. It is a distance of approximately 590 miles, and it usually takes 12 to 14 hours. Being in uniform generally means that someone will stop and give me a ride regardless of where I might be stranded.

I've made this trip several times, and I'm confident that I can get home by Saturday morning, have a full day and a half at home, and then hitch back to the base in order to make curfew at midnight on Sunday. It is a long haul and a lot of time hitchhiking on the road, but well worth it to a homesick, lovelorn sailor who is just beginning to become accustomed to being away from home for long periods of time.

I set out on my weekend jaunt and catch a ride all the way to Washington, D.C. Several connections later I arrive at the Breezewood entrance to the Pennsylvania Turnpike. By now it's close to midnight and the temperature has dropped dramatically. In the bitter cold I manage to catch a ride heading westbound, but the driver informs me that he's only going as far as Butler, Pennsylvania. He doesn't want to drop me off at the exit in the middle of the night because I'd be in grave danger of freezing to death—it's well below zero, and the winds are blowing fiercely. I'm wearing a dark blue Navy peacoat, and standing in the dark unable to be seen by the drivers heading west on the turnpike could be disastrous. This friendly driver insists on dropping me off at one of the service-plaza restaurant stops on the turnpike just before his exit a few miles ahead. I agree.

I head into the restaurant at around 3 A.M., get a cup of hot chocolate, and then head out to try my luck at catching a westbound vehicle—in the middle of the night, in the middle of what feels like nowhere, in the midst of the coldest weather I have ever experienced. On my way out to the ramp in the freezing darkness, I pass another sailor walking back to the restaurant. He has had no luck in securing a ride and tells me, "It's bitter cold out there, buddy. I wouldn't stand there too long; you could easily get frostbite if you're not careful."

I acknowledge him, wish him well, and head out to the turnpike. I stand there for 15 or 20 minutes—no luck. Almost frozen stiff, I decide to head back to warm up. When I enter the restaurant there's only one person in the place: the sailor who spoke to me a few moments earlier, warning me not to stay out there too long. Imagine my surprise when I realize this sailor is my brother!

Jim is stationed in Norfolk, Virginia. He too had decided to hitchhike home to see our mother and his fiancée, Marilyn, for the weekend; he too had been dropped off at the same exact spot. I had no idea that Jim's submarine was even in port. I hadn't had any contact with my brother in months, since his whereabouts on the sub were considered classified information. My own brother had spoken to me and warned me to be careful without even knowing that it was me. Together we stand in shocked disbelief at the mysterious forces that were at play in order to have this scene be a reality.

We meet the driver of an 18-wheeler who's gassing up and tell him of the incredible "coincidence" that's just transpired. This synchronistic event that brought Jim and me together in the middle of nowhere under these impossible conditions so impacts the truck driver that he drives us, out of his way, right to our front door at 20217 Moross Road in Detroit early on Saturday morning.

I Can See Clearly Now

I cannot begin to tell you how many times Jim and I have shared the above story in the past 50-plus years, and the conclusion is the always same: it's just one of those bizarre coincidences that show up and defy a rational explanation. This event was deeply meaningful to the 19-year-old sailor I was. It introduced me to the world of synchronicity, quantum physics, and the idea that there are no accidents in a world governed by a Divine intelligence.

Today I look back at all of the events that had to come together perfectly for my brother and me to have that encounter in the middle of the night so many years ago, and I am no longer surprised. My life has been crammed full with these kinds of happenings—but this was the first big one that really caught my attention and changed the way I looked at things forever.

I can see clearly that I had to rid myself of all doubts about the possibility of all things coming together in Divine order and in Divine time. My writing and speaking have been dominated by this grand idea of *synchronicity,* which is a term coined by Carl Jung to explain what he called "meaningful coincidences." The synchronistic incident that brought this to Jung's attention occurred during a session with a client who was relating a dream. As his client pondered the significance of a beetle in the dream, they both heard a noise—which turned out to be a beetle on the window attracting their attention. I now see that this synchronistic event with my brother, which goes way beyond logical thought and defies the incredible odds against such a thing transpiring by chance, was needed so that I could open myself to the possibility that all things are connected and on purpose. I personally needed to be liberated from my own excessive rationalism at that time in my life.

In order to eventually write and speak about the world of Spirit I needed to know at the young age of 19 that there are no accidents or coincidences in a universe that is truly created and guided by invisible forces that elude rational explanation. I now see that we have no idea how anything gets created in this physical universe and that everything originates in something called Spirit, which no one can define or come close to explaining—including our greatest scientific minds.

There is every reason to believe there is intelligence behind life. As Max Planck, a great scientific mind who received a Nobel Prize in Physics, noted: "All matter originates and exists only by virtue of a force which brings the particle of an atom to vibration and holds this most minute solar system of the atom together. We must assume behind this force the existence of a conscious and intelligent mind. This mind is the matrix of all matter." This being so, then all of that intelligence is innate in each creation of that intelligence, which means it is in everything and everyone and it is directing the entire play.

This intelligence is so stupendously mysterious that it is able to create worlds and galaxies so vast as to stupefy even the most open-minded imaginations. An intelligence that can keep the entire universe in perfect balance and create a rose from scratch, an intelligence that is in all things—"The spirit that gives life," as Jesus said. This invisible intelligence can and does create miracles every second of every day. Bringing two brothers together in the middle of the Pennsylvania Turnpike is a minor achievement compared to creating life from nothing and assembling an infinite number of heavenly bodies to comprise an entire universe. I cannot conceive of a watch without a watchmaker, so it is impossible for me to believe this universe exists without an intelligence that is the *matrix of all matter*—a creator.

When I look back at this experience of synchronicity that occurred in 1959, it appears clearly to me to have opened my eyes to the possibility of a Divine design that contributes clues to our destiny. I felt then that both Jim and I were involved in a collaboration with fate, and I began considering my contribution consciously. I wanted to align my life with this miraculous invisible energy. I began choosing a mind-set that was aware that I was much more than a mere human form—that I was Spirit itself—that the life inside me was truly Divine. As I stepped back and observed from this place of total belief in my own magnificence and my connection to this grand invisible Spirit, I began to be a co-creator of more and more synchronistic events.

This experience was the first that I can remember that startled me into seeing that life wasn't exclusively factual and physical. I was and still am convinced that an event of this nature is not an accidental happenstance. From that day forward I began to think in new ways. I did not share this newly awakened awareness with anyone at the time. But I knew that I was involved in something much bigger than just going through the motions of life as it was being handed to me.

I began to hear the silence that seemed to gently murmur about my inner life and of seemingly miraculous happenings. There was, it seemed clear to me, a synchronistic tie-in to everyone and everything—all of life was interconnected. I thought of the drivers who dropped Jim and me off at that turnpike rest stop and I began to see them as a part of the drama of my life, and me as a part of theirs. This was my opening to an awareness of the Divine force moving through our lives.

From my perspective of looking back at this event so many years later, I see clearly that I was beginning to liberate myself from the chronological cause-and-effect way I had been trained to think. I was beginning to cultivate a mind that's truly open to everything and attached to nothing. It seems that the 19-year-old me welcomed discovering this theme that eventually would permeate his life's work—surrender and know that it is all just the way it's supposed to be.

Albert Einstein was right: "There are only two ways to live your life. One is as though nothing is a miracle. The other is as though everything is a miracle." Or as Buddha said, "If we could see the miracle of a single flower clearly, our whole life would change." This miraculous event allowed me to see clearly and begin co-creating my own life, and teach others how to co-create their lives as well. As I look back now I give thanks for all of the participants who collaborated to bring about this wondrous awakening in me.

13

It is the summer of 1960 and I am a communications specialist aboard the largest ship in the world, the USS *Ranger.* We're home-ported in Alameda, California, following a six-month tour of naval bases and hot spots in the western Pacific—including Japan, Hong Kong, the Philippines, and Hawaii—and now we're back in the continental United States.

All of a sudden, this announcement booms over the loudspeakers on the ship: "You will report to the flight deck and stand in a formation that spells out 'Hi Ike' as President Eisenhower flies over our ship in a helicopter."

I'm in a state of outrage over this order to gather with several thousand of my colleagues and participate in this absurd spectacle so that one man can look down and see this message, spelled out by a group of sailors wearing white hats. No way can I be one of a group acting like a flock of geese doing what they've been told to do, for no sensible reason that I can grasp.

I detest this mentality, and find such inane activities profoundly insulting and an affront to my dignity. I am a petty officer third class—a skilled professional with monumental responsibilities. I am totally unwilling to be herded into a group to stand in the hot sun dotting the "i" in "Hi Ike" in order to make a political statement for the Republican party during this election year.

It's a constant struggle for me to maintain my own singularity and still function within an organization that does everything it can to suppress any thoughts of individuality. The name of the game is groupthink. The rules are: do as you are told and ask no questions; forget your pride, your ego, your desire to have a mind of your own; obey all orders, and suppress any thoughts of disputing offensive orders. I know I have less than two years to serve and then I will be free of this mentality. I want an honorable discharge. I want to go to college and become a teacher. I want to make it through the rest of my enlistment avoiding any confrontations over my inner pride. But—and this is a big but—I simply cannot allow myself to participate in this charade.

For the past two years I've successfully avoided most of the military exercises that cause umbrage to my soul. I've learned how to be in other places legally when those mortifying inspections are called, and I've spoken about it to no one. I know not to make waves and draw attention to myself—I call it being *quietly effective.* I know what is an outrage to my soul, and I don't need to make a federal case about it. I despise inspections, so I find out when they're scheduled and get myself assigned to do something else while they take place. When I'm told I must carry a gun and stand guard duty, I get a permission slip to be elsewhere. I detest guns and instruments of death. I don't want to make a speech about it; I simply don't want to have these vile killing devices on my person at any time. I'm pleased with myself for figuring out how to stay within the system and still eschew the parts of the system that so violate my own personal inner standards.

As 2,000 enlisted sailors head to the flight deck to be told how to stand in the formation that spells out "Hi Ike," I head in the opposite direction—down, down, down into the lower decks, where I can sit in solitude until the madness above me subsides. There are too many people for anyone to miss me; no one will ever know that I am missing. Nor will they ever know how much contempt this provokes in me.

I just can't figure out why people who feel just as strongly about this as I do simply go along and allow themselves to be used in this manner. On the other hand, I reason, if everyone handles these kinds of situations as I do, then it would be impossible for me to do as I do—so in many ways I'm grateful for those who just go along and conform. It allows me to slip out of sight unnoticed and still maintain a shred of dignity without explaining myself to people who choose to conform.

I meditate quietly and read a novel that's currently on the best-seller list. I am immersed in the story of Atticus Finch fighting the system and battling prejudice. This is my third reading of Harper Lee's *To Kill a Mockingbird,* though it was released only a few months ago. This is not a book you read once and then put away.

Atticus Finch is an individual of towering integrity, a heroic Southern lawyer in Alabama who stands up for what is right. I am enthralled as he tells his daughter, Scout, that he could never hold his head up in front of his children again if he didn't take this case. He explains that he must take it even though everyone thinks he is wrong. As I reread *To Kill a Mockingbird* below decks, I'm pleased with myself for not going along with the herd of sailors above. I feel encouraged about my choice to listen to that still voice within me that says, *You don't have to be just like everybody else . . . there is another way.*

I Can See Clearly Now

I can still see myself sitting in an isolated boiler room nine decks below the flight deck reading Harper Lee's book. There's the 20-year-old me, awed by a fictional character defying the pressure to act just like everyone else, and listening instead to that implacable voice within him beckoning to him to follow his heart to be the person he was destined to be.

The theme of that "Hi Ike" story threads itself through all of the items on my résumé over the past 40 years. I feel that the persistent, insistent inner calling to resist conformity was Divinely designed to display my life purpose to me. I've never known a person who, after talking to them for an hour or so, didn't feel that they had a Divinely inspired mission. I felt it profoundly throughout my life. And I know now that the experience I had with Harper Lee's Pulitzer Prize–winning novel and my clamoring to escape the scene unfolding on the flight deck of my ship was a signal moment in my life. It is as clear to me today, some 50-plus years later, as it was when I returned to my sleeping quarters after everyone was dismissed from their ludicrous assignment up top.

I think often of these words of St. Paul: "Do not be conformed to this world, but be transformed by the renewal of your mind" (Romans 12:2). And the great Sufi teaching that instructs us "To be in the world, but not of it." I have written often of the idea that we are not our body, but rather infinite beings who keep occupying a new body every moment of every day we live. As I escaped the inane requirements that the military placed on my body, a part of me knew that I too was in this world as a body, but I was not of this corporeal world of form. I was going beyond form—being transformed right there on board my ship.

I can see that those strong impulses to be quietly effective and avoid activities that seemed preposterous to me were early training exercises for teaching me self-sufficiency. At this point, I'm deeply grateful that Harper Lee's *To Kill a Mockingbird* showed up when it did, and for the decision by the powers that be to conduct that "Hi Ike" ceremony! My consciousness needed those incidents to inspire me to start writing essays that eventually became books that encourage millions of people around the world to have the courage to listen to their own inner callings.

About a decade ago, when my son turned 13 years of age, I wrote him a letter about what it meant to reach this age and become a man, as is taught in many spiritual traditions. I ended by giving him this sage wisdom: "If you follow the herd, you'll end up stepping in shit." The shit I refer to is living with yourself when you ignore what you know to be right and true and instead follow the "offal" instructions of others who are afraid to leave the herd and want you to be just like everybody else.

14

I have been assigned to a post on the island of Guam in the South Pacific for the last 18 months of my enlistment. I've been promoted to petty officer second class and am supervisor at the naval communications center near the city of Agana.

I've been reading daily editorials and stories in the *Guam Daily News* about a discriminatory policy on the naval base. Civilians working in the retail stores have the privilege of shopping at these outlets and thus are able to take advantage of the sizable discounts offered for all military personnel on active duty—unless you are a civilian employee who happens to be of Guamanian descent. Then this privilege is not for you. If your skin is dark and you are a Guamanian, then you are excluded. Once again this kind of discrimination surfaces in my life. This time it's sanctioned by the U.S. Navy—the military service for whom I work as well.

One Saturday morning, I notice this ad on the back page of the paper:

> This is an invitation to speak your mind. A $75.00 first prize for the winning letter on the policy of the U.S. Navy's ban on shopping at the Navy Exchange for civilian employees who are of Guamanian descent.

I know that if I enter this contest I will win the prize—it will be my first payment for something I've been doing daily for the past several years. I have an extensive collection of essays that I have been writing on a wide variety of topics.

Writing essays is more than a hobby—it's become a passion. I discover topics everywhere. Behavior that I could never in a billion years participate in myself catches my attention—for example, a news clip of people wearing silly hats and chanting a candidate's name at a political convention, jumping to their feet at an applause line, demands an essay on the inclination of average people to behave foolishly when they're with others who do so.

I feel it is so important to trust in your own individuality and live from a perspective of being extraordinary rather than ordinary. I've written several hundred essays, without any idea what to do with them, or even why I write them. It is simply my passion, and that inner calling is working overtime in me as I finish out my enlistment here on this island in the South Pacific.

I send in my entry for the letter-writing contest that very evening. Two weeks later I receive a phone call from the newspaper advising me that I submitted the winning entry. I had obviously taken the position of supporting the local Guamanian civilians and railing against the Navy policy of excluding people from special privileges on the basis of their national origin and skin color. I receive $75.00, and my picture appears on the front page of the *Guam Daily News* in my Navy uniform holding my prize. And then all hell breaks loose.

I receive dozens of angry phone calls, including one death threat. It seems that the civilians who are mostly relatives and dependents of armed forces active-duty personnel are very upset at the idea that Guamanian civilians would be given the same entitlements that they enjoy. Racial prejudice is evidenced by the epithets directed at me for supporting these "savages" and "non-Americans."

I am in shock. My letter simply stood up for the equal rights the Constitution guarantees, as well as for simple fair-mindedness. Why should anyone have special benefits that are denied to others simply because of their place of birth? If any civilians are to be granted these advantages, then all civilians should be. It seems so clear and simple to me.

I am called before the Commander of the Naval Forces Mariana Islands and told that I violated the Uniform Code of Military Justice, which I'm informed requires me to submit my opinions to my superiors for approval before making them public. Because I went ahead on my own and expressed an opinion that contrasted with existing Navy policy, and because I was photographed in uniform accepting money for writing that opinion, I could be considered for a possible court-martial. I could be reduced in rank and possibly given a less-than-honorable discharge from the armed forces. All this for a simple letter expressing an opinion that just seemed so obvious to me.

I have a couple of weeks to stew over this before the Commander of the Naval Forces makes a decision, so I immediately spring into action. I write letters to the editors of *The Detroit News* and the *Detroit Free Press,* two newspapers that I delivered door-to-door when I turned ten, in which I detail what is taking place here on Guam. I also write a lengthy letter to the President of the United States, John F. Kennedy, spelling out the discriminatory policy that is in place here on Guam. I tell him how I am being threatened for expressing views that he spoke so eloquently about in his inaugural address a year ago. I make copies of these letters, but I do not mail any of them.

I am summoned by a young ensign who is an assistant to the admiral who is the Commander of the Naval Forces here in the Mariana Islands. He begins to give me a lecture on what could happen to me, and tells me that I have committed a grievous violation and am being considered for a serious reprimand and possible further retribution.

I am polite, but firmly resolute. I totally believe that the Navy is way out of line and practicing discrimination, something that the Commander in Chief has vowed to eliminate in our country, and I assume this means the armed forces as well. I tell this officer that I am not afraid of their threats—and although I do not want to jeopardize my upcoming discharge date, and I definitely do not wish to be court-martialed for winning a letter-writing contest on why this kind of bias is improper and even illegal, I will not back down.

I show him the copies of the letters I have written and tell him softly but firmly that this could become a huge eyesore, not only for Commander of the Naval Forces but for the entire U.S Navy—which up until only a year or so before was still practicing segregation policies on their ships at sea and their bases abroad, and I was a witness to this outrage throughout my enlistment. I tell him if I am to be court-martialed, then I will definitely be sending these letters when the proceedings commence.

This is all being said in a very civil and friendly environment. I'm convinced there's absolutely no intent by my superiors to take this matter to a court-martial. I believe I'm being bullied because of the large number of complaints they've received about an enlisted sailor who had the temerity to speak out publicly about long-established Navy policy.

I leave the ensign's office and never hear another word about the matter, though the threatening phone calls and letters continue to show up at my living quarters.

I Can See Clearly Now

Although I was just in my early 20s, I was being directed to be a person who could make a difference, who could stand up to authority for what I believe in, and do it fearlessly. I recall my outrage at the way a minority group of people was being treated unfairly, and I was to learn as a result of my own intervention in the matter that yes indeed, one person with a conscience who was unwilling to be intimidated could bring about change; and yes, when I was back in Detroit as a college freshman, I received a letter from a friend telling me that the discriminatory policy toward the Guamanian civilians had been revoked and they'd been granted the same privileges as all of the other civilian employees. This was a monumental experience for my own development. It stands out even today, 50 years later, as one of the paramount lessons I was to learn. After all, it did shape my entire writing and speaking career.

Somehow the universe conspired to place me on Guam for the final 18 months of my naval career. It was on that island that I felt an overwhelming knowing that I could not only be a writer, but I could earn a living doing so. When I mailed in my entry to the *Guam Daily News,* I had not a shred of doubt the prize money was mine. I felt an invisible Source of energy with me as I composed my response to the Navy's misinformed policy of maltreatment toward a minority group. When I was notified of my prize, I said to myself, "I can do anything with the power of the pen. I can not only change policies, I can impact people's lives with my writing." That little contest on the faraway island served as a linchpin for me to engage in writing in a big way.

Throughout my writing and speaking career, I have been telling audiences to above all else trust in themselves and never allow any force outside of them to take them away from what they feel to be their truth. Standing there in that admiral's outer office and presenting my case to that young naval officer was a key role I had to play. It was as if my Source of being was saying to me, "Here is a fork in the road. Which way do you wish for your life to go?" This wasn't something I was doing to make a point; this was to be a tipping point for me, and there was no way that I could retreat and give in to fear.

This experience contributed to launching me into a writing career. I feel that young ensign was placed there as a guide for all that I was destined to take on in the future. I watched his face as he smiled at my lack of fear over his plans for dealing with me in a harsh military manner. I knew that he was an ally, and I felt certain that he would do what I requested and make this silly thing disappear.

At the end of my military enlistment, I was given the opportunity to write for a newspaper and be paid to do so, as well as to test my resolve. I was given the opportunity to experience the power of fearlessness and unwillingness to compromise values, and be instrumental in overturning an immoral policy. I often give thanks to all of the individuals who aligned to bring this all about and launch me into the work that I have been doing for so many years. The person at the *Guam Daily News* who decided to run this contest; the forces that determined I was to be assigned to this isolated place; the people who called threatening me, thereby intensifying my resolve; the young ensign; and on and on they go.

From this perspective, I can see clearly that I was destined to open that newspaper on that Saturday morning on Guam and accept the challenge of the letter-writing contest. I am so grateful for every moment of that experience, which taught me *Don't ever give up, trust in yourself, know that you can change the world, be fearless, reach out and serve those who are in need. And don't ever let anyone restrict you from what you feel deep within you, especially when they attempt to intimidate you.*

15

Excessive sitting while working at the communications equipment combined with the tropical humidity has caused a severe soreness and some swelling to develop at the base of my spine. It's diagnosed as a pilonidal cyst, which is common in young men (in fact, this diagnosis is most prevalent in males under the age of 24). According to the naval doctor I see on Guam, they have an entire ward of young men suffering from this affliction.

I report to the hospital in Agana, where I'm assigned for the three days prior to the minor surgical procedure that will be performed on me. My duties are to assist with the treatment of the other young men who have had their surgeries: I will help cleanse wounds, change bandages, and help the impaired sailors with sitz baths.

On the first morning, I'm assigned to work with a young sailor who had his surgery the day before. He stands before me and drops his gown, and I see a sight I'll never forget. He's been cut down both sides of his buttocks, and raw meat is exposed at the base of his spine. I am told to dry and clean the wound after helping him with his sitz bath, and then apply an ointment to this bare oozing flesh followed by a bandage. There are at least a dozen or more men there, all of whom have had this surgery in the past few days, and those who are healing are assisting those who are immobilized and in quite a bit of pain.

I cringe at the sight of all of these wounds and at how much flesh has been cut away, leaving permanent impairments to their bodies. All I have is a soreness and some swelling, and I'm looking at what appears to me to be an assembly line of radical surgical procedures that will leave permanent damage if I go through it two days hence. I make a decision right there on the spot that this is not for me. I'm not going to let these knife-happy young doctors go to work on my ass.

I leave the pilonidal-cyst ward and make an appointment with the head nurse. I inform her that my swelling has disappeared and I have no pain, so I won't be needing their surgical intervention now or ever. I see the doctor and tell him the same story. He insists I stay one more night to see if my sudden miraculous healing holds up the next day after an examination. I stay the night, and all that night I visualize myself as healed. The thought of being cut in such a drastic way motivates me to go to work on my very first self-healing adventure.

The next morning I tell the nurse and medical team that I am healed—I have no symptoms whatsoever. I refuse to allow them to examine me any further, and I also spurn their efforts to get me to sign a surgical permission form. I am released, put on a bus, and sent back to the Naval Communications Station for duty. All the way back on the bus my ass still hurts, but I am noticing a considerable diminishing of the symptoms that got me to that madhouse in the first place.

For the next several weeks I take my own sitz baths at the barracks, and I practice a kind of visualization technique that I read about in a recently published book that I borrowed from the library. The title is *Psycho-Cybernetics,* by a medical doctor named Maxwell Maltz, and its premise is that the mind-body connection is the core of successful self-healing. He urges his plastic-surgery patients to pursue a positive outcome through intense visualization, and emphasizes that an attitude adjustment can create miraculous healings.

I diligently practice the principles that Dr. Maltz elaborates in *Psycho-Cybernetics*. Within four days my pilonidal cyst disappears and I'm symptom-free, with no need for any further medical treatment.

I Can See Clearly Now

I cannot begin to tell you how many times I've expressed my gratitude to the pilonidal cyst that showed up on my coccyx back in 1961, and for the three guys whose asses I had to treat during my one day at the naval hospital in Guam. This was my introduction to the power that the mind can play in healing all manner of medical diagnoses. Dr. Max Maltz's book became a bible for me during that crisis.

I think back to how I literally healed myself by intense visualization, and I can see that all of the people involved in my life during that experience on Guam were indeed some of my most significant teachers. After that crisis I resolved to use my mind to visualize myself as healthy and disease-free, and to stay away from the medical mindset except in the most dire of circumstances.

I can see clearly that I needed to have that frightening experience in the hospital in order to discover the wondrous and mysterious powers that are inherent in our consciousness. As I watched many of my young friends go off for their surgical fix, I talked to them about what I'd learned from Dr. Maltz. "Change your image of yourself," I'd tell them. "You can heal yourself! Honestly, I did it by seeing myself as already healed. Try it." But mostly they refused to listen because of the image they carried around of themselves as unskilled and inept when it came to their own healing abilities.

I can see clearly that the experience I described at the naval hospital when I was a 21-year-old sailor was absolutely necessary in order that I might ultimately become a teacher of the power of mind-body medicine. Once it was fully embedded in me, I spent the better part of 50 years using these techniques of self-healing through visualization. I encouraged many people to change their self-concepts and begin to see themselves as the miraculous Divine beings they truly are. Clearly, I was destined to believe and teach that *with God, all things are possible.*

I've shared stages all over the world with masterful medically trained physicians who join me in teaching the mind-body connection. Gradually the field of mind-body medicine has taken hold, and more people are receptive to relying on their healing abilities before pursuing drugs, surgery, and other invasive procedures. For me, this fascinating field of inquiry began back there on Guam where I had a Divinely inspired epiphany while staring at the bloodied rear end of a postoperative young sailor, and made a decision that there had to be another way.

I give thanks for that epiphany, as well as for Max Maltz publishing his classic *Psycho-Cybernetics* at precisely the right time in my life. Over 50 years later after a diagnosis of leukemia, I still use the techniques I learned back there on Guam in 1961, and I believe and teach the power of the mind to heal anything that we place into our imagination with a God-realized alignment. This is a lesson I have stressed in the raising of my eight children as well.

Looking back, I can see clearly why I had to have that terrifying experience at that time, and today it reaffirms what I know to be true: everything that shows up in our lives does so for a reason, though it sometimes takes 20/20 hindsight to view it this way.

16

It is the spring of 1961, and I am about to board a military prop plane to cross the Pacific Ocean. My uncle Bill Vollick, a schoolteacher in Hayward, California, is seeing me off after a two-week leave, which I've spent with him and his family.

During the past two weeks with my uncle (who was a radioman on board a destroyer in the Pacific during the hellacious years of World War II), I've enjoyed accompanying him and observing his teaching style. He is the most popular teacher in his school because he makes the subject matter come alive. I love watching him teach and seeing the affection his students demonstrate toward him. I am in awe. He is fun, smart, and deeply committed to his work, as well as all of his young students.

We spend evenings together quizzing each other on all manner of subjects. We banter back and forth, and I attempt to stump him and his wife, Barbara, with quizzes that I've concocted. I love the intellectual and philosophical back-and-forth that takes place every evening. I love the atmosphere of being in the company of well-read, stimulating people. And I love my uncle, who is by far the most influential man in my lifetime. For me, he's a role model, an intellectual—yes, even a quasi-father.

Before boarding, I make a promise to myself. I say out loud, "I'm going to spend the next 18 months on Guam preparing myself to attend college and become a teacher."

I am alive inside with anticipation and excitement. I want to teach. I *will* teach. I will go to college and get the credentials necessary to make this dream a reality. There is no doubt. I have found my calling, and my uncle Bill is my inspiration.

I have a year and a half on Guam to prepare myself for what I will be doing when my discharge date arrives on September 4, 1962. Eighteen months to figure out a way to get admitted to a university, which could be a major challenge since my high school transcript is not one that is predictive of being ready for college matriculation. I commit myself to figuring out a way to be able to pay the tuition and textbook expenses, as well as convince the university that they should overlook my high school records and take a risk and admit me as a full-time student.

I decide on my first day on the island that I'll save 90 percent of my salary for the remainder of my time in the Navy, and live on the other 10 percent. All of my meals are paid for, I have no rent to pay or clothes to buy, and I do not drink alcohol or smoke cigarettes. I am determined to have saved enough money to cover all of my tuition expenses for four years of university study, plus be able to purchase a used automobile at my discharge. I'm certain I'll be able to get a part-time job when I enter college.

I receive my first paycheck and take the shuttle into the town of Agana, open a savings account, and deposit all but 10 percent of my pay. I am thrilled—I'm on my way! I see myself as a college student, and I know that I will absolutely not be deterred from this commitment.

Each month for the next 16 months I resolutely go through this ritual, watching my bank account grow and having a great time proving to myself that I'm capable of amassing wealth even on the paltry salary of an enlisted man in the Navy. I watch with interest as many of my fellow sailors squander their money, getting drunk, living beyond their means, and barely making it from paycheck to paycheck. This is not my way—I'm in my own separate reality. I am living in a very different world from all of the people I am working with at the Naval Communications Center on Guam. I am living in the vision I have for myself.

The small library on the base provides me with a source of books to borrow and read during my free time. I read avidly, jotting down words that I cannot define. At night before going to sleep I look up the definitions of the words and write it all out in my vocabulary-improvement file. I am tenacious in this activity, and the file is getting thick. I frequently spend evenings perusing this growing list of word definitions, and notice that the new words begin appearing in my essays and the letters I write home. I am sounding more and more like a person who is educated beyond high school.

I spend a great deal of time at the library and decide that I will read a minimum of 500 books during my time on Guam and maintain a bibliography, which grows rapidly. I ravenously read everything the library stocks—my sleeping space in the barracks soon becomes overloaded with all of the books I'm reading.

I say nothing to any of my friends about my intentions. They see me as a bookworm and a private sort of intellectual. I'm merely acting on my inner vision to prepare myself for university study. I see myself as a teacher, a college professor, and I am acting on that inner picture every day.

I read books on every subject imaginable, preparing for the entrance exam to the university that coincidentally bears my name—Wayne State University—at home in Detroit. I particularly enjoy reading about people who have gone way beyond just being ordinary. Great writers, poets, philosophers, scientists, inventors, musicians, athletes—nothing is off-limits. The idea of living at extraordinary levels and transcending "normal" is most appealing to me.

A great deal of my free time is spent writing, and I've amassed a large collection of essays on a variety of subjects. These essays seem to just write themselves through me, and I feel the pen rushing across the pages as the excitement within me wells up at the idea of becoming a writer myself. I share my essays and my growing vocabulary list with no one—this is my own personal adventure. I seem to have figured out a way to get out of the present moment, and I actually feel as if I'm living the life I'm imagining so lucidly in my mind. I am a writer. I am an educated man. I am a teacher.

Finally, several of my close friends become interested in what my daily reading and writing are all about. I describe some of the ideas percolating inside of me, and I mention William Blake, Emily Dickinson, Plato, Friedrich Nietzsche, Henry David Thoreau, Ralph Waldo Emerson, and Thomas Wolfe, among many others. I talk about these great thinkers' lives and what they convey in their writing. I speak of existentialism, transcendentalism, and other strange-sounding *isms* to my small group of friends. As they begin seeing me as an expert in these subject areas, I do nothing to disabuse them of their faith in me. I am an expert because I'm willing to speak as an expert about my interest in these famous experts!

At my friends' request, I arrange to conduct a small group lecture. A half-dozen guys show up, and we have a discussion that I lead on Albert Camus, a French author and philosopher who had recently died. We talk about "The Myth of Sisyphus" and the idea Camus presents that "all great deeds and all great thoughts have a ridiculous beginning. Great works are often born on a street corner or in a restaurant's revolving door." We discuss the greatness latent in all of us.

To my surprise, my friends want more. The following week 12 people show up, including an officer who isn't supposed to fraternize with the enlisted ranks. I'm the resident philosopher at the naval base—simply, it seems, because of my willingness to live fearlessly and lose myself in works that are available to everyone at the library on the base. I love these evening sessions where we can talk about ideas that inspire me to my own greatness.

As the time of my discharge grows nearer, I get acquainted with the education officer at the naval communications center. He writes a letter to the admissions department at Wayne State requesting that I be allowed to take the entrance examination here on Guam and have it administered and proctored by him at the education office.

After several months of wrangling and (before cell phones or computers!) international phone calls, the arrangements are made and I'm scheduled for a full-day examination. At the end of the day of testing I feel quite confident that I did well. Virtually all of the vocabulary questions are words that have appeared in my massive vocabulary-improvement folder.

A month later I receive a response from the Wayne State admissions officer that I have spoken and corresponded with over the past six months or so. I have done exceedingly well on the entrance exam—however, my high school transcripts are not indicative of success at the university level. The conclusion is that I should attend a community college and then apply for a transfer upon completion of a two-year curriculum. This isn't the response I envisioned.

I speak to the education officer, who sends a glowing testimonial to the admissions office detailing the work I've been doing. He describes the study groups I've been leading and teaching, and my commitment to higher education. I make another international call and plead with the same admissions official who has been handling my case. After a great deal of discussion and negotiations, I receive a telegram informing me that they are going to make an exception because I am a veteran who has become a gigantic pain in the ass. They are going to admit me on a provisional basis and reevaluate my status after the first three quarters of the academic year.

I am admitted—I am ecstatic!

I Can See Clearly Now

Looking back I can see clearly that the 18 months I spent on Guam just prior to my enrolling as a full-time college student were incredibly instrumental in the life's work that was to be ahead of me.

There was something at the controls of my life that landed me in Northern California, where I spent many weekends and leave time at the home of Bill and Barbara Vollick. My time spent with my mother's youngest brother was Divinely arranged—of that I am now certain. These were my introductory lessons in the power of the idea of intention. I didn't want to become a teacher until I observed Bill in action, and from that day I was able to declare it as a present fact and to live from this inner mind-set.

It was this *intention* of myself as a teacher, inspired by Bill, that allowed me to go forward and declare myself as a teacher when I arrived on Guam. For me, it was a reality, nudging me to apply for university enrollment and demanding I actually teach classes on base. Intention provided the impetus to organize my entire life around an idea I implanted in my consciousness when I was a 20-year-old sailor with only a high school diploma. After thousands of public lectures on all manner of subjects covered in the 41 books I've written, I still see those four words of the intention I made back in 1961 imprinted on my inner screen: *I am a teacher.*

The universal mind appears to have known that I had to be so imprinted, and I am in awe of its magical power in me now and always. Teaching people to act as if what they desire to manifest is already a present fact has been a major theme of my life's work. When I held the idea of being a teacher in my imagination, the only thing I could do was act upon that intention. I am deeply grateful for the powers that brought Bill and me together at that crucial time in my life. We were destined to be lifelong friends. I am also appreciative of the fact that I was able to repay this beautiful man for what he unknowingly offered me when I was a young sailor going to an island in the Pacific where I would undergo a colossal transformation and shift from the direction my life had been taking.

While on Guam I persistently and determinedly acted from the inner affirmation of *I am a teacher.* My bimonthly trip to the bank to save 90 percent of my salary emerged from that intention. By the time I left the Navy I had amassed all the funding that I would need to attend college. I was able to purchase a previously owned Studebaker Lark, which lasted until I completed my master's degree. But more than that, I adopted a philosophy toward money and saving that put me on the path of making myself financially independent for a lifetime. Somehow the universe was teaching me how to live and fulfill my own dharma without allowing myself to become burdened by debt, a lesson that has served to keep me on purpose rather than figuring out how to resolve indebtedness that would have distracted me from my mission here, this time around.

Back there on Guam I was being nudged by the universal mind, which advises that wisdom is unrelated to one's potential personal greatness. Becoming an expert means being unafraid to declare yourself one, and then act on that inner declaration. These early lectures and study groups on existentialism and philosophy were the prelude to a career of being willing to stand before people and speak common sense because it was what I knew to be true deep within me. I was being directed by an invisible force back there in 1961 as I steadfastly pursued my intention to live up to my inner affirmation of *I am a teacher.* I refused to accept any response other than, *Congratulations! You are admitted to our university.*

I can't define that inner spark that wouldn't allow me to give up, but I know for certain that it is a piece of the Divine—a spiritual drill sergeant refusing to relent even when everything around me was saying, "Give up on it, Wayne!" That inner motivator kept pushing and has pushed me throughout my life, not because I'm special, but because it takes its orders from the intention that is in my imagination. That taskmaster acts on what we believe is already a present fact. Consequently, there's no giving up on a destiny that is and must be fulfilled.

When I arrived at the university in September 1962 to enroll as a freshman, I went to the admissions office and looked up the official who'd been so kind in bending the rules so that I might be admitted as a full-time student. I'd often thought about the courage of that gentleman to make an exception and allow me to attend the university. He told me that he was simply acting on a hunch. An invisible signal if you will—indeed, the same invisible energy that was pushing my buttons back there on Guam to not give up was pushing his buttons to overlook the rules. After my first academic quarter my provisional status was removed, and there were no asterisks next to my name anymore.

Then on May 4, 1970—the same day as the horror show at Kent State University in Ohio, where four students were killed (and nine wounded) by National Guard troops who'd fired live bullets into the crowd of young students who were protesting the fiasco in Vietnam—I passed my final exams and became Dr. Wayne Dyer, adjunct faculty member at my alma mater. In eight years I had gone from freshman to professor.

With gratitude for all that had transpired, I was able four decades later to pledge one million dollars to a scholarship fund for "unqualified" students to enter the university in the memory of the admissions officer who had done the same for me. What do I know for sure? There are no accidents in an infinite universe in which Spirit is at the helm of all decision making.

When I received my orders to depart from my ship, the USS *Ranger,* I'd only been aboard for a little over a year. It was unheard of to be transferred after such a short tour of duty, especially since I was a short-timer, meaning I only had 18 months left of my military obligation. Clearly it seems the invisible hand of destiny was at work—I was fated to spend that last year and a half on Guam, where I came face-to-face with my future, which in some mysterious way had already been played out. All I had to do was listen, get out of the way, and allow myself to catch up.

In a universe where everything is happening at once, there's no past or future, and everything exists simultaneously. I didn't know it at the time, but I was living what Lao-tzu expressed so succinctly: "You are not doing anything, you are just being done." A big hand figuratively reached down and plucked me off of the ship and put me down on Guam, where I was aligned with all that I needed to fulfill a dharma that I had signed up for, long before I appeared on this planet in 1940. Had I stayed aboard the USS *Ranger,* I would have lived out another dharma, and you wouldn't be reading this book.

I can see very clearly that it is and was and will be all perfect. As Rumi said, "Sell your cleverness, and purchase bewilderment." I am bewildered and awestruck by the perfection of my spending four of my developmental years in a military organization that represented the exact opposite of all I've taught and strived to become. Divine perfection also plunked me down on a South Pacific island where I could foster my readiness for a new way of being.

I have come to know, from a much clearer perspective, that there are no wrong roads to anywhere. I continue to look back with awe and astonishment at the perfection of it all.

17

I am a 22-year-old veteran attending college classes for the first time, and it feels like the happiest time of my life. I love walking between classes on campus, looking at all of the buildings in the heart of the city where I grew up. This is a great honor for me after spending the previous four years on board a ship or in the barracks at the military installation. I am beyond ecstatic. I love attending lectures and can't imagine wanting to cut any classes. I arrive early every morning and spend a great deal of time in the huge library . . . as well as looking for a parking space every day! But I have no complaints.

The thing I feel the most is pride. I've never had the idea of attending higher education imprinted on my consciousness by my family —that wasn't an expectation. It was my own personal choice to take this route at this time in my life.

I have a close to full-time job working as a cashier for the Kroger Company retail grocery chain. I'm grateful for the opportunity to work evenings, study late at night, and attend school during the day. My tuition is fully paid and I've accumulated enough in my savings to cover my school expenses until I graduate.

It is my second academic quarter at Wayne State University. Although these school quarters only last for 11 weeks, a great deal is packed into them. The previous quarter I received above-average grades in all four of the courses I completed, which included English 101, American Literature; where I loved discovering Theodore Dreiser, William Faulkner, Ernest Hemingway, Mark Twain, and F. Scott Fitzgerald. Now I'm taking English 102, which is a composition class. I feel that I will have no problems whatsoever—after all, I'm a writer! I've been writing since I was a preteen, I've completed a novel, and I have a file full of essays I've written.

This glow of eagerly anticipating having my writing legitimized by a college professor teaching at a major university is dimmed dramatically, however, when the young graduate fellow assigned to teach this freshman English course announces: "Everything you write must be submitted according to APA style. You will lose points for any and all inconsistencies; and if you ever use the word *interesting,* you will receive a failing grade on your paper." The weekly essays required for this course must be footnoted and supported by something someone else has already written.

He's not interested in what students in this class think or write? Students are to be guided by a manual that's designed to make everybody write and sound just like everybody else? No creativity, no opinions? I find it almost impossible to believe, but it seems to me that Joachim Ries, who's teaching this class, is obsessed with *The Publication Manual of the American Psychological Association.* Every paper must meet the exact standards laid out in the manual. Grammar, punctuation, bibliography citations . . . everything must adhere to a certain format, and no opinions are to be expressed by students.

My first paper, which is an interpretation of a poem, receives a failing grade. Red scratch marks throughout the paper point to my mistakes as Mr. Ries sees them—improper annotation, punctuation, and footnotes—and I've had the audacity to interpret the meaning of this poem in a way that Mr. Ries finds incorrect.

I am incensed. I despise the idea of having everything I write criticized and rejected for what seem to me irrelevancies. I write to the poem's author, who is a professor at a small university in Wisconsin, and include a copy of my paper, which details my personal interpretation of what he wanted to convey in his poem. I too am a poet. I wrote many poems during my years on Guam, and am deeply interested in the works of Rumi and Hafiz, two Sufi poets from Persia whose words bring a soothing elixir to my soul.

I receive a warm letter from the professor of poetry congratulating me for my interpretation. He loves the paper and is touched by what I got from his poem. This man was thrilled to write to me—poets obviously do not receive very much mail!

I take my response from the poet to Mr. Ries, who's obviously very upset with me, this inexperienced college freshman who dared to question him and his grading system. I've not ingratiated myself to my instructor, who sees me as insolent and refuses to even consider changing my grade.

The weeks go by, and for our final exam, we're assigned a term research paper due the last week of the quarter. I write a paper on the 1956 Hungarian Revolution and the role that János Kádár, a Communist sympathizer, played in that conflict. This is of particular interest to me because when it happened, I was a 16-year-old high school student trying to follow this event as best I could. I'm proud of this paper and think it is very well written—and I follow APA style to the letter.

Mr. Ries is still upset over my attempts to have my grade improved on my first paper. He's a graduate assistant who takes umbrage at the idea that one of his freshman students would take exception to any of his pronouncements or grading procedures. Now he tells me that my 57-page research paper on the role of János Kádár in the recent Hungarian revolution is not my original writing. I must have plagiarized, in his opinion, even though he has no evidence of such a transgression He gives me a *D* on the paper—and when my final grade arrives in the mail a week later, I find that I have a *D* for the course as well. A passing grade, but a less-than-satisfactory grade.

I am beyond angry. I have plagiarized nothing. I have been writing papers and a novel for over six years. I'm being punished for what I consider a high quality of writing.

I make several attempts to meet with Mr. Ries in the next quarter. He refuses. I ask the department head to hear my case. He listens attentively. I show him my research paper and the accusation of possible plagiarism, and he informs me that there is nothing he can do.

He's not in a position to overturn the grades that a staff member gives, and tells me that I can retake the course and have the *D* superseded by my subsequent grade.

I think back to my leaf-collection fiasco and remember having to retake biology and how I let my pride inconvenience me, just to prove that I was right. I decide to drop it. The *D* stands as my only unsatisfactory grade over an eight-year time period from when I was a freshman to the completion of my doctorate.

I Can See Clearly Now

My days as a college student, especially those earliest days, taught me a powerful lesson that has permeated my writing and speaking throughout my life. I've spoken often of the metaphor of the wake of a boat—that the wake is nothing more than the trail that is left behind, and it has no power in the present. It does not and cannot drive the boat. It is a trail that has no influence on the boat whatsoever.

Attending and excelling in those university classes taught me more than the subjects I studied. Walking about the campus, I became aware that my past did not have to dictate my future. The enthusiasm I was feeling and the success I was having in the university setting were certainly unanticipated based on my past. Using the boat as a symbol of my life, the wake of that boat was not the driving force of my life. I no longer needed a personal history; my past was just that—past—no longer a factor for me. I was doing well regardless of what my high school record indicated—regardless of the facts of my background and upbringing. I needed to know this firsthand from experience, and somehow I was led to this realization.

From my first day on campus I never looked backward, and understood that I could be anything I put my attention on—that anything I could place into my imagination I could achieve. But I had to experience this truth before I could teach it—and you can trust me on this, every day as I walked that campus in an exhilarated state of awe, I was seeing that the wake of my life was indeed nothing more than a trail that I had left behind. I was now in charge of the direction my life was to take. My experience with Mr. Ries in English 102 is now seen by me as another one of those great learning experiences that showed up disguised as an embarrassing and anger-producing event. A part of me seemed to think I was back in the military, being told not to think for myself, just do as I was told and write according to a manual.

APA style is basically the uniform code of military justice for college students that says: *Write according to a code devised by the American Psychological Association. Don't be creative; don't think outside of the box; write a paper that looks just like every other paper ever submitted to a college professor.* Writing by these dictates results in books or papers that remain unread. Citing sources and footnoting everything creates dreary, researched, data-based writing that doesn't come alive for the reader. Books written in this style are read mostly by other academics, and contribute primarily to enlarging the vast supply of unread manuscripts gathering dust on library shelves.

I wanted my writing to excite readers—to inspire them. I wanted readers to want *more,* not feel that they can't wait to finish! Being forced to write in such a noncreative style, fitting in to a preestablished format, gave me a valuable experience. It taught me what I didn't want for myself—it allowed me to experience what I definitely did not want to be. I discovered right there in English 102 with Mr. Joachim Ries that I wanted to write for a large audience, not a pedantic, erudite collection of academics.

I felt the pain of having to stifle my own creativity in order to please and fit in to a preordained style of writing. Yes, I succumbed and went along, but in doing so, I was motivated to do this writing thing the way my heart described it to me. I went through the motions, but my imagination was stoked every day by my desire to write in the exact opposite way than I was being forced to write for a college requirement by a rigid graduate student. It seemed that this man had opted to drink all of the institutional Kool-Aid, and that busywork had captured his soul.

From a distance I can see clearly that my episode with the Wisconsin professor and poet was a product of my living almost exclusively from my ego at that time. I wanted so desperately to prove that I was right, even though all of my efforts were obviously self-sabotaging. Rather than coming from a place of understanding and love, I chose to put all of my efforts into making my college teacher wrong. This is the action of an ego-dominated fool! It is akin to talking rudely to a uniformed police officer when stopped for a traffic violation, regardless of whether you feel you are in the right or not. I was so outraged that this man would find my interpretation of a poem to be wrong that I reacted by striking out at him and even attempting to embarrass him by giving him proof of my superiority.

I can see clearly now that I needed to have a series of these kinds of misfortunes throughout my life. I finally got the message that has been a central theme in my life's work: *When you have a choice to be right or to be kind, always pick kind.* Living from your highest spiritual sense is the essence of what it means to be a self-actualized person.

I was viewing Mr. Joachim Ries as an enemy whom I had to overwhelm, even if the only result would be a Pyrrhic victory. In the Navy I learned to be quietly effective, and it had always worked for me. At Wayne State I was busy fighting a losing battle against the system. What I know today is to treat everyone with love and kindness, even when they're behaving in ways that I dislike. I had to learn how to allow my highest inner self to become the dominant influence in my life. The only way that I could get this lesson was to have my ego tamed.

I must admit that it made me feel great to prove to myself and Mr. Ries that I was right on this matter. But being right should have taken a backseat to being kind and keeping my eye on what my real goals were for that English class. Those goals involved completing the class with a good grade, removing one more obstacle from my larger goal of actualizing my *I am* presence, which had already declared that *I am a teacher!* With these kinds of setbacks I was being groomed to teach about the absurdity of relying upon the ego and what a truly ill-fated choice it is to do so.

And now I can give my honest assessment regarding that one *D* grade that seemed to be a speck of poison on my otherwise illustrious-looking college transcript. I can see clearly that I totally deserved that unsatisfactory grade. I created it, and take full responsibility for it.

I egged this man on. I saw him as a competitor and a threat to my self-image as a competent writer. I put him in a position where he was going to do anything he could to retaliate against my supercilious attitude.

Yes, I earned that *D*—and even though it is now half a century later, the presence of that scarlet letter on my college transcript is an enduring reminder to always make the choice to come from kindness and love.

If the Wayne Dyer in his 70s were to talk to the Wayne Dyer in his 20s, he would remind him of the great truth that he had been teaching throughout his professional career: *Live so as to be detached from outcome. Do it all because it resonates with your highest self and responds to your beseeching inner voice—not because of rewards that might come your way.* That *D* grade on a transcript is totally irrelevant to a highly functioning person. I'd advise that 22-year-old version of myself to be content with knowing that he'd written a great paper and take pleasure in the feeling that comes with the joy of writing and expressing yourself. This is a lesson that I have had to learn the hard way.

We live in a world that places an inordinate amount of pressure on defining success in external terms. I've spent many years in a profession where so many chase after success in these ego-defined terms: *How much money do I make? What position is my book on the bestseller list, and how many weeks has it been there? Did I receive a promotion? Did I get the job I sought? What did the reviewers think of my book, and how many copies did I sell?* These and hundreds more ego-driven thoughts are typical of authors who fixate on external indices of success. Over the 50 years I've been immersed in this business, I've learned to let go of them.

My preoccupation with that unsatisfactory black mark on my transcript was a great learning experience as I look back. Taming the ego, which defines itself on the basis of its reputation and what it accomplishes and owns, has been one of the top lessons of my life. The fact that my experience as a 22-year-old college freshman in an English composition class stands out indicates the importance that attempting to curb the demands of the ego has played in my life.

I can see clearly now that the grade of *D* shrinks in significance from the distance of a 50-year observation tower. The fact that I could interpret a poem and understand it as the poet so indicated, and that I had the energy and the willingness to invest myself in writing a detailed scholarly research paper that was thought to have been plagiarized because it was so well written, far superseded the trivial mark on a transcript that has absolutely nothing to do with who I am or what I have accomplished in this lifetime.

I needed to learn this lesson well. Detachment from outcome was my ultimate objective, and this early experience was one of the necessary episodes I needed in order to bring this message home clearly so that I could ultimately become a teacher of self-actualization.

18

I am driving my Studebaker Lark home from the university after a full day of classes. I am nearing the end of my sophomore year after having attended summer school. I want to graduate as soon as possible to get on with my teaching ambitions, so I'm taking additional courses each quarter and plan to attend school full-time on a year-round basis to make this idea a reality.

It is Friday afternoon, November 22, 1963. I am approaching the Edsel Ford Expressway (I-94) on Crane Street and am just on the entrance ramp when I hear this shocking news on the car radio: "We interrupt this program to announce that the President of the United States has been shot in Dallas a few moments ago. It is expected that it is fatal."

I pull over on the entrance ramp and sit in stunned silence. Tears are rolling down my cheeks. I feel as though a bullet has torn through me and left me too shattered to drive. I can't catch my breath. I am taking the news blaring over the radio very, very personally. I loved this President dearly. He spoke so eloquently of the many injustices that he wanted to see corrected. He stood for eliminating the horror shows of segregation that so impacted me while I served my four years of active duty. He exuded hope for a better world, and he was willing to take on the forces that wanted to keep the same old prejudices and hatred in place. I marveled at the courage he showed in his campaign when he promised executive, moral, and legislative leadership to combat racial discrimination and school segregation.

Only a few months before I watched with pride as the Alabama National Guard, at President Kennedy's orders, provided for the safety of two black students to enter a building at the University of Alabama and register. I watched as Alabama's Governor George Wallace stepped aside, and a whole new era of equality was ushered in.

On June 11, 1963, I heard President Kennedy give this speech on television:

> The heart of the question is whether all Americans are to be afforded equal rights and equal opportunities, whether we are going to treat our fellow Americans as we want to be treated. If an American, because his skin is dark, cannot eat lunch in a restaurant open to the public, if he cannot send his children to the best public school available, if he cannot vote for the public officials who will represent him, if, in short, he cannot enjoy the full and free life which all of us want, then who among us would be content to have the color of his skin changed and stand in his place?

That speech marked a turning point for our country—the beginning of the drive for passage of what became the Civil Rights Act of 1964.

I sit in my car on the entrance ramp to the freeway remembering how those two young African-American students looked as they went to register for classes. I recall my friend Ray Dudley being denied a seat at a restaurant in Havre de Grace while dressed in the uniform of the United States Navy only a few years ago, and I am saddened for the loss of those hopes that the President offered.

I read of JFK's heroism during World War II in the book *PT 109* by Robert Donovan, and how his actions saved the crew after his ship had been cut in half by a Japanese torpedo. I devoured Kennedy's own book, *Profiles in Courage,* in which he focused on the careers of eight senators in the U.S. Congress who had shown great courage in the face of constituent pressures. I had such high hopes for this kind of courage to be applied to so many social issues in our deeply divided country. I recalled the fear that gripped the nation during the Cuban missile crisis and how this young, courageous President stood up to the Soviet Premier Nikita Khrushchev and averted a nuclear disaster.

I believed in this man. I felt close to him. I'd written him during my involvement in the incident on Guam where the indignity of prejudice was raising its ugly face in my life. JFK was the man I thought would right this mess if he was informed of it.

I slowly begin to pick up speed and enter the freeway, heading east to my home where I'm living with my mother, until my upcoming marriage next year.

Later I'm working at Kroger's grocery store on the evening shift from four till nine. Everyone checking out at my cash register is in shock—very few are able to speak. I look into a woman's eyes as I hand her her change and when our eyes meet, we both break down in tears. The silence permeates everything. No one can speak without tearing up. I am impacted by this tragedy in a way totally foreign to me. It feels as if my life is going to make a big shift as a result of the events of this day.

I Can See Clearly Now

I've included this historic incident because it influenced the direction of my personal and professional life. That day in November 1963 did initiate a huge shift for me in many ways. Up until then, virtually everything in my life that was impacting my future was of a personal nature. My experiences in foster homes or an orphanage, in high school, and in the Navy were my "Wayne Dyer moments" of awakening to a new direction and a new consciousness in my personal life. The assassination of President Kennedy didn't just kill a man I admired tremendously; it killed something in me as well.

I began then and there to think about a plan for a life that would have a historical and global effect. It was no longer just about my impending career as a teacher. I began to think in terms of how I could impact the consciousness of the entire planet. I saw myself from that day forward as a man with a voice of compassion for a higher good. I didn't know how or even what my role might be, but I knew that one person with a conscience could make a difference and I was that person. Why not? I thought like JFK did long before I had ever heard of this man. I tingled as I thought of giving a voice to these ideas and having that voice heard around the world. I began to see myself as a world leader—not a political leader—but a person who was filled with compassion for everyone, and a person whom others were willing to listen to.

As I look back on the assassination of President Kennedy, now 50 years later, I can see that he was destined to give up his life in order to have his own dharma fulfilled. The Civil Rights Act was not headed for passage in 1963. The likelihood of JFK being reelected was shrinking because the South was rebelling at his uncompromising view on racial intolerance and voter rights. Filibusters by Southern senators were almost assured. But when JFK died and the nation mourned this great man, the entire mood of the country shifted. Under the new President, who was reelected in a landslide in 1964, the winds of change began to blow much more robustly.

Politicians who vowed "segregation forever" began to shift under the pressure of a more enlightened and awakened population, and actually voted for equal rights and moving toward a Great Society. I believe that there are no accidents in this spiritually ordained universe. The death of President Kennedy that day opened the door to long-overdue civil rights, voter rights, health care for the elderly, improved schools, and an awareness that equal rights were not just words to be spoken, but actions to be taken by all of us. This was the only way that the consciousness of our country could shift.

I was also caught up in this new awareness. A rising tide raises all boats, and I felt metaphorically raised by this tragic event. I, like so many others, marched for civil rights and protested a looming war in Vietnam. As a teacher in the inner city of Detroit, and later as a spokesman for ending world hunger through the Hunger Project, I sought changes to our unjust and unnecessary attitudes. My life as a writer and speaker focused on elevating people from thinking of themselves as ordinary and limited, to trusting in a new awareness that within everyone resides a no-limit person who can accomplish anything they place their attention upon.

President Kennedy's vision for a country populated by citizens who want to give and to serve more than take and receive, is a vision that I share as well. That he had to die in order to move the entire country in a new more compassionate direction is a part of the perfection of our universe. It can be argued interminably, but nevertheless it is so. He *did* die, and we all became better people as a result. And I too began my journey toward being a better person, and a career centered on service and compassion and love for everyone. My life might have had a different emphasis and direction had the events in Dallas that day not occurred.

19

I'm in my senior year of college. I've attended close to 100 lectures in these four academic years, never once cutting a class. I am committed to this full-time student regimen, and so happy, proud, and lucky to be here in the first place that voluntarily missing even one class is never even a consideration.

While I love the atmosphere of this university built right in the middle of a teeming, large inner city, I am flabbergasted by what appears to me to be apathy on the part of the teaching faculty. It is rare to find professors genuinely excited about their subject matter or interested in inspiring the students. I notice how much disinterest is omnipresent in so many of the classes I take. Thoughts like these stream through my consciousness repeatedly: *It seems to me that all of these professors are just going through the motions of doing their job. So much boredom—so little excitement for what they are teaching.*

I think back to my uncle Bill Vollick, who was my inspiration for wanting to become a teacher. His classroom was a joy because of the laughter and excitement he inspired. Bill loved his students, and he loved his subject matter. He was living out his own dharma and everyone was having a good time. The key word here is *love.* I think, *That's what seems to be missing in these classes. Everyone is going through the motions; there's no love here. The students dutifully take notes on items that might appear on the midterm or final examination. Otherwise they're so obviously blasé about this entire business euphemistically called higher education. The teachers aren't teaching—they're presenting material and simply going through the motions themselves. They're doing a job, showing up most of the time, although often cutting classes themselves, and seemingly oblivious to the ennui that permeates the entire classroom.*

I notice this lack of enthusiasm on the part of almost everyone involved in what seems like a game that is being played out. I watch and ask myself, *Can't they see that no one is excited about what they're saying? They have a captive audience—the students have to be here and can't leave until class is dismissed. Why aren't the professors making this subject matter and this class come alive?*

I imagine myself having the distinct privilege of being in front of the class as a teacher with this same captive audience. I play this fantasy out in my mind almost daily when I'm in a classroom full of students who are being bathed in a lukewarm learning environment. I imagine myself making the room come alive and presenting the material in a compelling fashion. I see myself teaching students to be motivated and inspired and learn the curriculum even if they think the material is unimportant. This is a fantasy that I experience every day.

I watch the teachers with some disdain, the same way I did a few years back in high school. I actually feel sorry for them because they seem so trapped in living out their routine day after day, year after year. In high school there were several teachers at the end of their careers who just put in their time until retirement. I see some of the same thing at the university and wonder, *Where is their pride? How can they be in front of a class and not want to entertain their students and get them excited about learning this subject?*

I vow to myself that this will never be me. I love making people laugh, and the memorable teachers I've had all had this wondrous ability to infuse their teaching with humor. I promise myself that when I speak in front of a group—any group—the audience is going to love being there. I will not just go through the motions and do my job in order to receive a paycheck every two weeks. I will keep the love alive—the love for what I teach, the love for my students, but most significantly, the love I have for myself. I'm determined to honor who I am and never become a teacher doing my job in a listless charade of indifference. That's a blasphemous image that I would abhor were I to subject myself to such ignominy.

Each day, in classroom after classroom, I'm captivated by my own imaginative ruminations on how I would make this material come alive. I'm motivated by an intense desire to bring excitement, fun, and humor to the experience of learning.

Ultimately I am assigned to Pershing High School, in the Detroit public-school system, to do my student teaching. I am to teach honors economics to a group of 35 graduating seniors, and my supervising teacher is Mr. Zigmund Boytor. I have been truly blessed—Zig Boytor is a master teacher, a man who embodies all that I aspire to become. He is loved by his students and considered to be the best teacher in the school by his principal.

After the first two weeks, Zig gives me free rein; I am the sole teacher for the remainder of the semester. Economics can be an incredibly dreary subject, or at least it was for me in the two courses I was enrolled in as an undergraduate. But now I have an opportunity to put into practice what I have been imagining over the previous four years sitting in so many humdrum classrooms. I am in heaven!

I love this semester more than any up until this point. I love this class, I love the students, and I even grow to love economics! I'm thrilled when the class presents me with a leather briefcase and a beautiful card expressing their enthusiasm for the course and for me—the teacher! I am profoundly touched. I am enthused. I am a teacher, and I am on my way to being an orator as well.

I Can See Clearly Now

While I was sitting in an endless array of classes where apathy seemed to rule, both on the part of the professor as well as the students, I didn't realize that this was my early training ground for being a public speaker. As I look back, I can clearly see myself sitting in the classroom incredulous at the dullness that seemed so unnecessary. *Why,* I would wonder, *doesn't the instructor make this exciting? Isn't it obvious how tedious this is to everyone in the room?* Now I know, from a distance, that I had to have these feelings of frustration. They were awakening something in me that couldn't be silenced and ignored. I was destined for a role as an orator in my life.

I needed to get ready back then, and the surest way to prepare me was to provide me with a forum in which I had to participate in something that was distasteful to me. Once again, it is that old theme of having to experience what I didn't want to be, in order to truly know what it was that I wanted to do. This, like every experience of my life, was a bountiful blessing in disguise. Those inner musings I was hearing and feeling were my wake-up calls.

When I talked to my classmates about these feelings, they looked at me with bewildered expressions. To them, this was the system; boring lectures are part of what college is. Little did I know that my internal outrage was a voice from the universe saying to me, "Observe this carefully, feel the pain, and make a commitment based on what you are feeling to learn from this and become a brilliant, entertaining, compelling speaker."

Having spoken in public forums for almost four decades, to audiences paying their hard-earned money to attend, I feel blessed to have had the opportunity to be in classes in high school and college that provoked those inner voices saying, "Pay attention and make a commitment to make your messages come alive. Be enthusiastic and watch your audience for clues to see if they are paying attention and enjoying themselves; if they're not, then change what you are doing on the spot."

Over the years I've written and spoken often of the importance of passion in one's undertakings. To be apathetic to me means to have lost connection to my Source. A person standing in front of an audience without enthusiasm for his subject and his actions is disconnected from his spirit; that is, the God within. In fact, the root meaning of the word *enthusiasm* is "the God within."

Throughout decades of speaking before large groups of people I've learned that when I surrender and allow myself to be guided by a Divine Source, everything seems to fall into place. While I'm being introduced as a speaker about to take the microphone, I repeat this line from *A Course in Miracles* to myself: "If you knew who walked beside you at all times on this path that you have chosen, you could never experience fear or doubt again." This has been my reminder to hold the image of my alignment with the creative Source of the universe and speak from my passion. What was happening to me in those passionless classrooms was that I was being prodded by my spirit to stay in rapport with my inner sense of awe and appreciation for all that I am—and in doing so, I could become a speaker that people would want to hear.

I can remember as an undergraduate student thinking that I would like to excel at whatever I undertook, particularly in writing and speaking. I'd heard that writers were generally not great speakers, and that those who excelled at oratory were generally not great at expressing themselves on paper. I've learned over the years that greatness is really a function of what I choose to believe about myself and my abilities. I know that I have the capability of excelling at anything I choose.

There is nothing written in stone that says if I am a professional research expert that I must therefore lack competence at speaking before an audience. I took up tennis at the age of 31 and decided on the first day I played that I loved this game and could become a highly skilled player if I put in the time. And I did, for over 35 years. Similarly, in undergraduate school I knew that my ability to reach any level of prominence was unrestricted. I would live my passion, loving what I did, and there was nothing to hold me back except my own beliefs in my limitations.

I can see one thing quite clearly as I look back at myself in those classrooms observing the monotony all about me. From this perspective I understand that every experience of my life, regardless of how I chose to process it at the time, had something extremely valuable to teach me. There are lessons in every moment, and I now know for sure that there is no such thing as an uninteresting subject or an ordinary moment. There are only disinterested people. I learned by example many years ago not to be one of those disinterested people. I feel that to be bored is an insult to one's highest self, which is by definition the God within.

20

The year is 1968; I am married and have a year-old baby girl named Tracy, who was born in the midst of the riots that decimated a large portion of the city of Detroit. I'm also in the doctoral program at Wayne State University after completing my master's degree two years ago.

Since I have both bachelor's and master's degrees from Wayne State, one of the requirements of my Ph.D. program is to complete several semesters at the University of Michigan to give me some diversity in my overall educational training. I am currently enrolled in a summer-school course here called "The Psychology of Perception," in which there's a heavy emphasis on the advantage of using hypnosis in the treatment of perceptual impairments. I used a form of self-hypnosis to quit a smoking habit that I picked up in undergraduate school, and I'm looking forward to receiving hypnosis instruction and practicum experience.

The professor of this course, a highly energized and very competent scholar, did a group hypnosis on us yesterday. I was in a state of bliss—my mind was in an enhanced state, and I felt peaceful. I was totally aware of everything taking place and did not sense that I had given up control, yet I found myself following his suggestions willingly, doing everything that was suggested to me without questioning anything. I felt as if I didn't have to do what I was being told to do, but I did it anyway.

Today we are to witness an experiment in mind-body control. A woman in her early 40s has agreed to be the student who will undergo a hypnosis experiment with our professor as the experimenter. He places her in a chair at the front of the classroom and puts her in a hypnotic-like trance. He then explains that the human body cannot make a clear distinction between extremely hot and extremely cold temperatures. He tells us—along with the hypnotized woman, who looks totally normal and unaffected by any hypnotic suggestion—that a blindfolded person touched by a super-cold instrument or a red-hot instrument generally cannot tell which kind of touch they've received. He explains that extreme hot and cold can feel identical.

We are all attentive as the professor continues explaining the psychology of perception and that the nervous system simply reacts. Hot and cold are merely perceptual variations depending upon the makeup of the person being touched.

He blindfolds the woman and proceeds to touch her with an ice-cold metal instrument and a blown-out match still hot to the touch. First cold. Then hot. Then a variety of mixed-up trials. The woman is about 75 percent accurate in her guesses as the experiment unfolds. Then he takes off her blindfold and discusses the results with the class.

The woman is still in a hypnotic state. He tells her that he is going to show her which extreme-temperature utensil he is going to use and instructs her to simply say hot or cold quickly as she is touched. He shows her a frozen utensil and then a red-hot pin that he says he will touch to her inner arm, and she is to say out loud how each touch impacts her.

He places the blindfold over her eyes again and takes out the ice-cold metal pick. Very softly he says, "This is the cold one; tell me how it feels." She says it is cold and is a bit startled. Then he takes the red-hot pin and places it near her face so that she can feel the heat, and says, "I am going to touch your inner arm only slightly, and I want you tell me your immediate reaction." After the pin is placed close to her face, she is convinced that he's about to touch her with the red-hot object. The professor sets it on a glass ashtray on his desk, and instead touches her inner arm with the eraser on the end of a pencil he's taken from his shirt pocket. The woman is startled and a slight blister forms on her arm—even though she was only touched by a room-temperature pencil eraser.

A stunned classmate says, "Did you see that? It's unbelievable. I can't believe that she did that with her mind. I am flabbergasted."

My eyes are wide open, as is my mouth, as I observe firsthand the astonishing power of the mind over the body. By her belief and nothing more, this woman was able to produce a blister on her arm!

The professor explains that much of our perceptual activity is controlled by the beliefs we hold. He describes the placebo effect, wherein experiments are done with sugar pills that arthritis sufferers believe are arthritis medicine—and the sugar pills alleviate the arthritis!

Just as I had experienced with my pilonidal cyst when I was in the Navy, I'm again seeing the way our beliefs can be key to healing. Even more than this, I am wondering if outside influences or culturally entrained ideas might be irrelevant in the face of this infinitely powerful mind of ours. *Perhaps,* I ponder, *we can convince ourselves of our own abilities to manifest anything.*

I Can See Clearly Now

That summer day in 1968 was a tipping point in my life. It tipped me over the edge of one reality that I had believed in for 28 years and landed me in a place of unimagined potentiality.

Though it was a relatively new field of inquiry, I had done quite a bit of reading on the mind-body connection, particularly in the field of medicine. However, my intellectual inquiry hadn't prepared me for what I witnessed in the classroom at the University of Michigan that day. I can see clearly now that I needed to be there to have this new awareness firmly implanted in both my conscious and subconscious mind. It is one thing to read about something; it is quite another to experience it directly.

If this is possible, I wondered that day in class, *then what else is the mind capable of achieving that most people believe to be impossible?* This one incident at the University of Michigan that summer day in 1968 was the birthplace of my teaching about something I came to call "no-limit living" a few years down the road. But way beyond my becoming a teacher who passionately wrote and spoke on this subject of being unlimited—because of the limitless power of our minds to imagine anything and then make it a reality—was the impact this experience with the blister and the eraser was to have on me personally.

I made up my mind that I was capable of creating anything that I put into my imagination and kept there enthusiastically. I decided that I didn't have to have colds, or fatigue, or financial shortages, and for the most part I was able to manifest pretty much everything I imagined. It was as if a lightbulb went off inside me when I saw the shocked look on the face of the woman when she observed what her strong belief had accomplished. I reasoned that if she could believe so strongly in something that she could create a blister with that belief, then there was no reason I couldn't begin to train my mind to believe in all manner of staggering accomplishments.

As a result of that one episode of hypnosis, I later incorporated this concept into my public lectures. I encouraged people to cultivate a way of believing that could overcome the conditioned belief in their limitations.

I have always felt that a major hand of destiny placed me in that classroom in 1968. As I sit here writing today, more than 40 years since that demonstration in the early years of my doctoral studies, I have such a clear picture of all that transpired that day, as if it happened only this morning. This was life-changing for me because I knew that that could very well have been me creating the blister with my own mind. Little did I know as I walked into that classroom that day that the class was to provide me with an image that would personally and professionally affect my life from then on.

This image was so strong that it impacted me; all of my children, who were raised to have a mind that was open to all possibilities; and my many students and millions of readers, in 47 languages around the globe. One seemingly innocuous classroom demonstration rippled out into infinity, influencing countless others to trust in themselves and the power of the mind to make anything happen.

I reasoned at the time that if enough people accessed the potential of no-limit thinking, the entire course of human behavior could be changed for the better. Why not? This invisible mind of ours seems to affect everything in the physical universe, so why not dream big and work toward a world where massive numbers of us truly do think and act in this new way? I know this sounds a bit grandiose, but that's what was going through my mind that day when I left class a changed and idealistic young doctoral student.

Yes, I see clearly from this vantage point that the body is the servant of the mind. I had heard it, read it, and paid very little attention to this phenomenal idea until I experienced it right in front of me. Even events in our lives that appear to be mundane can, if we are willing to pay attention and be astonished, impact our lives and the lives of others. The blister-and-eraser event was to be a monumental experience, influencing all that I was to create in the years ahead. From that day forward I began to become much more aware of how I was using my thoughts.

Because I had witnessed firsthand the power of a thought to create a physical manifestation, I couldn't get the idea out of my mind that every thought I had contained a kind of enormous potential for change. I remember walking to my car after that class, thinking that I would one day write an entire book on this subject . . . not knowing then that the demonstration I had just been a party to would launch me into writing a small library on the amazing power of our mind. The image of the woman in the classroom never left me. Almost half a century later, it still shines brightly on my inner screen.

21

As I pursue my Ph.D., I'm employed as a guidance counselor at Mercy High School in Farmington, Michigan. I love this school where some 1,000 girls are matriculated in a college-preparatory curriculum run by the religious Sisters of Mercy. I love my job, which is to provide counseling and guidance services for approximately 300 students in grades nine through twelve.

It is the Wednesday after Labor Day, 1968. In the auditorium last night I spoke to the parents and presented the school's plans for the academic year. The opportunity to give a speech and entertain the audience made for a compelling evening, and I am still on a high from it.

Nancy Armstrong, one of my students, tells me, "My mom heard you speak last night, and she wants me to give this book to you as a gift of appreciation. She told me to tell you that she loved your speech to the parents." Nancy explains that her mother is a member of the Book-of-the-Month Club and received this large volume as a bonus for purchasing a certain number of books. Mrs. Armstrong doesn't think she'll ever read it—and because of the content of my talk the previous night, she's certain I'll enjoy having it for my personal library.

The book is titled *The World of Psychology, Volume II, Identity and Motivation,* edited by G. B. Levitas; it was published in 1963 by George Braziller. It is a compendium of 41 essays written by a diverse collection of authors, including Plato, William Butler Yeats, Friedrich Nietzsche, Aldous Huxley, Margaret Mead, Carl Jung, and many other prominent contributors. The mix is exciting—poets, psychologists, literary luminaries, and philosophers. It is right up my alley, as I thoroughly enjoy reading poetry, essays, commentary, and the like. In my amateur way I've dabbled in these forms of writing since I was a kid.

I call Mrs. Armstrong and thank her for her thoughtful gift. Then I realize I have four hours free before I need to be on campus at Wayne State. I'm meeting there with my doctoral advisor, Dr. Mildred "Millie" Peters, to discuss my plan of work for the remaining two and a half years of my doctoral studies. I've already decided on the direction I want to take. I simply need Dr. Peters to okay my plan, which outlines all of my upcoming course work, my practicum and internship requirements, and my doctoral dissertation theme. I'm interested in Carl Rogers's client-centered therapy and B. F. Skinner's work on behaviorism and have decided to pursue areas of research that focus on their modalities.

I pick up the compendium that Nancy gave to me this morning. I flip to Part VII, "The Whole Man," and see that there are offerings by John Stuart Mill, Ralph Waldo Emerson, Robert Browning, and C. E. Montague. But one especially catches my eye: "Self-Actualizing People," by Abraham Maslow. I am inexplicably drawn to the article, which is 28 pages long, and will require a couple of hours to read thoroughly. I turn off the phone after deciding that I must read this before my 7 P.M. meeting with Dr. Peters. As I read, I have the strangest sensation that my life is about to make a radical shift.

The essay describes people whom Dr. Maslow calls "self-actualized." He defines these rare and unique people this way:

> What a man can be, he must be. This need we may call self-actualization. . . . It refers to the desire for self-fulfillment, namely, to the tendency for him to become actualized in what he is potentially.

Maslow describes the innate inner calling of these kinds of people to become everything that they are capable of becoming, and how difficult to impossible it is for them to stifle this drive. As I read on, he describes in detail the specific characteristics of self-actualizers, who are dramatically different from average people. Maslow suggests that they are often labeled as selfish or unconventional and, seems to me to say, that their actions and attitudes should be exalted and commended rather than suppressed and squelched.

Maslow notes that the self-actualized person has a strong desire for privacy; vehemently resists enculturation, but always has a freshness of appreciation; and has a genuine desire to help the human race. Yet "when it comes down to it, in certain basic ways he is like an alien in a strange land. Very few really understand him, however much they may like him."

I am enthralled—highlighting almost the entire article. I feel that I am reading about qualities I've always felt deep within myself, but have often been criticized for. I am so fascinated by what I'm reading I feel as though I am in the midst of an oceanic mystical experience. *This is it. This is the direction I want my advanced studies to take.*

As I read the conclusion I know that I too must be what I can be, and marvel at the coincidence of receiving this gift just before finalizing my plans with my doctoral advisor. Yet, on some other level I know that Nancy bringing this book from her mother is somehow connected to the necessity of my reading this essay today. I reread Dr. Maslow's conclusion again and again. And I know I no longer want to focus on what I was so sure of before reading this essay. I am absolutely certain about what I want to study now.

I make a copy of the last paragraph to take to my meeting with Dr. Peters.

> In this, as in other ways, healthy people are so different from average ones, not only in degree but in kind as well, that they generate two very different kinds of psychology. It becomes more and more clear that the study of crippled, stunted, immature and unhealthy specimens can yield only a cripple psychology and a cripple philosophy. The study of self-actualizing people must be the basis for a more universal science of psychology.

My heart is beating fast; I feel as if I am about to enter a new phase of my life. I show Dr. Peters my plan of work all typed up and ready for her signature, and then I tell her about what I have just read. I am bursting with enthusiasm about this idea of focusing on the highest-functioning people and drawing conclusions about who we can become, based not on average people but on extraordinary self-actualizing people.

I want to write about what I have just digested. I see so many of my own atypical personality traits and inclinations in Maslow's description of self-actualizing people. I've always been independent of the good opinions of others, followed my own predilections, and been outside of the box in my thinking for as long as I can remember. I love the idea of having high standards that are not based on what the culture dictates, but on what I feel within myself to be possible.

I ask Dr. Peters, one of the most self-actualized people I have ever been blessed to know—a woman who earned a Ph.D. when very few woman were even considered for such elevated scholarly status, a woman who always encouraged me to follow my own instincts regardless of what the system seemed to dictate—if I can change this plan of work sitting on her desk and pursue this area of self-actualization in my doctoral studies. Without hesitation, she says yes. We tear up the old plan and I begin a whole new chapter in my life.

I Can See Clearly Now

The laborers of fate were working overtime that September day in 1968. I had given that talk to the parents because the school principal was feeling sick and asked me to fill in for her at the last minute. Had that not occurred, my entire life might have looked very different than it does from this vantage point almost five decades later.

When Nancy handed me that compendium of great spiritual masters' teachings, I felt inexplicably drawn to it. When school let out around two o'clock, I sat at my desk debating whether to head down to the university library or go over my doctoral plan of work one more time in my office. That black book sitting on my desk seemed to have an energy all its own, urging me: *Pick me up and read me; I have something very important to say to you.* When I came across Dr. Maslow's article on self-actualizing people, it spoke to me as well: *Read me and do it right now.*

I can see clearly now that these kinds of almost desperate callings are the work of something bigger than myself, but to which I am passionately connected. I have come to trust in these messages and synchronistic collaborations with fate.

At the time it was all happening I simply went along with how I was being steered without giving it too much thought. Today I am confident that on some level Nancy Armstrong, her mother, my school principal, the person who made the Book-of-the-Month Club bonus decision, and many others were, in some mystical fashion that eludes my intellectual understanding, participants in showing me my path. I believe in it. I trust it, and now from this vantage point, I am much more able to tap into it while it is taking place. It no longer takes years for me to have this insight—everything and everyone are connected to each other and to the Tao or the universal one mind from which all things originate and return.

After that fateful meeting with my beautiful advisor, Dr. Peters, she actually created an entirely new curriculum in the doctoral program in order that I might fulfill what I felt burning so hotly within me. She designed the new program for many incoming doctoral students, and at least 12 people signed on. I was able to be part of an internship doctoral program that focused on using small group-counseling therapy sessions to train people who were inclined toward embracing the tenets of Maslow's groundbreaking work on self-actualization. I would no longer simply check off requirements for a doctoral degree; I had a focus that filled me with passion.

Abraham Maslow became a towering figure in my life. He was the inspiration for me to look at psychology from a 180-degree-turnabout position. Rather than studying what was weak, infirm, or limited in clients and make an assessment based on overcoming ailments, I began looking for the highest qualities of self-actualization and encouraging clients—and ultimately readers and listeners—to seek their own innate greatness and aspire to these pinnacles. I reasoned that if some among us could be self-actualized, then so could I and anyone else who understood that it was possible. This became a major focus of my professional life and the compass I set for myself to live the principles that Maslow delineated in his writing.

Dr. Maslow spent his lifetime researching what constituted positive mental health. Most psychology that I studied before my introduction to his writing concerned abnormality and illness; in my doctoral studies and virtually all of my writing, the idea of self-actualization and humanistic psychology became the central focus. I was destined to spread this idea of each person having the ability to cultivate his or her own magnificence.

Throughout my life I felt that I had something unique within me —when I read Maslow's essay I knew that I had to make this the focal point of my doctoral studies and beyond. I can remember feeling familiar with what he described as the characteristics of self-actualizing people. Later, when I was writing *The Sky's the Limit,* I devoted entire chapters to elaborating on the ideas that were inspired by this mentor of mine who spoke to me through his lectures and particularly his writing. And I wrote *What Do You Really Want for Your Children?* as a guide for parents who want to raise self-actualized children to be humanistically oriented adults. All based on what this man taught me.

Dr. Maslow died of a heart attack on June 8, 1970. I received my final degree on the same day, and would from then on be known as Dr. Wayne Dyer. It's as if he had passed the baton on to me and said, "I've explained this idea of self-actualization to the academic world; now you take the baton and teach it to the masses."

Many books and thousands of lectures later, I can still see me receiving *The World of Psychology, Volume II* from Nancy Armstrong's mom and then letting myself be guided by those forces that are always at work in all of our lives at all times. That book continues to be a treasure—it is on my desk nearby as I sit and write some 45 years later.

This collection of profound observations by some of the scholars most beloved and revered by me was the inspiration for a similar kind of book that I produced in the 1990s called *Wisdom of the Ages.* I wrote 60 essays based upon the offerings of 60 distinguished scholars over the past 25 centuries and how their teachings could impact the reader today. Many of those erudite people were contributors to the book that contained that essay on self-actualization by Abraham Maslow. *Wisdom of the Ages* also became a PBS television special that aired throughout the country in prime time for many years and was watched by millions of people. All because of the events that transpired in my office back in the year of 1968.

It is so clear to me today that everything—every event, and every person—is in some inexplicable way connected. There is no *time;* 1968 and 2018 are all one, even though our body-mind sees them as separated by 50 years. We are all connected to everyone and everything in the universe. What I do affects everyone, and all of my thoughts and deeds are not only listened to by the great Tao but make an impact independent of time constraints. I can't begin to give a literal or linear explanation for how and why the events described in this section transpired, but from this vantage point I can see clearly that not only my life's journey but the lives of millions of people were impacted by my reading that essay by Dr. Maslow that September afternoon.

Today, anytime I feel compelled to do something—something that I experience passionately—I pay attention. When I recognize that it is a calling from my soul, I know for certain that this is something that I must do. It is God calling me in a way that is uniquely and bewilderingly mysterious. It is that calling that I pay attention to that pushes me every day to write these vignettes.

I am connected to you, dear reader—though we may have no physical linkage, there's an energy flowing between the two of us. Neither of us knows how mind-altering it may be, or how far-reaching its extent. I know this for certain as I see more and more clearly.

22

It is the final year of my doctoral studies. For my internship practicum, I'm leading beginning doctoral students in group counseling while simultaneously doing research for the publication of my doctoral dissertation.

Dr. John Vriend, a relatively new faculty member at Wayne State, is a member of my doctoral committee. He received his own doctorate at NYU, where he was involved in an approach to counseling and therapy called *rational emotive therapy (RET)* taught by Albert Ellis, who's written many books and conducts workshops and training at the Albert Ellis Institute on East 65th Street in New York City.

John hands me a book and says, "I want you to read this very slowly and very carefully. It will alter your views on how to help people in a new and enlightening way." What John gives me is *A Guide to Rational Living,* one of more than 75 books that Dr. Ellis has written for the public.

As I read the small book it speaks to me like nothing else has in my training, course work, and personal reading, in terms of how to assist clients in attaining their highest self. This is the same *self* that Dr. Maslow wrote about so poignantly and convincingly. What attracts me is that Dr. Ellis is providing the specifics for teaching people how to attain the pinnacle of Maslow's hierarchy of needs: self-actualization.

The essence of RET is a basic understanding that unrealistic and irrational beliefs cause most emotional problems. The job of the therapist is to help the client strive to change irrational beliefs, challenge self-defeating thinking, and actively promote rational self-talk. The core unrealistic beliefs that most people carry from childhood into adulthood that cause emotional disturbances include: *(1) I must perform well to be approved of by any significant others in my life; (2) I must be treated fairly, and if not, then it is a catastrophe and I simply could not bear it;* and *(3) Conditions must go my way, and if they don't, then it is horrible and I will be distressed and unable to bear it.*

I devour this book and its central theme: *We are responsible for the way we feel, and have within us the capacity to change the way we view the events in our lives.* In simple, commonsense language Dr. Ellis is offering therapeutic tools that prove to clients and therapists that it is unnecessary to be emotionally disturbed or upset. He repeatedly emphasizes that *I must do well, You must treat me well,* and *The world must be what I want it to be* are neurotic ideas that he lumps under the category of "musterbation."

I'm completely taken by the simplicity and logic that Dr. Ellis teaches. I replay the taped recordings of him conducting therapy sessions with people suffering from all manner of serious emotional disturbance and begin to use these techniques with many of my own clients at the university and at the high school. The results are astounding.

I'd been attempting to do counseling that involves client-centered therapy, a psychoanalytic method where I'm essentially a reflective listener. So far I've felt frustration for my clients (and myself as well). But as I begin to be interactive and present an alternative to my clients, positive changes take place almost immediately.

I feel happier and am able to actually talk myself out of some lifelong thinking patterns that aren't serving me. I take this book with me wherever I go and I read it over and over, studying the logic and seeing that most emotional upsets are caused by a set of insane beliefs, that when changed result in a disappearance of the unsettledness. I'm fascinated by how Dr. Ellis weaves in the teachings of Dr. Maslow on self-actualization, Buddha and Lao-tzu and all of the Eastern philosophers, and Epictetus and Marcus Aurelius from ancient Roman times. This little book is the most powerfully influential book I have looked into.

Dr. Vriend, who introduced it to me, is not only on my doctoral committee and a staff member in my professional studies, he's becoming a close friend as well. He gives me guidance—but even more, gives me permission to enter into friendly disputes with my clients over the nature of what disturbs them, and to fearlessly show them how their thinking is really the cause of their emotional turmoil. So I tell them, "Change your thinking: attack the logic that supports your continued annoyance and basically change your philosophy, and you will improve everything about your life. By changing the way you process any and all events as they crop up in your life, you can live a happy, fulfilled life devoid of emotional disorder."

I take notes on this new way of helping people and especially myself. I bring this approach to my teaching, to my counseling, and to my training sessions at the university in my internship. I drink it in—I live it. I write notes to myself about a book I would love to write one day that combines self-actualization, rational emotive therapy, and the ancient Eastern and Western philosophies that I've been studying for over a decade now. I am grateful every day to Dr. John Vriend, who brought this amazing book to me and insisted that I read it slowly and carefully.

I am now very clear on the path my future counseling, teaching, and writing will take. But more than that, I'm thrilled that I have a new tool for my own life. Never again will I blame anyone for any emotional upset that I experience. Blame is gone from my life. I know that if I change the way I process any event—and I always have this power, even as a young boy—then I can get myself righted almost immediately.

I Can See Clearly Now

A Guide to Rational Living was placed into my hands by a man who went from being my mentor and colleague to my closest friend, a man who was sent to me at precisely the right time in my life. Many years later John told me that he felt inexplicably compelled to introduce me to the idea of rational emotive therapy while I was one of his doctoral students. He'd had a vision that it would influence my future writing when I left the familiar territory of Wayne State and embarked on my own professional calling.

I carried Albert Ellis's favorite quote from Marcus Aurelius in my wallet for many years and have used this idea in my speaking and writing for over 40 years: "If you are distressed by anything external, the pain is not due to the thing itself but to your own estimate of it; and this you have the power to revoke at any time." This is quite a departure from what behavioral and psychoanalytical schools taught, which was that our disturbances can be traced to cultural and familial factors, that we are often powerless over these external influences and thus must learn to adapt and work through these early traumas.

I was so drawn to this kind of thinking—that we are responsible for how we process any external event—it's what I intuitively knew way back in grade school when I urged my friends to not be fooled by adult efforts to manipulate them emotionally. Now I had been introduced to a process and an interactive methodology for helping others opt for their own greatness. I currently had three astounding sets of ideas percolating within me: The great ancient philosophical teachings of the East and West; the concept of self-actualization and living at extraordinary levels and the reality of creating miracles; and a methodology for interpreting all of this in a practical way, for anyone to bring about any desired changes and overcome any and all ingrained obstacles.

I began to think about writing a book in the future that would incorporate all of these modalities and still appeal to the masses. I could see that this was more than *The Power of Positive Thinking* by Norman Vincent Peale, which I'd already read. I felt I had a way of presenting commonsense ideas that anyone who wanted to could use to change self-defeating attitudes and live from their own greatness. They only needed to be willing to change the way they think, and conceptualize themselves as able to actualize their greatness.

As I look back on the people and events that were instrumental in shaping my thinking, two people stand out. One is Abraham Maslow and his radical idea that there are people among us who do reach exalted states of awareness and live exciting lives impacting the world they live in and the people around them. When I read Maslow, I wanted to be one of those venerable souls that he called self-actualized. However, Maslow believed as a result of his research that this lofty perch atop the hierarchy of needs pyramid was limited to a select few. Albert Ellis's rational emotive therapy closed the gap that existed in my consciousness about who could become self-actualized.

After reading and studying *A Guide to Rational Living,* I was convinced that this noble calling was available to all. It became increasingly clear to me that we simply need to just get out of our own way and overcome the conditioning we've become accustomed to believe is how our lives are supposed to be. Then we can reprogram our self-concepts and live from a new perspective. Once we eliminate the erroneous thoughts, it's a joy to begin choosing our own greatness, our inherent birthright, if you will. I look back with deep gratitude and respect for all that I learned from the work of Dr. Ellis just as I was launching myself into the world of publishing and speaking.

Although I never emulated his harsh and often crude therapeutic style, I was proudly influenced by Dr. Ellis's logic and all that he had to teach about overcoming emotional roadblocks to a self-actualized life. I feel a guardian angel whispered in John Vriend's ear to place that life-changing book in my hands some 45 years ago. Since that time I have never taken lightly any book that seems to just show up in my life—particularly if I feel some kind of special energy associated with the book at the time.

God works in mysterious ways, and what seems like an insignificant coincidence can be the impetus for a monumental shift as a result of what appears to be an inconsequential act of giving. From this vantage point, I can see that John's gift to me was one of those magical life-altering moments.

23

I am in my final academic quarter of my doctoral studies. The year is 1970, and I am on schedule to complete all of the multitudinous requirements for my degree. My dissertation is almost complete, and I will defend in May—just 90 or so days from now.

I am in an advanced seminar on case study diagnosis and review, which is a required course for completion of my degree. There are six students in this seminar, which meets every Thursday evening from seven to ten. Our professor is the most famous man on campus, and it is truly an honor to be sitting with him. I've taken two courses with him already and found him to be the most memorable professor of my eight years of higher-education study.

I consider myself fortunate to be in this seminar, as it is the most sought-after one at the university. Admission is by lottery because there are several hundred applicants and it's only offered once a year. I'm almost certain that my advisor, Dr. Mildred Peters, a close friend of this professor, had something to do with the fact that I was a lucky lottery winner.

Each week we present case studies to the people in the seminar room sitting around a large table. The students offer their thoughts and diagnostic assessments, and the professor then gives his appraisal. We all take notes furiously as he speaks; we are in awe of this man with an international reputation for his erudition and diagnostic brilliance.

The man of letters who teaches this seminar is Dr. Fritz Redl, known as the "father of modern psychoeducation." He's published many books, the best known of which are *Children Who Hate* and *Controls from Within*.

Dr. Redl was born in Klaus, Austria, in 1902 and earned his doctorate at the University of Vienna, studying with Anna Freud and August Eichorn. He left Austria in the late 1930s because of the Nazi occupation and their treatment of scholars when they occupied a country. He is also known for his work with delinquent boys and for teaching that love and affection are absolute requirements in the treatment relationship. To that end, he takes us to visit Pioneer House, which he founded in Detroit as a residential treatment center for psychosocially lost young boys.

I have grown to love this man in so many ways. He oozes compassion, and always entertains and uses humor in his presentations. I've devoured his writing and feel I have a very special relationship with him. He's taken me under his wing—frequently inviting me to meet alone with him and discuss some of the cases I am presenting in the seminar.

Here in this weekly seminar, the true genius of the man is displayed every Thursday evening. I so love my time with this great teacher who brings incredible insight to every case study we present at the seminar. He speaks with reverence of the work of Abraham Maslow and encourages me to think of every single person as a Divine being capable of self-actualization if treated with love and affection, even if they don't deserve it. Throughout the entire semester, Fritz Redl repeatedly emphasizes this: *even if they don't deserve it.*

Dr. Redl is a highly unpredictable man, well-known for his unusual sense of humor. His classes and seminars are always fun and entertaining but also laced with his commitment to love and affection as two essential components of the therapeutic relationship.

At the midpoint of the academic quarter, we find these words written on the blackboard:

> This is your midterm exam. You have 30 minutes to write. Your answers will determine whether you remain in this advanced seminar.

He looks at the six of us, all sitting there with our open blue books, dutifully ready to write for 30 minutes, and he hands us a paragraph that reads:

> A self-actualized man arrives at a dinner party in which everyone is dressed in rather formal attire. Evening dresses and suits and ties are worn by everyone. He is wearing a pair of dungarees, tennis shoes, a T-shirt, and a baseball cap. What does he do?

Dr. Redl looks at us, tells us that he will return in 30 minutes, and leaves the room abruptly.

The six of us cast curious glances at each other, and with puzzled looks on our faces begin to write. After precisely 30 minutes, our professor returns to the room and asks each person to read aloud what they've written. We all say pretty much the same thing, trying to sound scholarly and regurgitate back what we learned about this idea of self-actualization: *He wouldn't bring it up, he wouldn't explain himself, he'd simply act as if nothing were bothering him. He would engage in conversation and be himself even though he wasn't dressed the same as everyone else. He wouldn't judge the situation or feel uncomfortable about it because he never judges others or himself by appearances. He wouldn't be bothered by the fact that he stood out, he wouldn't apologize or excuse himself.* All of our blue books pretty much convey these kinds of responses to the midterm question.

After Dr. Redl has listened to each of us, he picks up his briefcase and slams it down on the seminar table in feigned indignation and outrage at our answers. "You have all failed this course. You haven't yet learned a thing. All you had to do was to write three words on your paper." He takes his chalk in his hand, turns around to the blackboard, and writes in large letters: HE WOULDN'T NOTICE. He then leaves the room for five minutes while we sit there smiling sheepishly and staring at each other.

Dr. Redl returns to the room, sits down, and announces that there's really no midterm in this seminar! We spend the next couple of hours discussing the huge distinction that exists between people who are classified as average and those who are self-actualized.

I Can See Clearly Now

It has been well over 40 years since I took that seminar, and I've never forgotten the lesson in those three words that Fritz Redl wrote on the blackboard that Thursday evening. *He wouldn't notice.* They have stuck with me and influenced me in a multitude of ways. Those words penetrated me at the time, and after all these years I can clearly see how they've permeated my writing, my teaching, and, yes, my soul.

Self-actualizing people see the unfolding of God in everyone that they meet. They go beyond appearances. They are friendly with anyone and everyone regardless of class, education, political belief, race, or religious affiliation. As Maslow pointed out, "As a matter of fact, it often seems as if they are not even aware of these differences, which are for the average person so obvious and important."

When I left the university and was driving home that night, I made a commitment to myself that this was going to be my way for life. I would do all that I could to abolish any judgments I made based upon appearances. Dr. Redl always emphasized the quality of love, acceptance, and affection for all, in both the therapeutic relationship and our own lives. He used to say to us that therapy is for better or for worse—and if we as supposed helpers were operating at lower spiritual levels than our clients, we would not only be incapable of helping them, but they would leave their counseling sessions worse off than they were before.

After that experience of what I called "my fake midterm," I realized that I learned more from that little exercise than I ever could have from my reading or research. This was a signature moment for me, or what Fritz would have called a "peak experience." At the high school where I was employed, I took pride in being the one faculty member who had no judgments toward any of the students. The nerds, the troublemakers, and the undisciplined were as welcome in my office as the shining stars who always looked, smelled, and performed in an aura of rosy excellence—I stopped noticing any differences between them. The same thing held true in all of my interactions. I had always prided myself on being nonjudgmental and free of prejudice, but now I realized that I'd noticed appearances in a big way.

Throughout my academic years I encountered so much *going through the motions* behavior on the part of faculty and my fellow students that I was motivated to be different—in some way that could be defined by myself as *better.* Meeting Fritz Redl, this international spiritual superstar from Austria, was a kind of peak experience in a reverse way. I was enamored of this man's true charisma. I loved his lectures so much that I actually attended them when I wasn't registered for the classes. I was learning from him just by being in his presence. His high energy was infectious. He made me want to be a better therapist, a better teacher, and most significantly, a better human being. This was a man who cared, especially for the underdog. He spent much of his time reaching out to the disadvantaged and those who had been labeled delinquents.

Dr. Fritz Redl's lessons to me are evident throughout all of my writing, beginning a year later in 1971, with the publication of my first textbook. He was masterful in front of a group, whether it be 1,000 students in his large lecture-hall classes or with a group of six doctoral students, or even in a private conversation in his office. He loved his work. He loved his subject matter, and he truly loved those who had more than two strikes against them. He saw the potential greatness in everyone and always looked past the outer and peered in to that inner space where the spirit is at play. He was a giant of a human being, a man I wanted to emulate in so many ways. He taught me one of the greatest lessons of my life: *to see the unfolding of God in everyone and when it comes to external appearances, to be a humanistic teacher who wouldn't even notice.*

I am ever so grateful for this man's presence in my life, and for the way I see so much more clearly because of him. Rest in peace, my beloved teacher.

24

It is 1971. For the past four years I've enjoyed working as a counselor in a fantastic high school, where I occasionally take on the role of acting principal. My salary is satisfactory, and I can increase my income by directing the driver-education program on evenings and weekends.

All of my doctoral-degree requirements are completed, and I could easily stay in Detroit with a terrific career ahead of me. If I remain here I could eventually head up the counseling department, have a business on the side that pays more than my full-time job, and have the added pleasure of being an adjunct professor at Wayne State University on a part-time basis. I've been teaching graduate courses at Wayne State once a week, and I love the feeling of being Professor Dyer. Only a short time ago I was a freshman, wandering around the campus trying to figure out the confounding registration procedures at a university with over 45,000 students, and now I'm accorded the title of professor, with all of the prestige that accompanies such a lofty position (at least it feels lofty to me).

I've been teaching at Wayne State part-time for the past four academic quarters, and I have a wonderful relationship with the head of the department. My evaluations are great and I've applied for a full-time position, but there is no opening at this time. However, I am under consideration for a professorial appointment at a large university in Wisconsin. A gentleman named Bob Doyle has also just telephoned to tell me, "You have been offered a full-time teaching position as an assistant professor at St. John's University. Are you willing to move to New York City?" I know for certain that I want to teach at the college level, which means I am faced with an opportunity, and a major life decision. Accepting this offer from Dr. Doyle, who is the department head of educational counseling at St. John's, represents quite a struggle for me.

Detroit is the only place I've ever known, other than my four years spent traveling the world in the Navy. This is the only place I've ever called home. I am married with a daughter who is four years old, and my two brothers and my mother also live here. My wife isn't enthusiastic about uprooting herself from her own family and moving to a distant city. She works as a dental assistant, makes good money, and she too has only known Detroit as her home for the 31 years of her life.

I know I'm being called to a new phase in my life that I've been working toward since deciding on this academic path, but there's a part of me that wants to stay where I am and work in the setting that is so familiar to me. I wrestle with this dilemma every day. I am considering moving to a place where I know no one, for a considerably lower salary than I'm earning now, to pursue a dream that everyone else feels is a foolish choice. I am in a quandary day and night, and I only have a few more days to decide or the offer will not be there.

The job market is very tight at this point in time. There are very few openings at universities for professorships anywhere in the country. No one is hiring, and here I have two offers sitting in my lap after just one interview with both of these major schools. I feel blessed, but I live with inner pandemonium every day. I'm a mess because of my indecision and doubt. The easiest thing to do would be to tell myself, *Forget about changing locations; it's too stressful, and besides, you have everything going your way in Detroit. So why mess it up by uprooting yourself and your family to pursue a dream that is simply too difficult to implement?*

The second dilemma I face concerns which of the two professorships I should take, if in fact I'm bold enough to finally conclude that I am going to dislodge my family and do this thing that is causing me so much stress. I am much more familiar with the Midwest, and Wisconsin is much closer to home than faraway New York City. I present this dilemma to my principal at the high school, and she adds more anxiety to the situation by offering to give me a considerable raise in salary if I'll consider staying in my present position. Now I have to decide if I am going to take a university professorship, and which city I'm going to go to—or should I just take this sizable increase in pay and forget about all of this other foolishness, and finally settle down once and for all? The time is drawing near. I must make a decision tomorrow.

I go to a semiprivate cubicle in the university library that I use almost daily throughout my years of graduate study. I am able to access a quiet place within myself and meditate for over an hour. When I'm suddenly startled back to ordinary awareness, I'm directed by an inner voice to go across the street and talk to Dr. Mildred Peters. She was with me all the way through my doctoral studies, rearranged the doctoral-program curriculum for me four years ago, and was like a parent as well as a guide for me.

I go see Millie and explain to her what is going on. She hears me in her beautiful, soulful way and asks me two questions that resolve all of my dilemmas right on the spot: "Will you be able to live with yourself, Wayne, if you don't take on the one that represents the biggest challenge? It's what you've always done. This is your calling—why are you at war with your highest self?"

I realize that the only reason I am in a quandary is because I've allowed fear to occupy my inner world. In my heart I have always known and affirmed that *I am a teacher.* I love being a professor. I've known from the time I went for my first interview with Bob Doyle at the American Personnel and Guidance Association (APGA) National Convention in the spring that this was my destiny. I knew I would be offered the professorship even before my interview, and if any doubt existed, it was gone after our first meeting together.

This was a done deal—but in my mind I'd begun to *disasterize* about the potential consequences of leaving behind what was so familiar to me. I'd written an essay on something I called "The Fear of the Unknown," and now here I am living out that fear instead of trusting in the loving feeling I experience when I picture myself as a college professor in the Big Apple.

When Millie reminds me that I love the idea of challenge, I realize that is precisely what New York represents to me. I hear the words of the popular song within me: "If I can make it there, I'll make it anywhere." It is an ecstatic feeling—New York is the greatest challenge I could undertake. It's the Big Apple, and I *am* going to make it there!

I call my wife from Millie's phone and ask her if she is willing to do this with me. She is reluctant but agrees, knowing that it is something that I must do.

Two months later we're living in New York. I am in the biggest city in the country teaching master's-degree students in the department of educational guidance and counseling during the summer session. I'm thrilled to have my own office, a full schedule of classes, and my own parking space! Leaving the only life I've ever known behind me has been one of the challenges of my life. I have wandered into the unknown, and I'm thrilled to have finally mustered up the courage to leave the familiar behind.

I remember my grandfather working in the same factory, living on the same street, for an entire life. I could sense a deep feeling within him that he was unfulfilled. I recall working as a resource teacher in Detroit and having a conversation with a friend who told me that he only had 13 more years to work at the school and he would receive his gold watch and his retirement benefits. I recall the sick feeling I had when I contemplated doing the same thing for 13 years just so that I could retire in comfort.

I am so pleased that I have made this gigantic shift in my life. It is all so foreign to me—the traffic, the customs, the accents, the rush, rush, rush of it all—but I am at peace and know I can make it here.

I Can See Clearly Now

As I look back on those days when I felt so much inner tension over not being able to make the decision to leave the familiar and head into the unknown, I can see clearly that there was something very powerful working within me that simply could not be ignored. I came here with music to play, and the idea of getting to the end of my life and dying with that music still reverberating within me was more than I could bear. I trust in these inner feelings and believe that they involve a kind of Divine guidance, which in this instance sent me to Dr. Peters.

Millie knew precisely what to say to me at that time, just as she is here guiding me as I write these words. I feel her presence almost every day, smiling at me even though she left this material world many years ago. She knew that I had a big dharma to live out; in fact, she often told me that I had greatness within me and was destined to be a big voice for transformation in our world. She is truly an angel now, someone I speak to when I have big decisions to make, and I know that she was an earthbound angel for me throughout all of my years as a doctoral student back in the 1960s.

I can see clearly now that there are guardian angels who show up in our lives at crucial times. From this vantage point it is obvious to me, even though it wasn't at the time, that Dr. Mildred Peters was sent to me by celestial forces that knew I would need a guiding light in order to make the big decisions of my life. I recall so many times when I thought about giving up on my lofty ideas and Millie would just show up and steer me in the right direction that my destiny demanded.

On that day in 1971 I was in such inner turmoil about where to go and how to make it all happen. This woman, who I swear had the ability to look into the future, took away all of my reservations with her penetrating gaze and set me straight. The outcome of that decision to date includes 41 published books, 10 public television specials, over a thousand public lectures, and hundreds and hundreds of recorded programs, which have helped millions of people improve their lives. I can see it all from here, as I have a vision of Millie smiling at me right now, that I was blessed to have not only an exceedingly competent professional advisor, but one who was to be with me for all the rest of my days.

Something that I know today that I wasn't aware of 40 years ago is the learning gained from *A Course in Miracles. ACIM* teaches us to make decisions by asking ourselves, "Am I doing this from fear or love?" When we are in fear, there is no room for love, and when we are in love, there is no room for fear. When I removed the fear from my inner world, I felt a deep sense of peace. In other words, I was able to come from love. Sans fear, I was able to look at New York City as a great adventure rather than something to dread.

Fear is a mental exercise that's a habitual response lodged in the subconscious mind from early childhood that arises when we anticipate the unknown. I know from my perspective today that love is what's left when I let go of fear. I have applied this wisdom from *ACIM* in making major decisions throughout my life. When a push-pull comes up that involves indecision and doubt, I remind myself that the anxiety is an emotional response, and therefore it must be coming from either love or fear—and since love is not stressful, it must be a fear that is at play. I then simply go to a loving place within, and the indecision is resolved. I find that if I let myself get quiet and meditate on the issue, the loving guidance shows up, and for me that loving guidance often takes the form of someone who has been a heavenly presence for me in my life.

It is obvious from a distance where I can see clearly now that I had to go to NYC. Had I gone to Wisconsin or stayed in Detroit, my life, and yours possibly as well, would have looked different than it does today. It was conquering the fear that allowed me to follow my dream when those mental obstacles surfaced.

I live by the ancient adage that I truly understand today, "Fear knocked on the door; love answered, and no one was there." As one my greatest teachers, Ralph Waldo Emerson, once observed, "They can conquer who believe they can" and "He has not learned the lesson of life who does not every day surmount a fear." On that day, I learned one of the great lessons of life.

25

I am a full-time professor teaching graduate students at St. John's University. This is my second year, and I still love being in this academic world. I'm free to teach my courses as I choose. I teach mostly schoolteachers who are interested in becoming school counselors; I also supervise five or six doctoral students as their advisor and direct their research toward their doctoral dissertations. I have a private counseling practice as well. However, a great deal of my time is spent writing articles for professional journals.

My department head, Dr. Bob Doyle, has told me, "In order to receive a promotion and ultimately tenure, you must demonstrate your academic proficiency by publishing in professional journals and textbooks." It is 1973, and I'm part of a system known as "publish or perish." If I don't have publication credits I will lose my job, and professional jobs are in very short supply.

I'm doing the kind of writing I abhorred when I was a college freshman writing in APA style in order to please a graduate teaching assistant in English 102. I want to write for the masses—I want to publish my own books on living a self-actualized life, and I have a million ideas running through my mind on what would make a popular best-selling book. I particularly am attracted to writing a handbook that invites people who see themselves as ordinary to create a new vision for themselves. I want to encourage readers to discover their potential for living at extraordinary levels of awareness. Dr. Maslow wrote about this potential in *Toward a Psychology of Being,* published about a decade ago—a book that's always in my briefcase. Even so, I dutifully send in articles to many journals and compile an impressive résumé of professional writing.

I apply for a promotion to associate professor after completing my first academic year. I am rejected for advancement but encouraged by the committee who considers such requests to continue in the same vein. I am frustrated with this kind of activity in my life. I love my teaching responsibilities and am popular with the students. I put a great deal of love and effort into my teaching activity, and I love being in front of a classroom. I practice the vow I made a decade ago when I sat in on so many monotonous lectures. I do all that I can to make my classroom come alive. I use humor and anecdotes, and I demonstrate the kind of counseling I would like to see my graduate students practice. I bring in tapes of prominent therapists and generally make my classroom an exciting place to be. My class size is approximately 30 students, but it's not unusual to have as many as 60 people show up, since my class attracts many guests invited by my graduate students.

I begin to tape-record my lectures. In the back of my mind I know that the material I teach and the methods I employ will appeal to a general audience as well as the schoolteachers desiring to become helping professionals in the field of counseling. I want to have a record of these popular lectures for my personal use when I'm ready to write for other than stodgy lettered periodicals—hopefully in the near future.

I complete my second academic year, and this time the promotion committee decides that I'm worthy of the title of associate professor. I have now co-authored a book with my colleague in Detroit, Dr. John Vriend. The book is written by the two of us and a series of other professionals and is titled *Counseling Effectively in Groups*. I am now a published author, and this publication credit allows me to be called "associate professor of counseling psychology."

The following year I write another textbook with John, published by AGPA Press. The American Personnel and Guidance Association is the professional association for scholars and professionals in this field, a prestigious organization within the academic community. This book is titled *Counseling Techniques that Work,* and it will be well received in that it is a required textbook in classes in graduate schools throughout the country.

I'm busy writing a third textbook that I've agreed to co-author with John Vriend. I write furiously every free moment that I have and send the original manuscript chapter by chapter to him for editing—but I cannot get him to respond. John has become more and more preoccupied with his drinking. When I telephone him to discuss the manuscript, he's frequently incoherent and talking the kind of inebriated talk that I recall so vividly from the days of living with my stepfather many years ago.

I write the entire book, titled *Group Counseling for Personal Mastery,* but I cannot get the man whom I've agreed to co-author with to cooperate on what I consider a sensible schedule. I decide that I don't want to be in a position of depending upon someone else for the completion of my writing anymore. I am a lone act and will no longer partner up with anyone.

I abandon the idea of publishing this book at this time and begin to focus all of my mental energy on writing my own book. Not for the academic community, but for the general public. I've read Dale Carnegie, Napoleon Hill, and Norman Vincent Peale and feel that I can offer a book that goes beyond their inspiration and advice. I love and admire all of these men and what they have offered—I see them as pioneers in a fascinating club that I intend to join.

I've written three textbooks, the last one as yet unpublished, but I know it will be one day. Approximately 25 articles I've written have appeared in professional journals, and I co-produced a 12-cassette tape series titled *Counseling for Personal Mastery.* I feel that this leg of my journey is now complete, and my vision is changing.

The academic world, while stimulating and rewarding, more and more is becoming insufficient. I love the classroom and the students, but the politics of university life leaves me cold. Committee meetings, office politics, pressures to gain tenure, administrative demands that seem trivial, and a mountain of paperwork and notices in my in-box are all squelching my creative juices. I'm through with writing that has a limited audience and is being done for status and promotion rather than self-fulfillment. I am feeling stifled in many areas of life and I realize that I need to get away from this environment temporarily.

I know this is a fabulous job that many would give almost anything to have, but I feel called to a new chapter in my life. I know the signs, and I also know that I can't ignore them without paying a heavy price. I remember reading a question that's tugging at my conscience now: *Have you lived 75 years, or have you lived one year 75 times?*

I am in the throes of a shift that I cannot and will not ignore. I do not want to do the same thing over and over, compiling a résumé of repetition. I need to expand. I need to call the shots. I especially need to be free of the stale, insipid requirements that are imposed upon me as a requisite for the privilege of being employed as a university professor.

I Can See Clearly Now

As I look back upon my years as a college professor, I know now how important it is to avoid the pitfall of evaluating success and happiness on the basis of outer measures.

I had everything going for me in my early to mid-30s. I had a job wherein I was almost certainly going to be granted tenure, which means a guaranteed job for life, in a profession where such security is a rare commodity. I had great evaluations by all of my students and my supervisors at the university. The dean frequently reminded me how much I was valued and appreciated for the recognition I was bringing to the university. I had amassed an enviable publishing résumé, with future textbook contracts sitting on my desk awaiting my signature. I had the coziest working arrangement one could ask for. I was only required to be on campus two days a week, had a great relationship with my colleagues, and had a thriving therapy practice.

This was a plum of a job to be sure, yet there was something burning inside me, demanding my full-time attention. My outer world looked great, but my inner world, where I do all of my living, felt incomplete and restless.

I was reminded of Leo Tolstoy's eponymous character in his famous story *The Death of Ivan Ilyich.* On his deathbed, Ivan Ilyich looks into the eyes of his wife, the woman he despised because she had made so many of the arrangements of his life without consulting him and what he felt. And he asks, "What if my whole life has been wrong?"

That scene sent shivers through me. I couldn't imagine living out my life writing for academia, co-authoring with a man whose heart wasn't in it, and teaching courses in the same classrooms and attending the same college curriculum meetings for a lifetime. My life truly would have been "wrong," as Ivan Ilyich feared on his deathbed. I didn't know it then, but that was my highest self, trying to get my attention in an effort to get me to live fearlessly.

26

Wayne State University offers a graduate program in counseling psychology to eligible military personnel and their dependents in Germany. Rather than have the students come to the university, this ongoing program brings the university to the students. I am asked if I would consider teaching in this overseas program for two academic quarters, and I say yes. It is the spring of 1974 and I am on a leave of absence from St. John's University in the divided city of Berlin.

This is my first time in Europe, and I'm thoroughly enjoying the freedom I feel from all of the disquieting requirements associated with my university position back in New York. I am teaching a full academic load in Berlin, and I love this job and this adventure in a very big way.

Germany has always fascinated me. My mother's two brothers were both in the Second World War: My uncle Stuart—whom I lived with during my eighth year, along with his four children—had been a Nazi prisoner of war for two years. My uncle Bill—my inspiration for going on to college and becoming a teacher—had served in the Pacific on a Navy destroyer. I have heard the horror stories of the Holocaust and seen the films of the death camps, and I have always found it incomprehensible that such evil could have ever taken place, particularly during my own lifetime. Perhaps in ancient times, but not while I was a little boy in an orphanage does it seem possible there could have been camps erected for the purpose of exterminating an entire population of people, just because of religious and cultural differences.

I struggle with how this country of civilized people allowed such a malignancy to run rampant among them. Everywhere I go I talk with German people, and I ask the same question: "It was only a few years ago—how could this happen?" No one will talk about it. There's a collective shame evident in all of the men and women who lived through it.

I decide to learn more about this. I'm incredulous and obsessed with how such unprincipled behavior could infect an entire population. *What were they thinking? Why weren't they able to end this madness before it reached such epic proportions?* This is evidence of the groupthink mentality that I so abhor and have been battling on a small personal scale, and of how monstrous it can become.

I purchase William Shirer's history of Nazi Germany, titled *The Rise and Fall of the Third Reich,* which was first published in 1960. I read the whole book in a few days and am even more distressed than before. It seems that the course of human history has made blind obedience to rules the highest virtue of the German mind. I notice it everywhere. It appears that everybody does what they are told—no one questions supposed authority. If there is a rule, you obey it without question. I see this automatic submissiveness everywhere. No one in Germany ever seems to question anything.

My teaching schedule allows me time to travel, so my wife and I spend weekends visiting places within a brief train ride of our location. We go to Bavaria, Denmark, Sweden, Norway, Austria, France, Holland, and Switzerland. I find the differences between East and West Germany to be stark, and I cannot get the images of the Holocaust out of my mind. The trampling of all evidence of individuality, when sufficiently suppressed, brings about the madness of ethnic cleansing and makes genocide an accepted fact. I am beyond obsessed. I have to see this for myself. I make a decision to take the train to Munich and visit Dachau.

Upon arrival I tell a cab driver that my wife and I wish to go to the former death camp that's been preserved as a reminder of what took place only 29 years ago so that the world might never forget. The cab driver, a man of 55 or so, refuses to take us to the camp. He obviously took part in some way in those horrors during his 20s, and his shame is so great that he chooses to lose a fare rather than visit this place.

Another cab takes us to Dachau—the first concentration camp opened in Germany. Built in 1933 for political prisoners, it was later turned into a crematorium and mass-murder facility for the evil visions of the Nazi party. Rather than thinking for themselves, the German people did what they were told to do on a scale so large that it took millions of them to carry out the sinister orders of a madman and his loyal henchmen.

As we walk through the grounds of Dachau I am overwhelmed by sadness and despair. I feel the pain of the hatred that was carried out right here—yes, here, in the ovens and gas chambers, human beings were slaughtered day after day, for many years, all within sight of a thriving city a few kilometers away. This is the ultimate result of people being brainwashed to vilify others who think or worship or act in ways unlike the majority.

I sense the air is getting more and more difficult for me to breathe. I feel as though I am going to vomit. The fear and desperation is still here in these old barracks, and shower stalls, and ovens—even in the pavement I'm walking on. I feel as if I am here for a reason.

The inner disruption is more than a normal reaction to such a horror show. I know I am changed forever. I was conceived on the day that this war began—the first of September 1939, when Hitler invaded Poland. I was born nine months later, on the tenth of May 1940. I feel that in some mysterious way I was intended here, and I can't get this idea out of my mind. I was called to this godforsaken place that is now a Holocaust memorial museum, and it is leaving a lasting impression on me.

A week later I take a train to Amsterdam and visit the home where Anne Frank hid in the secret annex, and wrote her famous diary that became a worldwide phenomenon when the insanity of World War II was brought to a close. I walk up the stairs and again feel the pain that still emanates from the banister, the floor, the entire building—as if this shameful energy hasn't dispersed. It's still right here in the home that's now a museum in memory of the Otto and Edith Frank family, as well as the countless victims who were slaughtered during the same years I was a little boy growing up safely in a foster home across the ocean. I don't just look at the photos and read the mementos; I connect with the fear of those who lived right here. Again, the air is thick, I can't breathe, I have to exit to get some fresh air. Somehow I am connected to all of this. It happened while I was alive.

I don't understand my passionate desire to know about all of this. It is way more than a curiosity. I'm in this setting and compelled to visit other horrendous places where atrocities were performed with the willing aid of an entire population who had been brainwashed by a compelling speaker who spewed evil and hatred and convinced a vast collection of people that it was their duty to behave in these malevolent ways, even though it violated their own original nature. They voluntarily let themselves violate their own inner sense of love toward their fellow humans. How could this possibly have happened? It is unimaginable that this took place in my lifetime. I am shaken. I feel a calling to speak out—to write in a way that such a thing could never ever again come to pass.

I leave Germany to do a teaching assignment in Karamursel, which is located in northwestern Turkey on the Bay of Izmit on the Sea of Marmara. I cannot shake the images I've seen, and I'm deeply impacted by my experience of living in a Germany that a little less than 30 years ago was at war with the world.

During the long bus ride from Istanbul to Karamursel I feel as if I'm being transported back to biblical times. I see animals being slaughtered in the central markets of the villages, all manner of carts carrying goods, and the locals driving old American cars or riding bicycles. It is a far cry from Germany. I teach at an Air Force base for a ten-week quarter, and I'm enthused about the university being brought to our servicemen abroad. The students are appreciative, and I'm proud to be a faculty member here in this isolated place. My ten weeks go by quickly.

My wife and I are scheduled to leave Turkey and return to the United States in July, when I am to return to teach at St. John's University as a newly promoted associate professor. I'm uncertain about continuing to be employed on a full-time basis, but I've agreed to stay at the university for the upcoming fall semester beginning in September.

Living in a Muslim country has been enlightening in many ways. I love the people here. I love being close to nature and swimming every day in the Marmara Sea. Living in Berlin; then Glyfada, Greece, for a short time; and then Turkey has been mind-stretching. However, I am anxious to return home.

My wife and I arrive at the Istanbul airport under circumstances that are new for us. There are tanks, military soldiers armed with rifles, and weapons of many descriptions on the way to the airport and within the airport itself. It is July 18, 1974, and there's talk of war, and of closing the airport, which is jammed with people attempting to leave the country.

When I check in for our flight I'm informed that there will be no commercial flights in or out of Istanbul for the foreseeable future. I'm told that we might be stuck here for an indefinite period of time. People are panicked—the airport is congested with frustrated, angry, scared people. War talk is omnipresent. Turkey is preparing to invade northern Cyprus, and Greece is girding for a military response.

I walk through the airport with a different mental vision than everyone else, who all seem to be in various stages of fear and panic. I see myself flying out of here this morning. It is an intention that is affixed with Super Glue in my imagination—this image will not leave me.

I see some Americans standing in a line preparing to board a military transport plane going to Ramstein Air Base in Germany. I also notice a Turkish man who seems to be somewhat in charge of the boarding procedures. In this hectic environment he approaches people and asks them questions. Everyone he approaches shakes their head and leaves.

I approach this man, and he asks me where I'm going. I explain that I'm scheduled to fly to London, but my flight has been canceled. I tell him I have a military ticket, with a rather high-ranking GS (general service) rating, since I was a professor at an air base in Karamursel. He says that my ticket is no good anymore, but if I want to get out of Turkey he can arrange it on this flight heading to Germany and I can figure it out from there. There are only two seats left on this military transport—for $2,000 cash, he will get my wife and me on this flight and out of Turkey, which is about to erupt into war.

I see this Turkish man as an angel sent to me to fulfill my intention to get back home today. I give him all the cash I have, which is about what I've earned for my teaching stint at Karamursel. I'm about $200 short, but he accepts it and my wife and I board the last flight out of Istanbul. She is staring at me with her mouth agape—a few moments before she was panicked about being stuck interminably in a war-torn country, and now we're flying to Germany on a U.S. military flight that I had managed to somehow get aboard by bribing a local Turkish man in the midst of the chaos.

We land at Ramstein, get a commercial flight out of Frankfurt, and are back in the United States on July 20, 1974—the same day the Turkish military invasion of Cyprus is launched in response to a Greek military junta–backed coup in Cyprus. I sing the praises of the power that exists in making miracles happen when one is steadfastly holding on to an intention.

I Can See Clearly Now

The time I spent teaching abroad provided me with life experiences that were instrumental in all that I was to create for the next four decades. I spent a great deal of my earlier life, right from my first memories, rebelling against authority figures and institutions that were directing me to think and be just like everybody else. It seems as if I was born with this kind of recalcitrant reaction toward the mentality of groupthink. Living in Germany allowed me to see firsthand, on an experiential level, how dangerous such thinking can be, and how it can lead to the ultimate human degradation of genocide.

Every day I asked the difficult questions of anyone who lived through those gruesome years of World War II. I needed to hear from the former soldiers, the housewives, those who were children—I had to hear it from them. "Did you know? What did you think about it? Did you ever consider disobeying odious orders?" The answers were almost always the same: "We were unaware of it . . . we were too frightened to object . . . it's just the way things were . . . we did what we were told." I knew in my heart that virtually everyone had to cooperate in some way, because the grisly actions were so widespread and involved millions of people.

When I left Germany I knew I'd been changed forever. I had to be in this place at this time in order to have my consciousness imprinted. I would have to write and speak about the importance of self-reliance and the *self*—but not the human self, a higher self. I knew that what Thoreau had impressed upon me back in high school on the necessity of civil disobedience would now have to seep through into all of my future writing. These vile acts came about through erroneous zones of mental picturing that had to be changed. I could write about this with much more passion than had ever before been a part of my writing and speaking.

I look back now and can see the perfection in all of this. I incarnated on the day that horrific war began. I was obsessed with learning the truth of what the Nazis were able to accomplish while I was a child living in an orphanage. I had made my inner vow to teach *self* rather than *group* reliance. All of these influences were a part of the dharma that was my destiny. I left Germany determined, even though I didn't know when or how, to teach people to rely on their own original nature, which is comprised of love, kindness, gentleness, and above all, service to others.

In both Amsterdam and Dachau I experienced firsthand that energy is eternal. In those resurrected sites, open to the public so that we should never forget, I felt some of the pain, sadness, and fear that those who were being so mistreated were feeling. I have never doubted this. From this vantage point I can see clearly that I was breathing in the actual pheromones of fear while in Amsterdam, Dachau, and other such places. I have seen how animals who are being led into slaughterhouses where other animals have died in fear react the same way, as they sense that energy and emit pheromones of fear themselves. It's all energy. I gave up eating meat from slaughtered animals years ago, because when I ate that meat, I was also consuming fear.

I choose to do all that I can personally to be surrounded by and encapsulated by love rather than fear. My future writing was to focus on overcoming fear and an awareness of the permanent nature of energy and how it impacts all of us. I was to lecture and write on the idea of all of us being connected in Spirit—that's the nature of our universe.

I was so profoundly influenced by my visits and conversations in Germany. Walking through those vile sites I could actually feel in my gut and my heart a connection to these unfortunate souls. I felt possessed by something ethereal as I traveled about Europe in 1974. I know I was sent there to awaken my soul and inspire me to teach people how to overcome their erroneous thinking patterns.

As I relive my experience in Turkey as war was breaking out over the Cypriot issue, I recall how significant that day was to become for me. I had an image in my mind of escaping from the country that particular morning—it was so real that I acted on it as if it already were my reality. It was not a wish; it was an intention. And because I had used my imagination in such a way as to exclude any and all thoughts of it not working out, I discovered the power of intention experientially, long before I was ever to write about it many years later.

I must have told that story hundreds of times about how powerful a picture in your mind can be, especially when you act as if the picture is already a reality. Rather than look for reasons to verify why this was an impossible situation at the Istanbul airport, I acted on an inner picture. Once again I had been exposed to the idea that was to become a motto for me in my writing, and in my life: "There is nothing more powerful than an idea whose time has come."

My leaving Turkey that day in July 1974 was already an idea whose time had come in my mind, and the power came from my willingness to act only on that idea. This has been a central theme in all of my writing, and I obviously had to experience it firsthand in order to have it imprinted so vividly on my consciousness.

27

It's August 1974, and I'm in New York teaching a summer-school session at St. John's University. It is a shortened semester, with classes meeting twice weekly in order to make it equivalent to a normal semester.

I speak with my colleague Dr. Shirley Griggs, who is the director of a federal grant designed to determine if Southern colleges and universities are in compliance with the Civil Rights Act of 1964. She tells me that I could earn some extra money if I were to go to the Mississippi University for Women in Columbus, Mississippi; spend two days sitting in on classes, interviewing students and faculty; and write up a report at the end of the trip. I have just returned from Europe, where it cost me $1,800 to bribe my way home from Turkey, and I'm pleased to have an opportunity to make some extra money, so I accept.

Four years ago, I heard from a cousin on my father's side named Dorothy Phillips, who said, "Wayne, I've heard that you have spent a lot of energy in trying to meet your father. I'm just calling to tell you that he died in 1964 in New Orleans and his body was shipped to Biloxi, Mississippi, for burial. That's all I know."

Although my father had died and I'd stopped my search for him, my dreams of meeting him, and the rage I feel in these dreams, still persist. Now I have an opportunity to go to Mississippi on business, and I'm excited about the possibility of going to his grave and even reviewing the death certificate to see if I am listed as a surviving son. I've never seen this man, of course, nor do I know if he ever acknowledged that he had three boys, myself being the youngest.

I take the assignment offered by Shirley, and am looking forward to actually visiting my father's grave and perhaps creating some closure on this subject, which has perplexed me since I was a young boy.

The summer session ends on Wednesday, August 28. I fly to Columbus, Mississippi, on Thursday and do all of my required visitations and interviews that evening and the next morning. When I finish, I go to the only car-rental place on campus and rent a 1974 Dodge Coronet. I'm going to drive the 200 or so miles to Biloxi, spend a day or two there, return the car to the New Orleans airport, and fly home Sunday evening.

I notice that the Dodge has that new-car smell, and I see that it has never been rented before. The odometer reads 000.000.8 miles—a brand-new car delivered today to this location at the college. As I settle in behind the wheel, I reach for the seat belt and discover that it is missing. I get out of the car, take out the entire bench seat, and see the belt attached to the floorboard of the car with masking tape, the buckle encased in plastic wrapping and a rubber band around it. I rip off the tape and the plastic, and find a business card tucked inside the buckle. It reads: CANDLELIGHT INN—BILOXI, MISSISSIPPI, with a series of arrows leading to the inn. I momentarily think it's odd that this is in a brand-new car and I'm actually headed to Biloxi. Then I put the card in my shirt pocket and start my trip.

I arrive on the outskirts of Biloxi at 4:50 P.M. on Friday, August 30, and pull into the first gas station I see. I look in the phone directory hanging on a chain in the phone booth and call the three cemeteries listed in the yellow pages. After a busy signal for the first number and no answer for the second number, the third listing is answered by an elderly sounding Southern gentleman. I inquire if a Melvin Lyle Dyer, who died ten years ago in 1964, might be buried at this cemetery. The man is gone from the phone for a full ten minutes, and just as I'm about to hang up, he says, "Yes, your father is buried here."

My heart is pounding through my chest. I feel as if I'm finally going to have my visit with my father, even though it is in less-than-ideal circumstances. I ask the gentleman for directions, and he informs me that this place isn't a real cemetery but somewhere that indigent people are frequently buried . . . on the grounds of the Candlelight Inn! Stunned, I pull the card out of my shirt pocket—I'm three blocks away and there's a map embossed on the card.

Shaking, I drive to the little shack, where the gentleman shows me my father's death certificate. It has been filed away in a battered cardboard Coca-Cola box for ten years. The certificate is stained and musty, and I note with some degree of satisfaction that my name and the names of my two brothers are listed as his surviving sons. *He did know that he had a son named Wayne. I wonder who put it there and what he ever said to anyone about my brothers and me.*

The elderly man directs me to a grassy knoll above a driveway with a chain across it. He says I can stay there as long as I like and asks that I put the chain back up when I drive out. I park my car and walk to the grave marker on the ground that reads: MELVIN LYLE DYER 1914–1964. That's it. This is how we meet.

I stand there with tears rolling down my face. I am still filled with rage, thinking, *I should piss on this grave and leave.* But I don't. I have searched for this man ever since I knew I had a father. For the first seven or eight years of my life, I didn't know what the concept of *father* even meant. So many questions run through my mind now, and I am overcome by the emotion I feel as I stand next to this metal plate on the ground.

During the next two and half hours I converse with my father. I cry out loud, oblivious to my surroundings. And I talk out loud, demanding answers from a grave. As the hours pass I begin to feel a deep sense of relief, and I become very quiet. The calmness is overwhelming. I am almost certain that my father is right there with me. I am no longer talking to a gravestone but am somehow in the presence of something that I cannot explain.

Finally, I wipe away my tears and say my good-byes. As I walk toward the rental car and have the chain in my hand to block the driveway, I'm overtaken by an indescribable force and return quickly to the grave site, as if I am being propelled to go back.

I again speak to my father, only this time I say something very different: "I somehow feel as if I were sent here today and that you had something to do with it. I don't know what your role is, or even if you have one, but I am certain that the time has come to abandon this anger and hatred that I have carried around so painfully for so long. I want you to know that as of this moment, right now, all of that is gone. I forgive you.

"I don't know what motivated you to run your life as you did. I am sure that you must have felt many forlorn moments knowing that you had three children you would never see. Whatever it was that was going on inside of you, I want you to know that I can no longer think hateful thoughts about you. When I think of you now, it will be with compassion and love. I am letting go of all this disorder that is inside me. I know in my heart that you were simply doing what you knew how to do given the conditions of your life at the time. Even though I have no memory of ever having seen you, and even though it was my fondest dream to someday meet you face-to-face and hear your side, I will not let those thoughts ever hold me back from also feeling the love I have for you."

I stand at this lonely grave marker in southern Mississippi, and I say what I now feel: "I send you love . . . I send you love . . . from this moment on, I send you love."

In this pure-bones moment I experience feeling forgiveness for the man who was my biological father, as well as for the child I had been who wanted to know and love him. I feel a kind of peace and cleansing that is entirely new for me. I walk back toward my car, put the chain up across the driveway, and feel a brand-new sense of lightness.

The elderly Southern gentleman had given me the name of the man who delivered my father's body to this cemetery for indigents. I look him up and discover that this was my father's closest friend. He works as a projectionist at a Biloxi movie theater. On Saturday, August 31, I go there—*The Ten Commandments* is playing at the matinee.

I walk up the back stairs and knock on the door of the projection booth. I spend the afternoon with this man who tells me about the man who was my father. I learn very little except that he had mentioned his three boys on occasion, but it was very rare. I hear again about his alcoholism and wandering nature. I don't even care to know any more details. I walk out of the theater and drive toward the New Orleans airport.

I am a changed man. I have just participated in a miracle. I no longer hate my father. I know I was sent here to do this forgiveness thing, but I'm not sure why. I just know that something very mysterious is at work here. Something bigger than I am is moving the pieces around, and it conspired to land me here.

I arrive home in New York on Sunday, September 1. I have over two weeks before I'm due back at the university for the fall semester. I gather up all my recordings of my lectures from the past three years, along with the notes that I kept during the time I was in Europe earlier this year. I make a flight reservation for tomorrow, Labor Day, to fly down to Ft. Lauderdale, Florida. I am going somewhere that is sunny, warm, and on the ocean to write my book—the thing that has been dominating my inner world needs to escape and be born.

At the Ft. Lauderdale airport I rent a car for two weeks and drive to the Spindrift Motel, across the street from the Atlantic Ocean. I hole up in my room, listen to the tapes, and take copious notes. I decide I'm through with all of this mental and physical preparation—I'm ready to write, and begin a writing binge. I stay in that motel room writing every night until the sun comes up. On September 15, I fly back to New York to begin the fall semester.

I've written an entire manuscript using the same formula that has been working so well for me in my private therapy practice. Twelve chapters describe a rational, commonsense approach designed to assist anyone to reach the top of Maslow's pyramid: self-actualization. First, *identify the thinking* that is causing any kind of disturbance. Second, *label the behaviors* the client is demonstrating. Third, *establish the psychological reward system* for maintaining these behaviors. Fourth, *focus on alternatives* by designing specific strategies for eliminating those self-defeating ways of being. No fancy psychological system;

just plain old common sense with specific techniques for change. This has worked wonders in my counseling practice, and I'm certain my book will be well received.

After spending a few hours in a spirit of forgiveness for something that immobilized me for my whole life, it appears that what I've agonized over for years has taken flight in just two weeks' time. The writing seems to be effortlessly guided, and I have completed a handwritten manuscript. No title. No publisher. Only an inner knowing that those moments at my father's grave have infused me with a spirit that I've never experienced before.

I Can See Clearly Now

Today, if asked what is the most significant experience of my life, I respond with the events of August 30, 1974—being at my father's grave site in Biloxi, Mississippi, forgiving and loving him, and cleansing my soul of the toxicity that living with internal rage had brought.

I'm in awe of the synchronicities that came together to bring me to that grave site. I have no clever intellectual explanation for the presence of that business card in that brand-new rental car. I cannot give a rational account of why a cousin I'd never known called me four years earlier, why Dr. Shirley Griggs offered me that temporary assignment, or why I was called back to the cemetery plot and directed to send love where internal violence had previously resided. I take Rumi's poignant advice. I am bewildered by it all. Yet I know that something much more powerful was at play than a series of mere coincidences.

From a clearer perspective looking back at it all, I know that God's fingerprints are all over this scenario. I now realize that I was a mess in those days. I was working but feeling unfulfilled. My writing was stunted and for the first time, unrewarding emotionally. I had terrible eating and drinking habits, was overweight, and was in an unsatisfactory marriage. I was an angry man in many ways, and I was having frequent nightmares about my father. I would awaken in a cold sweat having met him in a bar in the nightmare, and I was always in a fist-fight with him, striking out in anger and demanding answers from a ghost who kept disappearing from view in my slumbering vision. I knew that I had bigger things to accomplish and yet I felt trapped by the circumstances of my life and unable to free myself from these self-imposed snares.

After my return from Biloxi, my life took on an entirely new flavor. My writing at the Spindrift Motel was pure joy. I would write all night, often frustrated in the morning when I'd see sheet after sheet of paper on the floor—my writing reverie had been so hypnotic that I neglected to number the pages.

Within a few weeks of returning to New York I began an exercise regimen that continues to this day. I got myself in top physical shape and began an eight-mile-a-day running streak that lasted for 29 years—with the exception of one day. I changed my dietary habits, and took on an entirely new attitude.

The book I wrote in 14 days after I dispelled the angst from my soul ultimately became the number-one-selling book of the decade, and it has now been published in 47 languages around the globe, with total sales somewhere shy of 100 million copies worldwide. It is called *Your Erroneous Zones,* and it speaks of the foolish errors in our thinking and how to live a life free of emotional turmoil by changing our habitual thinking habits. This was a book that I was destined to write. A lifetime of Divinely inspired experiences prepared me for the task, yet I was being throttled by inner self-sabotaging rage that had to be excavated.

I was directed to Biloxi to understand firsthand the incredible power of forgiveness. This idea is at the core of spiritual teaching and yet is one of the most ignored principles. Jesus reminds us in Luke 6:27, "But I tell you who hear me: love your enemies, do good to those who hate you." And in Luke 6:28, "Bless those who curse you, pray for those who mistreat you." These are only two of hundreds of such biblical admonitions. I can see clearly now there is great power in truly living this way.

When I was able to forgive and send love where hatred previously dominated, everything in my life shifted. The right words were there, the right people began to show up, the circumstances magically appeared, all scarcity dissolved, my health returned, my energy was reignited, and my life became flooded with abundance—all because of a profound moment of forgiveness that was orchestrated by forces beyond my human ability to explain. It was as if the universal Divine mind, God, or the Tao, if you will, saw that I was stuck in a quicksand that was destroying me—and it coalesced the necessary events in order to give me a giant branch to grab ahold of, and remove myself once and for all from the deadly pit that was snuffing out my life forces.

From this vantage point I can see that God is love, and forgiveness is a tool that's available to get us back to a God-realized life. I had always known that I had to write my own way on the subjects that were precious to me. Yet I was unable to break free of so many bonds that were holding me back. I had a life that would have been the envy of most people, yet inside I was teeming with discontent.

While I was in the midst of the events of that summer in 1974, I sensed that something was being awakened within me. I couldn't see the mystical hand of Divine intervention at work—this was only available to me as a clearer vision years after I was able to see from a distance what I was being led to do. In fact, many years later, I helped to write and produce a movie version of the essence of that experience in Biloxi, titled *My Greatest Teacher.* I gave it this ironic title because I believe today that it was my father, this man I've never known, who taught me the great lesson offered to us by St. Augustine: "Forgiveness is the remission of sins. For it is by this that what has been lost, and was found, is saved from being lost again." After Biloxi I have never been lost again.

I have written whole chapters on the power of forgiveness, and told the story of my coming to know my father to audiences all over the world. I have counseled thousands of people in person, on the media, and on my own radio show; and I created the movie I just referred to. Once I was found and saw how it offered me a U-turn in my life away from pain toward self-actualization and God-realization, I was never lost again.

Perhaps my favorite quote on forgiveness is from Mark Twain: "Forgiveness is the fragrance that the violet sheds, on the heel that has crushed it." Indeed we send love in response to hate and become spiritual alchemists. I didn't forgive my father just for his sake; I did it for my own and his as well. This I can now see with a much clearer vision today.

28

At the end of the fall semester in 1974, I am completing teaching two courses at St. John's University on counseling techniques that work and diagnostic skills. I've taped all of these lectures over the past three years and used much of the material in the first draft of my self-help book written a few months ago. That manuscript sits in my office as I consider what I should do about getting it published for the mass market. I am an unknown person and publishers haven't been eager to take a risk with me, even though I've written three textbooks and a gaggle of articles that have been published in professional journals.

I've made every effort to keep my evening classes both informative and entertaining. I think back to my days as an undergraduate student being so perplexed by the inability of the vast majority of professors to make the material come alive, to keep the audience entertained and on the edge of their seats. I love teaching and being in front of an audience—I especially enjoy making my classroom fun, injecting humor as frequently as possible.

Five students in my Tuesday- and Thursday-night lectures approach me, encouraging me to make this material available to a much wider and less academically oriented audience: "Dr. Dyer, would you please consider offering a series of lectures available to the public similar to what you're teaching here at the university?"

These students are completing their master's-degree program, and often they bring their friends and family to sit in on my lectures. They all live on the North Shore of Long Island and tell me they can guarantee a good turnout if I consider their request. It turns out that one of these students, Linda, works in Port Washington at the Education Assistance Center (EAC) as an administrator and tells me that the building is never used past six o'clock on Monday evenings. She'll make the EAC available at no cost if I'm willing to teach a course open to the public.

I agree, and come up with a course title for this four-week night-school offering: "Living a Self-Actualized Life." Linda plants a brief story in the *Port Washington News* inviting the public to four lectures on four consecutive Monday evenings beginning in February 1975. I am going to be giving a lecture to the public for the first time. Total cost for the course is $20. This is my first stipend for public speaking.

I arrive on Monday evening at seven o'clock for the first presentation to see that 25 students are sitting in the classroom! I end up with $500 in extra money, which is a huge amount of cash during a somewhat depressed economy.

I deliver the four lectures on topics such as "Overcoming Guilt and Worry," "Farewell to Anger," and "Breaking Free from the Past." These are all chapter titles in my completely written, but as yet unpublished, manuscript that's sitting in my office at the university.

At the end of the fourth presentation, the students petition me to extend the classes for four more weeks—they are loving these Monday-night lectures and do not want them to end. They also tell me that many of their friends are interested in signing up. So, on the first Monday in March, I arrive to teach my next class and find that the room is crowded to overflowing. Sixty people are jammed into the classroom, all with $20 bills in their hands. My Monday-night lecture series is a huge hit in the northern Long Island communities.

Within a year I have to leave the EAC because of space limitations, and I decide to rent the auditorium at Schreiber High School on Campus Drive in Port Washington. The place is packed every Monday night for the next year and a half, and when my book is published the following March, 1,200 people will be in attendance. I now earn more money from my lecture series than I make as a full-time professor at the university.

My Monday-night lectures in Port Washington are a huge community event, with people attending from all over the New York metropolitan area. It isn't long before I receive a letter in the mail from a Mr. Arthur Pine, who is a literary agent in New York City, telling me his wife, Harriett, is a close friend of someone who's been attending my lectures. Harriett's friend raves about the content and presentation style of the professor who is offering these classes to the community, and has suggested that Artie contact me to see if I might want to write a book using the format of these lectures for the general population.

I pick up the telephone and call Artie, who has a home in Port Washington. I tell him that I have a completed manuscript that I've been staring at for over six months, wondering what I needed to do in order to make contact with a publisher. Artie listens to me describe the book and how I want to keep it in everyday commonsense language for the general public. He loves the idea and invites me to meet with him in his Manhattan office the following week.

I take the subway into the city with my completed manuscript in my hand, and spend a delightful afternoon telling Artie all of my ideas. He says he cannot promise me anything since I'm an unknown commodity, and this would really be a first book since my previous books were written for a different market. Artie is skeptical, but he's taken by my enthusiasm and loves the rave reviews he's heard from his wife's friends who attend the Monday-night public lectures in his hometown of Port Washington. He says he'll call me if he's able to get me an appointment with a publishing house in New York.

I leave knowing that I will soon have my own book deal. I just know it.

I Can See Clearly Now

I now see that Linda and her four friends approaching me about offering a series of paid lectures to the community were angels sent into my life on a Divinely appointed mission. At the time I simply saw a fun new adventure—from a distance with a clearer vision, I see how this experience launched me in an entirely new direction. This was my first step in the direction of more thorough self-reliance in my life. I soon learned that I could stay in the profession of teaching, which I utterly loved, and not have what I considered restrictions, such as answering to administrators or the low pay that came with the teaching occupation. I could teach on any subject of my choosing on my own terms, and I discovered that this could be a lucrative way to make a living as well.

For decades now I've encouraged everyone to believe that making a good living at what you love is a possibility. If you stay on purpose and are committed to following your bliss, the universal one mind will cooperate with you in bringing this to fruition. The right people will show up, the obstacles will be swept away, the necessary circumstances will materialize, and guidance will be there. As the ancient Buddhist proverb reminds us, "When the student is ready, the teacher will appear." Likewise, when the teacher is ready, the students will appear! The key here is the word *ready.*

Had I decided almost 40 years ago that I couldn't do such a thing, it probably wouldn't work out, that people wouldn't show up, it was too much trouble, or the amount of money I would make was too small, I simply would not have been ready. Those five students and the availability of the EAC were teachers being sent to me. It was my readiness to see the opportunity and seize it that propelled me in the direction of saying "Yes, I'll go for it." Had I not said yes to this suggestion, my entire life would have unfolded in an entirely new way. I might have remained a college professor for the next 30 years, because I would not have seen firsthand that I could still teach and do what I love, *and* earn a grand living at it. I wouldn't have met the man who was to become my literary agent, guiding me into the world of publishing.

What I now know from this vantage point is that teachers are omnipresent in every moment of our lives. These teachers don't always show up as people; sometimes they arrive as what appears to be a coincidental coalescence of events, or an unexpected letter in a mailbox, or an interview on television. I have learned over these years not to look for the teachers, but rather to keep myself in a state of readiness and to stay in a state of gratitude for all of it.

I mentioned earlier the quote of Thoreau's that indicates if you follow your dreams, "You will meet with a success unexpected in common hours." I interpret this to mean that success will in fact chase after you if you stay aligned with the highest vision you have for yourself. This alignment process is key. Stay connected to your creative Source and you gain the power of that Source, because you and God are one. By taking advantage of that door opening at the EAC back in 1974, I opened a door into a grand ballroom of unlimited potentialities that would have otherwise been unseen.

I think back to the Monday nights when I was teaching my own course and it reminds me of the classes I offered to my fellow sailors on Guam when I was 21 years old. The pure joy I felt when I was following my own inner calling, and aligning with God, moved me away from having to let my life be guided by what others thought best for me.

I've often quoted the enigmatic writer Virginia Woolf whenever any of my eight children appear to be questioning what direction to take in their lives: "Arrange whatever pieces come your way." Such great advice. Take the pieces that show up for you, and arrange them in such a way so that you live fearlessly, and the one universal Divine mind will handle all of the details for you.

That wondrous hand of fate that knew what I had signed up for in this incarnation was directing things for me back in 1974–75. It sent me to Europe to help me define my mission, and it got me out of Turkey safely in order that I might see the power that my intentions had for accomplishing anything. It sent me to Biloxi to rid me of those inner impediments to my own greatness, and it brought into my life the awareness of my own potential for being independent as well as the people who would guide and direct me.

In 1974 I was looking at two doors to go through: one that ensured my stagnation, and another that opened me to vistas beyond even my own wildest imaginings. And the fall of 1975 was to offer me one more opportunity to arrange the pieces that were coming at me fast and furiously.

29

I have just completed my fourth year of teaching at St. John's University in the spring of 1975. I've also signed an agreement to have Artie Pine represent me in exchange for him receiving 15 percent of whatever I earn as a published writer. He's used a connection he has with the T. Y. Crowell publishing house, and I have the opportunity to present my completed manuscript to a senior editor there and see if they're interested in my book. As Artie says, "Go there and sell him on the idea of having them publish your book."

I arrive at my designated appointment in the heart of Manhattan and am told by a secretary to wait in the outer office. An hour goes by, and I'm finally escorted into the office of Mr. Paul Fargis. He apologizes profusely for keeping me waiting and begins the interview by asking me about my manuscript and what my plans for publication are.

Something is just not right, though. I've had a private therapy practice on Long Island for over four years, doing one-on-one counseling five days a week at my home office, seeing as many as 30 clients a week. As a result I've become adept at sensing when a person is deeply troubled, and I'm feeling that now in this interview. Paul exudes anxiety and stress—he looks as if he's been up all night and is attempting to mask his true feelings and get this interview over with, even though it had been arranged by Artie several weeks ago.

I immediately shift into a therapy mode, asking if he'd like to tell me what's going on as I may be able to help. Paul opens up about a personal issue he's dealing with, and we spend the next three hours talking about it. When we've finished, he once again apologizes to me as we shake hands and depart. I leave with my manuscript under my arm—the subject never came up after the first few moments of our introduction. I return home on the subway.

When Artie calls, anxious to know how the meeting at T. Y. Crowell went, I briefly tell him what happened. He is furious in a friendly way and upset with what he sees as my naïveté. He can't believe that I let this once-in-a-lifetime opportunity slip away. Artie had wrangled this meeting through a connection in the company, and didn't think he'd be able to get another appointment for me. This was my golden opportunity and I hadn't taken proper advantage of it.

Yet at ten o'clock the next morning, Artie calls from his Manhattan office, beside himself with excitement. Paul Fargis has just told Artie, "I don't care what is in that book of Dr. Dyer's—I want to sign him up as my author." He offers an advance that's almost equivalent to my entire yearly teaching salary at the university. I am overjoyed. I have a book contract with Funk & Wagnalls, a subsidiary of T. Y. Crowell—and I just doubled my income as well!

I Can See Clearly Now

Unbeknownst to me at the time, I was presented with one of the truly great opportunities that had ever come my way. I had the choice of letting ego take over and conduct that first meeting with a New York publisher. My ego would have ignored the obvious strain that Paul was under and proceeded full-steam ahead with its goals. I would have attempted to sell this editor on all of the reasons why he should consider publishing my book, which would have been ego's choice. The ego is all about winning, and drawing as much attention to oneself as is possible.

I've learned through the years that the inner mantra of the ego is always some variation of, *What's in it for me? Take care of me—I'm the most important person in the world.* With this kind of inner dialogue going on nonstop, the ego dominates most interactions—with less-than-satisfying outcomes. I can see from this vantage point and with a clearer vision that we are continuously being given chances for taming this aspect of ourselves.

The other choice I had in Paul's office on that day in 1975 was a wonderful opportunity to tame my ego by putting it on the back burner. The choice I was presented with that day was to ignore the prompting of my ego and listen to the inner mantra of my higher self. This mantra asks *How may I serve?* rather than focusing on *What's in it for me?* This was a major lesson for me, not just that day, but for all of my future writing and teaching.

Our original nature is love, kindness, gentleness, and service to others. This is what God looks and acts like—never asking for anything, always serving by providing fresh air, water, food, flora and fauna. All given freely. When we ignore our ego and listen to our highest self, we align with our Source of being, God, and consequently acquire the power of our Source as well.

When we come from an attitude of *How may I serve?* as I was unconsciously doing in Paul's office, the universal Source seems to recognize itself in that energy, and asks right back, *How may I serve <u>you</u>?* This is what was happening to me—my simple act of reaching out to another fellow human being in need brought a whole new world of unlimited abundance into my life without me even knowing it.

Several hugely successful best-selling books came out of that publishing contract, and my life was directed toward a dramatically different path than I'd been on. Taming ego's incessant demands for attention and self-serving has been a very big theme in my writing, my speaking, and especially in my own personal life.

I feel a Divine hand was dealt to me during those days in 1975. One fateful meeting and there I was, a 35-year-old unknown professor, ushered into an office with an invisible force whispering, *Take your pick—listen to your ego asking, "What's in it for me?" or the voice of your higher self asking, "How may I serve?"* This was truly one of the great lessons I had to learn, and I am so grateful that my previously seldom-heard higher self was able to drown out the usually victorious prodding of my ego.

I can see clearly that taming this loud swaggering me has been a lifelong challenge, and that day in Paul's office was an opportunity to begin that journey. I am forever grateful for all of those participants who joined with me to begin that odyssey.

30

During the fall semester of 1975, my plate is overfull. I have a multitude of assignments on various committees at St. John's University, a full teaching load, several doctoral students to advise, and a full-time counseling practice. Monday nights have grown into an event, with hundreds of people attending the class I conduct in Port Washington on living a self-actualized life. And *Your Erroneous Zones* is scheduled for publication in just a few months, so I'm in the first editing stages for the book. I love working with Paul Fargis—he's highly skilled and offers me a great deal of guidance in the editing phases of the first book I've authored alone.

My private therapy practice has grown so large that I no longer accept new clients. On my days away from the university I'm frequently scheduled with therapy appointments from 7:30 A.M. until well past 9:00 P.M. With papers to grade, dissertations to supervise, committees to sit in on, and many students to advise, I feel successful—but squashed.

Prior to my evening classes, my days at the university are beyond chaotic. My office teems with students needing to see me *now* with a legion of concerns, and my secretary, Mary, buzzes me continually to speak with someone who's on the phone.

In a couple of hours I'm scheduled to be in front of a full classroom of students, along with many uninvited guests who want to sit in on my lectures. I hear Mary asking several of my colleagues who are also holding office hours, "Has anybody seen Dr. Dyer? There must be one hundred people who want to see him, and I've looked everywhere!"

In the midst of this pandemonium—when the tentacles of bedlam seem to be coming at me from every direction threatening to pull me apart—I escape. I walk down the back stairs of Marillac Hall, step outside, and take a deep breath. I walk along Utopia Parkway for a few moments and enter the park, where I go to an isolated spot behind a clump of trees and sit on a huge boulder.

Five minutes away, my office is overflowing with people, all of whom want a piece of me. I smile inwardly at the enigma I'm living, as I close my eyes and listen to the sounds of nature. I feel the sun on my face, and bask in the healing energy it seems to bring to my anxiety-ridden stomach. I hear the sounds of birds, crickets, dogs in the park, and the wind as it moves the branches and leaves above me. I open my eyes slowly, appreciating the brilliant colors dancing through the trees as the magnificence of the autumn transformation plays itself out right before me—all done so effortlessly.

I spend barely 15 minutes in this spot I cherish, enjoying a brief escape from the chaotic energy of my office, and I'm ready to return. Refreshed, I walk back to the university feeling like a new person. The heaviness is gone—I feel as though absolutely nothing can get to me. I know I'm walking back to turmoil, but it no longer feels turbulent to me. I walk up the back stairs, enter the third floor through a seldom-used door, and stroll into the outer office space, feeling totally peaceful.

The students waiting to see me look different than they did when, unnoticed, I departed 20 minutes ago. I welcome each of them to my office and agreeably help resolve their concerns over grades, papers, and other university requirements that seem to them to be impinging on their desire to complete their degrees. My colleagues who need my attention no longer feel as if they're intruding; I can calmly handle all the phone calls now. The next two hours go by quickly, and I dispense with a host of details in a relatively stress-free fashion.

I think of my little area in the park as my serenity spot, making it a habit to visit there almost every day in the midst of the chaos that characterizes my office hours. I treasure my time in this tranquil enclave and the peacefulness I access there, content and envious of the creatures that don't seem to have to be in assigned places. I especially envy the birds flying above it all, soaring in the wind, oblivious to all that is chaotic on the earth below. But I realize that I've discovered that I have a place of freedom within me as well. I can soar above it all and look down at the tumult with a clearer vision, just by accessing my own eagle-in-flight imaginings.

I Can See Clearly Now

Now as I look back on the significance of my serenity spot, I see the important role this little escape place in the park provided for me back in 1975. This was before my true immersion into the blissful world of meditation, yet I feel that I was in some mysterious way guided to that spot near St. John's to introduce me to the idea of silence as an antidote to stress. It has been almost four decades since I sat on the park boulder, yet I can see it perfectly as I sit here writing today. I can see, smell, hear, and actually feel that serenity spot I retreated to all those years ago.

Meditation was to become an extremely important activity in my life—I was destined to become deeply involved in this ancient art of centering. Eastern teachers would show me how to teach others to practice *Japa,* an ancient form of meditation using the mantra of the name of God to reach exalted states of inner awareness. I was to be exposed to the magic of being a practitioner of Transcendental Meditation, and to be instructed in this practice by some of the world's renowned authorities on quieting the mind. I was also destined to create my own version of meditation and to write a book giving specific guidance on how to make meditation a daily practice in one's life. All of this was ahead of me—way ahead of me.

Yet I see clearly now the work of a Divine intelligence that was privy to my destiny, which was obviously obscured to me at the time. Divine intelligence was at work in the days I was prodded to leave my office and walk to the park. I look back at the bewildering energy that urged me to go to that spot on emotionally stormy days as a powerful experience directing the course of my life. My serenity spot, where I drank in the enchanting loveliness that was being offered to me, seemed at the time a great way to put aside the anxiety and let off a little steam. But from a distance I view it as a signal to me on that particular day to make a U-turn away from a life filled with unnecessary pressure.

I've often quoted the French philosopher, scientist, and mathematician Blaise Pascal, who said, "All man's troubles derive from not being able to sit quietly in a room alone." Though I'd thoughtfully considered his words many times, they didn't truly sink in until I experienced my troubles dissolving as I sat quietly in my own serenity spot alone. I was given the opportunity to know the truth of these sentiments from firsthand experience, and I remain eternally grateful to whatever Divine hand propelled me toward that sacred spot, where I retreated often. I was being given my introductory lessons on achieving inner peace in circumstances that drive others to madness, and learning to become a teacher of this wisdom for generations of new meditators and yoga practitioners.

One of the great truths that I've been blessed to receive and teach came several decades after my serenity-spot sojourns. It has become a trademark of mine and is imprinted on all my notepads. It says simply, *When you change the way you look at things, the things you look at change.* When I was involved in so many activities and attempting to find clarity in the midst of turmoil that defined my life, my escapes brought this truth home to me in a big way.

After spending a brief amount of time in nature, free from human distractions, and being in a silent inner space, I was able to go back to that helter-skelter office and change the way I looked at things. And sure enough—the things I looked at changed! My students were young people in need, not people who were causing me stress. My colleagues were friendly co-workers, not the source of more things to do. The phone calls were no longer interruptions, but simply part of the job that I'd volunteered to do. The whole place seemed to be an exciting enterprise with bustling energy, rather than a mind-numbing energy drain.

Today, when I read that observation about changing the way you look at things, I frequently go back in my mind to those peaceful retreats in the park adjacent to the university. This was my inauguration into becoming a teacher of the powerful idea that a few quiet moments in nature can bring about a radical shift in the most disagreeable of circumstances. And sure enough, I was about to embark on a new career of teaching others how to live from a place of peace and change the way they look at things.

31

I have completed my fall semester of responsibilities at St. John's University and been working almost full-time editing and rewriting *Your Erroneous Zones.* Paul Fargis, my editor at T. Y. Crowell publishing house in New York, has just told me, "Your book will be published in March, and we were able to get it serialized in a national publication. Congratulations!"

My book is developing into a guide for cutting through a lifetime of emotional red tape. I've written it not *because* of my advanced educational training, but more *in spite of* it. I'm confident about what truly works in helping people to bring about permanent change because I've worked with so many people of all age-groups and a wide variety of backgrounds and cultural influences.

In the past four years in my private practice, I've helped hundreds of clients learn how to manage their lives in healthier, more productive ways. They've come to me seeking to overcome emotional problems, and they've succeeded most often with a commonsense approach. I feel I can be most useful to readers of *Your Erroneous Zones* if I can eschew the more psychological route that's often the basis for training my doctoral students. I want to keep this book as simple and down-to-earth as I possibly can. I have a great deal of faith in the innate greatness of everyone.

I hear Buckminster Fuller give a lecture wherein he makes this statement: "Everyone is born a genius, but the process of living de-geniuses them," and I can't get this idea out of my mind. I want people to trust in their own magnificence. My experience doing therapy with clients and my exposure to Dr. Maslow have convinced me that everyone is a genius. In every counseling session I believe I'm sitting across from a genius who's unfortunately allowed him- or herself to become *de-geniused!* My book is about implementing these ideas without all of the excuse-making that theoretical psychological approaches provide.

I discuss my clients' problems, as they see them, very briefly. Most of my attention is on helping them think differently about themselves and their lives. I am calling this book *Your Erroneous Zones* because it's about teaching people to transcend errors in their thinking. So many people don't believe they have choices; they feel that their problems have been imposed upon them by external factors over which they have zero control. I see this as an error. I repeatedly offer my clients tools that will facilitate their discovering that they are the sum total of all of the choices they make. They resist at first, wanting to blame, and I point out this is a choice. I tell them that to do so is not just crazy, it is an error in thinking—that is their erroneous zone.

Change your thinking, take responsibility for everything in your life, and conquer your erroneous thinking. I practice a kind of softened rational emotive therapy, and I see colossal changes being made by my clients in a relatively short number of sessions. Abraham Maslow and Albert Ellis have been great teachers—their work impacts me in my private practice, in my writing, and in my personal life.

I insist upon keeping my message direct and simple throughout the editing process of my original manuscript that was written a year ago. It is common sense, more than pedantic psychological theory, which been most useful in my helping people to vanquish the errors in their thinking that have caused emotional disturbance and unfulfilled lives. I resist efforts by my publisher to *professionalize* my manuscript with an APA style of writing, or to use endless references to established research.

Fast-forward to March 1976. I receive a hardcover copy of *Your Erroneous Zones* by hand delivery at my office at St. John's University. I am thrilled beyond my ability to describe this feeling. My heart races with excitement as I contemplate what's been accomplished: The visit to my father's grave in Mississippi. The hundreds of lectures and counseling session I've recorded. The impact of Dr. Maslow and Dr. Ellis on my life. I am determined that I'll be able to make a huge impact with the messages contained in the pages of my book.

I reminisce about all of the hours of writing, beginning when I was much younger, and leading up to this moment sitting alone in my office holding a book that feels like the greatest treasure I could ever imagine. I carry it with me to my classes, but I tell no one about it. This is too precious—too gratifying for me to share it yet.

I recall Paul Fargis's words regarding my book being serialized in a national publication. Sure enough, the first of six installments of *Your Erroneous Zones* soon appears in *The National Enquirer,* a magazine that specializes in celebrity gossip and is sold in grocery stores throughout the country. I'm told that this weekly periodical reaches in excess of three million readers—in all of the articles that I've written for professional journals, I've reached a tiny fraction of that number. I feel that this is a huge audience of readers who will benefit far more than the readers of professional journals.

I begin receiving a great deal of mail from people all over the country, asking me for advice, and also telling me that my book is helping them with problems they're having in their families and love relationships. This national attention is all very new territory for me, and I begin to answer the letters.

My phone at the university is also busier than ever with calls as a result of the popularity of *Your Erroneous Zones.* One of these calls is from an administrator from St. John's admonishing me for sullying the reputation of the university by appearing in such a disreputable publication. I'm told that as a rising star, with published textbooks and journal articles, I shouldn't allow this serialization to continue. Advancement in my career could be jeopardized, as might any consideration for my acquiring *tenure*—a word I grow to despise. At the age of 35, the idea of staying in the same place for the rest of my life, doing the same thing, is an exceedingly unappetizing thought.

Not only do I refuse to put a halt to the serialization of *Your Erroneous Zones,* I look forward with pride to each new installment of my book, which is being read by millions of people. I feel strongly that many of these readers will discover ways to alter their lives in positive ways by learning to overcome their self-defeating, erroneous thoughts. I choose to ignore critical remarks, and I pay no attention to empty political threats directed my way from administrative higher-ups.

My colleagues give me a bit of good-natured ribbing about the serialization in this "gossip rag," but I don't mind. I'm happy knowing that I'm making a difference to some people in need, and that a book I wrote is being read by an audience so much larger than the very small number of people who read academic scholarly journals.

I Can See Clearly Now

As I look back at the time I was in the process of putting together the final package for my first solo book, I remember how strong the pressure was to produce a book that would stand up to any hint of scholarly criticism. *Your Erroneous Zones* is filled with suggestions for the reader to handle that very kind of thing themselves. To become independent of the good opinion of others and be free from the need for approval is precisely what I was teaching—this was one of the most common kinds of neurotic disorders that I had been helping clients overcome for years, and now I was the recipient of such efforts by others to secure approval of my book.

My publisher wanted this book to look more scholarly, with case studies and annotated references. I recall thinking back to Mr. Joachim Ries and his insistence on having me write according to a dry, unreadable, uninteresting style in a college freshman class, and how I resisted those efforts then, even at the expense of receiving an unsatisfactory final grade. I was adamant that I wasn't going to allow external forces, and standards written by academic types, to dictate to me ever again. Paul Fargis supported me on this, I think largely because he had seen firsthand that the methods I was writing about were effective in helping him personally.

This inner calling to resist the efforts of others to dictate to me how I should be as a person and particularly as a writer has played a big part in my development as a speaker and author. Every time I thought of giving in and shifting from the commonsense style of *Your Erroneous Zones* to a more "professionally acceptable" format, I heard a voice inside of me saying, *You know what works; you want to help people change for the better, not look good to a collection of scholarly strangers. Stay the course—keep it simple, talk straight to the reader. It works in your counseling office, it will work here.* From a distance with a clearer vision, I see this as Divine guidance, as an invisible intelligence that kept me on the path that I knew was right for me. It's about being myself, and recognizing that no one can do that for me. I was hearing this lesson loudly because I needed to experience it directly so I could teach it.

I had read most of the self-help literature that was extant in 1975, and I did not want to write another Dale Carnegie or Norman Vincent Peale book. I wanted to create my own genre, using a method that had been effective for so many clients who came to me for professional counseling. I knew in my soul that when people stop thinking erroneously and begin to take total responsibility for everything in their lives, true permanent change is possible. I was living proof of it, and this experience of holding my ground and not conforming and writing like everyone else allowed me to have the book I wanted to write. It had my name on it, and it was going to reflect what I believed no matter what.

I look back at the minor furor that was created at the university over the fact that my book was being serialized in a supermarket tabloid and I can see now how important it was for me to once again refuse to be swayed from my own firm stance on this matter. I had affirmed back at the age of 20 while in the Navy that *I am a teacher.* I didn't put any restrictions on this declaration. In my mind I was a teacher, and the more people I could reach with my message of self-empowerment, the more effective a teacher I would be. To me the logic was simple at the time: Write for an academic audience and professional recognition, and you'll reach maybe a few hundred people. Write for the widest possible audience in a tabloid and reach millions of people, all of whom will benefit the most from my teaching. This was a no-brainer.

My mission was to reach as many people as possible, so I was in heaven with the serialization of my book. I was not after prestige. I wanted to teach and I wanted people to purchase my book, because I knew in my heart of hearts that my time in the world of academia was growing shorter and shorter. I felt that this was a lucky break offered to me by a universal Source that knew it had much bigger plans for me than I could envision at that time.

I felt that *Your Erroneous Zones* was one way of reaching everyone, and I wanted everyone in this world to get the message that Buckminster Fuller expressed in these words:

> Never forget that you are one of a kind. Never forget that if there weren't any need for you in all your uniqueness to be on this earth, you wouldn't be here in the first place. And never forget, no matter how overwhelming life's challenges and problems seem to be, that one person can make a difference in the world. In fact, it is always because of one person that all changes that matter in the world come about. So be that one person.

I wanted to teach others to embrace this awareness to be that one person. More than that, though, I felt a deep yearning within me to truly be that one person myself, and I knew inside that I couldn't be that self-actualized person if I was afraid of what anyone else might think of me.

32

It is April 1976, and I'm renting a house on Kime Avenue in West Babylon, New York. I'm continuing with my busy private practice, along with my professional teaching duties at St. John's. I am also 100 percent determined that I'll bring the message of *Your Erroneous Zones* to the world.

I've purchased 2,000 copies, which represent approximately one-third of the entire first printing, directly from the publisher. A few blocks from my home I've noticed a radio station's call letters on the building: WBAB. I have no idea what kind of a format this station broadcasts, so I walk over one Friday afternoon and give the receptionist a copy of *Your Erroneous Zones.* I tell her I've just published this book, I live a couple of blocks away, and if they're ever interested in interviewing a local author, I'd be delighted to be a guest on their station.

The next day I receive a call from the station manager, who had seen my book with my phone number on the receptionist's desk. I am invited to be on the air that same day, as a guest they'd scheduled had suddenly canceled. I immediately accept.

That Saturday morning I spend a delightful hour being interviewed by a local disc jockey. It's my first appearance on any media and I'm hooked. We take a few phone calls, and I talk off-the-cuff about my commonsense approach to creating a joyful life. The phones light up—all incoming lines are full, and every caller wants to know where they can buy the book. I give the address of a local bookstore in Huntington, which I drive to as soon as the radio show ends. I ask the manager to take ten books on consignment from me, since the book hasn't been shipped from my publisher yet. The manager agrees—and I am now a writer, and a distributor as well! Within three days, this store has sold the ten books. I alert my publisher to make sure that the stores on Long Island are fully stocked, since I'll be on WBAB regularly now.

I've discovered my own marketing scheme: I can voluntarily visit small radio stations, do interviews, and generate interest in my book. My publisher is not nearly as excited about the marketing and promotion of *Your Erroneous Zones* as I am, but I am bubbling over with enthusiasm. After my WBAB interview I can see myself doing precisely the same thing, not just here on Long Island, but all over the country as well. The possibilities seem to me unlimited. I feel myself being pulled in a new direction. I will have to extricate myself from so many of the obligations I have to clients in my growing practice and particularly my responsibilities as an associate professor at the university.

On Monday, April 5, I arrive at Schreiber High School in Port Washington to give my weekly lecture. The audience has been briefed that my book will be available for sale after the talk, and my wife and I unload 500 copies from our car. The place is jam-packed—more than 1,200 people have shown up, and we sell all 500 copies almost immediately. I am beyond flabbergasted! There's something very exciting happening—I know I am on to something phenomenal.

The words *I am a teacher* flash across my inner screen. I can do this on my own. I can take total responsibility for all aspects of this enterprise. I can become my own bookstore if need be. I can market myself if the marketing division is not on board. I can distribute my own book. And most significantly, I can create the enthusiasm in potential buyers—not by selling my book, but by loving what I'm saying and selling that love. If they like what I'm saying, and if they like me, the person speaking, they will automatically want to purchase what I have written.

Someone who regularly attends the Monday-night lectures in Port Washington has recommended me as a potential guest to the hosts of an all-night call-in radio show at station WMCA. Candy Jones, the famous World War II model married to radio personality Long John Nebel, telephones me and asks, "Would you be willing to come to the radio station and stay for the entire all-night broadcast?" Of course I say yes.

I arrive at 11:30 P.M., and Candy, Long John, and I become involved in a high-energy discussion. We take phone calls, and I begin to give advice on the air to all measure of humanity in the New York metropolitan area. Truck drivers, insomniacs, lonely widows, unhinged late-night fanatics—the phones go crazy. Before I leave for home at 6:00 A.M., I'm asked to come back again the following week.

Both Long John Nebel and Candy Jones give *Your Erroneous Zones* an enormous amount of publicity and are doing outright commercials telling all of their listeners to go out and buy this important book, and to demand that their local bookstores stock it.

I return the following week to co-host the show with Long John, as Candy is otherwise occupied. Long John has been diagnosed with advanced prostate cancer and he's obviously in a great deal of pain, sitting on a specially designed pillow to alleviate some of the discomfort. He leaves me alone at the microphone, along with the person who answers and screens the calls.

I am thrilled to be on one of the largest stations in the largest city in the U.S., with five hours of time to take calls and tell people about my recently published book. When I leave, the phones have been ringing all night and I'm told that my appearances on WMCA are garnering exceptionally high ratings. I become a regular on the Long John and Candy Jones radio show, and every time I appear, my books sell out in all of the New York metropolitan bookstores.

I find myself being asked to appear on a wide variety of radio stations as a guest. The appearances are always unplanned and spontaneous. However, despite the inner glow of excitement I feel at being able to reach so many people and to see my book sales climbing, I also feel myself being pulled in one more direction. Staying up all night and talking on the radio is one thing—but then having to see clients all day, or show up at the university refreshed and ready to meet with students, attend committee meetings, and teach a full load of graduate classes is not a prescription for a long and healthy life.

It is now May, and *Your Erroneous Zones* has been out for two months. I have been unable to transfer my enthusiasm for the book to the powers that be at T. Y. Crowell, although Paul is extremely supportive of all of my efforts to get it the recognition that he and I feel it so richly deserves. I have my sights set on doing a national tour, even though it's been made clear to me that the publisher does not have the funding for such an undertaking.

Your Erroneous Zones has been designated as a "list" book. That designation means it's scheduled to be on the spring list of new releases, and if it sells out the first printing of approximately 6,000 books, it will be viewed a success . . . and that will be the end of the story as far as the publisher is concerned. I have a very different vision, which means that I'm designated a highly motivated, excitable first-time author, naïve and inexperienced in the ways of big-time New York publishing.

I know what I am compelled to do, and I cannot entertain any other vision. I inform all of my clients in my private therapy practice that I'll be closing my practice at the end of the month, as I'm unable to continue at the pace I've been keeping.

My clients are disappointed; however, they knew when they began with me that my practice wasn't about purchasing a friend. I believe in short-term counseling with an emphasis on coming up with practical solutions to self-sabotaging thinking and behavior. My attitude is, *Come to my counseling sessions and leave with new skills. We are not going to spend endless hours going over early childhood traumas.* This is not my way. It can be very valuable to engage in long-term psychoanalysis, just not with me.

On May 30 I close my practice, and am free of the need to be in a specific place several days a week. I'm able to breathe easier—but I still have more ties to sever before I can do what I feel is calling me with unabated exuberance.

I Can See Clearly Now

Opportunities to fulfill one's own dharma are omnipresent when there's an inner picture of one's intention firmly planted in the imagination. I look back at my actions in 1976 as *Your Erroneous Zones* was just being published, and I can see clearly how the universe was aligning me with the people and the circumstances I needed in order to allow me to continue in the direction I was headed—even though I had no idea of what the destination might look like. I've learned to practice this kind of awareness in even routine activities like finding a parking place. Parking places appear more often when my inner intention is on *finding a place to park,* rather than *there are never any parking places around here at this time.*

The inner vision that says yes to life and is open to all possibilities impels you to look about with a more intense vision, to anticipate things working out, and to jump on even the slightest omen that indicates you're being guided. This is all about alignment, which I've written about extensively in the years since *Your Erroneous Zones* was first published. I didn't know it at the time, but by holding firm to an inner picture, I was aligning myself with the one Divine mind—of which I'm a fragment—and allowing this great Tao to offer up experiences in the physical world that matched up to my own Divine destiny.

Once I began to pay closer attention, I could see the magical synchronicities manifesting. At that time I attributed it to good luck or bizarre coincidence. Now I can see more clearly and I know better. I must have walked by that WBAB sign a thousand times before I looked at it with new, more awakened eyes. The teacher was always right there, but it took my new alignment to now view it as a golden opportunity.

I was guided to knock on that door, and there was an invisible connection between myself, the receptionist, the station manager, the guest who canceled, the people who were involved in that guest needing to cancel, the disc jockey, and on and on into infinity. The same holds true for all of the people involved in bringing me to station WMCA and everything else that is taking place in my life right up until this moment.

The key to my seeing more clearly is *alignment*. By maintaining a burning desire with an image that's like an inner flame that is impervious to any distractions, I began to look outward at every circumstance as an omen. It wasn't luck that pushed me then; it was my willingness to hold on to an inner vision until it became an intention—and then to humbly follow my instincts and say yes to every break that came along. By being active and fearless, I was allowing doors to open that would have remained locked or, worse yet, unnoticed.

I now realize that I do not want to ignore even the slightest internal passing thought regarding an idea I'm pursuing. The thoughts are communications from the Divine mind where all things originate—even our thoughts. I see that the burning desire I was experiencing within me was not at all about becoming wealthy or famous or even selling a lot of books. It was a knowing within that this was my calling. I had to answer that calling or else I would have become dead inside, wondering why I felt so unfulfilled. As I said yes to this calling, I knew what to do. I knew I had to close my practice and free myself up. I knew that I could be effective on the media because I was given all of those opportunities to go on the air. Every time I said yes to another interview, or to staying up all night, another door just seemed to magically open with new vistas for me to explore.

In the Tao Te Ching, Lao-tzu speaks about the importance of thinking small, not big: "A journey of a thousand miles begins with a single step." Had I been thinking big back then, I would have passed over that tiny little WBAB radio station two blocks from my home. Yet a simple knock on the door of a station with maybe ten watts of broadcasting power led to so much more. What I see clearly is that a baby step leads to the second step. I was being urged to take little steps by a force in the universe that directs everything and everyone. Great things began with a single step.

I've always loved the film *Coal Miner's Daughter,* the story of Loretta Lynn, the country singer from Butcher Hollow, Kentucky, becoming a legend. She went from radio station to radio station tirelessly hawking her recordings in hopes of just getting one played on the air. And I love my friend Joe Girard's well-known quote, which I have lived by myself: "The elevator to success is out of order. You'll have to use the stairs . . . one step at a time."

I am grateful for having had the inner knowing to be willing to take that first step.

33

I've just completed the spring semester at St. John's University, and I am contemplating what to do for the summer of 1976 and beyond. I have either attended college or taught university courses every summer since 1962. I've been offered a full slate of classes to teach beginning next week, and I must give a decision within the next few days.

I'm driving westbound on the Long Island Expressway (LIE), heading toward the university to turn in some final grades for my graduate students who have been in an internship that I've supervised the past semester. I've been making regular appearances on a variety of New York–area radio stations, and the sales of my book have tapered off but are still quite steady. Suddenly I am overcome with emotion. I recall the trepidation I experienced just five years ago as I was struggling with the decision to leave Detroit and come to the Big Apple. I see Dr. Peters's calm face as I reminisce about her advice to me at that time.

Here I am again, having to decide between two choices—one that offers safety and security, and the other, the unknown. I've written a chapter in *Your Erroneous Zones* titled "Exploring the Unknown" that includes Robert Frost's poem "The Road Not Taken." Last night on the radio with Long John Nebel, I quoted the last lines of Frost's poem:

Two roads diverged in a wood, and I—
I took the one less traveled by,
And that has made all the difference.

Suddenly, without warning, clarity comes over me in a way that I haven't experienced since I talked to Millie Peters back in 1971 in Detroit. I am overwhelmed by the lucidity I feel. There's no conflict. I pull over onto the shoulder of the LIE with tears running down my face. I have the distinct feeling that I've been enveloped by a loving guiding spirit.

This is what Dr. Maslow called a *peak experience,* a term describing an ecstatic state that's especially joyous and has an ineffable mystical/spiritual essence. These are the moments, according to Maslow, lasting from seconds to minutes during which we feel the highest levels of happiness, harmony, and possibility. He once called these "supernatural episodes of enhanced consciousness." I am in this supernatural state right now, right here on the Long Island Expressway. I have been directed to take the road less traveled by, and I know what I am going to do—no, what I *absolutely must do.*

I don't call my wife or daughter; I seek no advice. I've seen the light on this matter and I need not obsess over it another day, not even another hour. I *see* with a capital *S.* It is already a done deal. I ease my way back onto the expressway, pull into my parking space next to Marillac Hall, and go to the second floor and tell the dean's secretary that I would like to speak with Dean Sarah Fasenmyer. I assure her that it won't take more than a few moments. I excitedly tell the dean that I'm resigning from the university effective the end of this semester, which is three days from now.

She asks me to perhaps take the summer off and gain some clarity on this matter. "Please reconsider," she says. "You have the potential for a great future here. You are a rising star and being associated with the university will be extremely advantageous for you."

I agree that this is a risky move in a very uncertain time and I'll lose the benefits that come with a professorship—medical retirement, IRA contributions, and job security. I listen attentively, but I have already peered into my future and seen it now as if it already were a present fact. I tell the dean that I know the risks and have weighed them carefully, and I'm terminating my employment. I am alive with excitement.

I leave the dean's office and walk up the one flight of stairs to my office. I call my wife and daughter, and they are both filled with enthusiastic jubilation for me. I tell my department head, Dr. Bob Doyle, and he's shocked—but also supportive. He tells me how crazy it is to give up so much security for a dream that might not pan out. He reminds me of the potential financial consequences, with no guaranteed income and no benefits, especially since I have a family to consider. I cannot be dissuaded. I think back to that supernatural peak experience of pure exhilaration that swept over me just an hour ago, while sitting in my car as thousands of commuters drove by me on their way home or to work. I am no longer a commuter; I am on my own finally. Everything that I do from here on in will be on my terms.

My colleagues congratulate me, and my secretary sobs, telling me how much she has loved working for me these past five years. I clean out my desk, submit my final grades, and walk down the three flights of stairs and head to my serenity spot a few blocks away.

I go into a deep meditative state of silence. I ask for nothing. No help . . . no guidance . . . nothing. I spend the last 30 minutes of my career as a professor at St. John's University sitting atop a boulder, listening to the birds and the wind rustling through the branches. I am in a state of awe. I give thanks for whatever it was that came over me a couple of hours ago, and gave me such luminous grace and clarity. I am for the very first time in my life, at the age of 36, self-employed, and I am flying by the seat of my pants, bewildered by the possibilities.

I Can See Clearly Now

The quantum moment I experienced on the Long Island Expressway, and the subsequent actions that were initiated almost instantaneously, retain their vividness to this day. I have written about these quantum moments as being the kinds of peak experiences that have the potential to shift awareness into a higher state, where conscious contact is made with our highest self and we are propelled into a new direction instantaneously. These epiphanies and sudden insights have been the topic of much of my writing because I have come to see them as visitation from a higher realm. I wrote earlier of my experience at my father's grave as one of these quantum moments, or what Dr. Maslow called almost supernatural moments of insight that are often life-transforming.

There are four characteristics of these quantum moments that I've described in my movie and book titled *The Shift*. First, *they are always surprising*. The moment of insight in my car on my way to work just seemed to come out of the blue. Second, *they are vivid*. Even today, so many years later, I know precisely what I was wearing that day, and I can tell you the color of the interior of my Oldsmobile Cutlass. I can still see the construction markers on the expressway, the cars going by, and I can smell the fumes from the endless stream of vehicles. Third, *quantum moments are always benevolent*. I can recall how completely blissful I felt as that angelic cloud wafted over me. My skin had gooseflesh, or what my daughter calls "the tinglies." Fourth, *they are enduring*. Need I say more—nearly 40 years later I recall this event as if it happened an hour ago.

Something indefinable showed up for me that June day in 1976 and assisted me in making an uncomfortable shift in my life. It has happened on several occasions when I was on the edge about what direction to take in my life. I trust in these peak-experience moments and not only rely upon them, but invite them into my life. The more I've become confident in what my life's purpose is about, the more I've been able to access this kind of vivid, emotionally charged energy. Clearly moments such as the one I experienced on the day of my resignation from the university are components of living a more self-actualized life.

As individuals begin to align with their original intent and live a life on purpose, they invite in their highest guidance. I have come to know that the only way to access the assistance of the ascended masters is to become like them so that they can recognize themselves. It does no good to pray for guidance and help if we're living an ego-centered life.

At that moment in my life all I wanted to do was to share the magic I was feeling by touching the lives of so many people through radio call-in shows and the mail I was receiving from all over the country from the serialization of my book in a national periodical. I wasn't ego driven—yet I had no idea that I might be receiving some kind of inexplicable spiritual counsel from the heavens. I was aligning with the one Divine mind that's responsible for all of creation because I was focused on serving rather than receiving.

I can see that I was just beginning to live from the new awareness by becoming more like those who live to serve in Divine love. They see themselves in that energy, and can and will guide us to a more God-realized path.

From this perspective of looking back, I feel that I have been in some kind of ascended-master training program. I had to go through the long period of time in the grip of my own false self—that is, my ego—but when I was able to dismantle ego's hold on me, I could feel the difference within me. I forgot about myself and focused on reaching out and serving just because it felt good to do so, with no consideration for the material benefit that might arrive to me.

Resigning from a secure position of professor, and taking the road not only "less traveled" but "never traveled" by me, was inaugurated by a spiritual visitation that I'm still unable to fully explain. I did not know at the time that *Your Erroneous Zones* was the first of 41 books that I'd write over the next 38 years, or that I was destined to impact the lives of millions of people all over the planet. I'm certain that the one Divine mind, the great Tao, God—or whatever label we place upon it—was fully aware of the dharma that I'd signed up for, and agreed to carry out, and it must have known that I couldn't do it from the comfort and safety of a professorship at a major university in NYC.

In the sixth chapter of *Your Erroneous Zones* I stated that "only the insecure strive for security," and I opened that chapter with this quote from Albert Einstein: "The most beautiful thing we can experience is the mysterious. It is the true source of all art and science."

I was about to embark on a journey to teach these ideas to those who were striving for the always-elusive security. I am certain that the ascended hosts watching over me and guiding my path were aware of this major insecurity and knew that it was imperative that I get on a path of walking my talk rather than merely talking it.

34

I am on the phone with a vice president at my publishing house, T. Y. Crowell, to ask how well my book is selling. After checking, he says, "When your book sells out of its original first printing, we will be moving on to the summer list. You should consider this a success for a first-time author."

I feel that *Your Erroneous Zones* will basically die on the vine before it is ever given an opportunity to ripen, and I become a gigantic nuisance to all of the powers that be at my publisher's headquarters. I talk to the publicity people, and they tell me that there is no budget allowance for promotion of my book. I talk to the people at marketing, and they tell me there is no marketing plan for my book. I make calls to the people responsible for distributing my book to the bookstores, and no one returns my calls. Everything feels as if it is at a standstill.

I'm in the midst of a kind of gridlock that is very new to me. Everything is too big—too many departments not communicating, and then blaming each other for inefficiency. I'm anxious to make something happen that's in accord with my vision for myself and this book. However, I seem to be running into roadblocks with everyone I encounter. I decide to take matters into my own hands. I figure if they sell out of the first printing while the book is still on the spring list, they will be forced to go to a second printing.

With one phone call, I become a bookstore: Wayne Dyer Books, West Babylon, New York. I call as a bookstore owner and order all the remaining copies of the first printing to be sent to my store (my garage). Two days later, I call the same vice president and ask him to please check on the status of my book. He is exasperated with me, since I have been a persistent pain to him at least twice weekly since *Your Erroneous Zones* was published three months ago in March.

The VP checks his records to give me the on-hand inventory report, expecting it to be the same as it was when we last spoke a few days ago. He comes back and tells me that the book must be gaining momentum because the entire printing has been sold on a non-return basis. I ask what he's going to do about that, and he presses the button to order another printing. This time it's considerably smaller, though: perhaps 2,500 books.

I now have over 4,000 books in my garage; one week later, I buy up the entire remaining second printing as well. My publisher is being forced to go back for a third printing, and now they are beginning to take notice. Meanwhile, I continue to do radio shows and sell my books at my Monday-evening lectures in Port Washington.

I begin to visit as many bookstores as I can in the New York metropolitan area. I take copies of *Your Erroneous Zones* and ask them to stock the title on consignment. Then whenever I appear on a local radio show, I mention the names of the stores that are stocking my book. I do commercial announcements for the book whenever I take a call on a talk-radio show, and I tell the listening audience precisely where the books are being sold, which makes the bookstore people very happy indeed. After a return visit to the various stores that have agreed to sell my book, I no longer have to play the role of distributor and money collector, as they're now purchasing *Your Erroneous Zones* through normal channels.

I have become my own bookstore, I have my own marketing plan in operation, and I take care of the distribution and delivery as well. Paul Fargis, who is also caught in the huge bureaucracy of New York publishing, is aware of what I'm doing, and talking to me about writing a follow-up book. This feels premature to me—I'm only in the beginning stages of my efforts to share the message of *Your Erroneous Zones* with the world. I tell Paul that I'll write a second book next year.

I'm now preparing my own publicity plan, as I've talked to the head of publicity at T. Y. Crowell and she too is a bit rankled by my continual pestering. I am perceived as a brand-new author who clearly doesn't understand how New York publishing works, as well as someone who doesn't really know his place. I ask about how to make this book available to the entire country. I am told that there is only one way to reach everyone in the country via the media, and that is to make appearances on the nationally syndicated shows such as *The Tonight Show, The Phil Donahue Show,* the *Today* show, and so forth.

A young woman named Donna Gould who works in the publicity department is assigned to me. Donna loves the book and she loves working with me, but she too is hamstrung by the fact that no money has been allocated for publicity for *Your Erroneous Zones.* I cannot travel, because there is no travel allowance. And no one on these national shows is the least bit interested in putting an unknown psychologist on their show, especially with a first book. Donna is young and full of energy, but she is powerless to override the system that she works in.

I write a long, impassioned letter to the director of publicity informing her that I know of a second way to reach everyone in America via the media, and that is to go to them directly—myself. I don't want any financing; I will pay my own expenses. I will tour this country on my own. I will go to the smaller markets with my books in tow, and I will distribute, market, and deliver just as I've been doing successfully in the tristate area for the past several months.

My publisher has never come across an author quite like me. They try to discourage me, but that inner flame is truly a burning desire—it tells me to forget about all of the resistance I encounter, and to listen and follow the inner callings that will not be silenced. I must do this thing on my own. I am through fighting and complaining about the bureaucratic snares; I am going to do this thing my way, and I know I'll be guided all the way. I am bursting with enthusiasm.

Donna Gould agrees to work with me from home—she is an angel. She tells me that if I show up in a medium-size city such as

Columbus, Ohio, she will make the calls to see what newspapers and TV and radio shows she can book. I will pay whatever I can for her services, but she is essentially doing this because she believes in me and the message I have to offer.

It is the middle of June 1976. My daughter, Tracy, is eight years old; I talk to her about going on a wondrous adventure to visit cities all over the country, north, south, east, and west. She is game. My wife is game. It isn't long before the car is packed and loaded with books for distribution, and my wife and I take Tracy and her friend Robin on a cross-country adventure.

I am going to visit as many places as I can that are willing to have me as a media guest, with Donna making the arrangements for interviews whenever possible. My plan is to do several radio shows and announce on the air that my book is available at specific bookstores that I've scouted out in advance. After the show I head to these stores. Often it is my wife who has called inquiring about buying the book this fascinating author on the radio is discussing. They have already received several requests and are willing to take the books on consignment when I arrive at the bookstore with a dozen or so books.

My days are filled with driving, checking into hotels, and going from station to station after finding their location on a well-used map. It is normal for me to stay in a city for several days and to do 12 to 14 interviews in a day—often staying up all night doing late-night call-in radio. Donna is unbelievably efficient. The more interviews I do, the more the word begins to spread that I can do compelling interviews. I have become a media therapist, and there's no shortage of radio stations that are willing to have me as a guest on their talk shows.

We head across the country, with me doing a large number of interviews in every city we stop in. The book is beginning to be noticed by my publisher, as orders from all of my interviews across the country are starting to pour in on a pretty regular basis. *Your Erroneous Zones* goes to a fourth printing, and Donna finally manages to get permission to work with me from her office at T. Y. Crowell during the day. The publicity department has been given some money for my book. And then I receive that fateful call from Howard Papush at *The Tonight Show.*

In September my agent, Artie Pine, and my editor, Paul Fargis, tell me that *Your Erroneous Zones* will be making its first appearance on the *New York Times* bestseller list the following Sunday. For me, this is the equivalent of being an actor and being awarded an Oscar.

I Can See Clearly Now

From this vantage point of looking back at my frustration with my New York publisher, I can see now what a great blessing they gave me in the form of their indifference. I was given the wonderful opportunity to take my life into my own hands, and as a result I would have absolutely no one to blame when things didn't go the way I wanted them to go. I had been practicing this lesson my entire life, but here it was presented to me in a very big way.

When I was told that my book was essentially headed toward oblivion if I allowed other people to be in charge of this entire operation, I had a choice. I could say, "Okay, I guess this is the way that big-time New York publishing operates. I'm just a little cog in a big wheel, and I'll take whatever they decide is the way things are going to be." I had experienced a modicum of success, and I could say thank you and just let it all fade away.

My second choice was to refuse to allow anyone's opinion to get in the way of what I had placed in my imagination, and to take total responsibility for every single aspect of this journey I was undertaking. In the letter I wrote to the director of publicity I included a very special quotation that I have always loved: "When Alexander the Great visited the greatest spiritual teacher of his time, Diogenes, and asked if he could do anything for the famed teacher, Diogenes replied, 'Only stand out of my light.'"

I was not asking T. Y. Crowell to pay for any of my expenses, nor even to offer me any assistance in booking interviews. All I wanted was some assurance that they wouldn't become an obstacle by being recalcitrant and holding back book production and deliveries because I was flying outside of the flight pattern that they had filed for their authors.

I had an inner conviction about what I intended to do. I knew that I could not simply stand by and allow all of my dreams to be wiped away because others, who were more experienced, felt that they knew better—knew the way. I asked them to please stand out of my light and let me be guided by my own vision.

I also used another of my all-time favorite observations, by the German scholar Friedrich Nietzsche, in my letter: "You have your way. I have my way. As for the right way, the correct way, and the only way, it does not exist, there is no 'The way' to do anything."

What I see clearly today regarding those interactions I had with my publisher over how *Your Erroneous Zones* was to be marketed, distributed, and publicized is that I was offered a first-rate chance to begin my new writing career by trusting in my own self first and foremost. A great learning experience was being presented to me.

At the time I was a bit frustrated that I wasn't getting the cooperation that I desired, but I never for a moment even considered abandoning the "this is my way" inner vision that was burning brightly within my imagination. Rather than making a big issue about all of this, or even blaming the system for not being my ally, I went straight to the picture I had planted in my mind and decided to make this entire thing a joyful, fun enterprise. I was having the time of my life in the New York area making all of this come alive, and I saw no reason whatsoever that it wouldn't work in every corner of the country (and the world as well) if I kept my vision and followed my inner promptings.

I didn't have all of the answers on how one should do the legwork in order to make a book a big success, but I did know what I had learned from my immersion in the self-actualization research of Abraham Maslow, and after counseling with hundreds of clients—it was imperative for me to remain independent of the good and bad opinions of others. As my friend Maya Angelou once observed, "A bird doesn't sing because it has an answer, it sings because it has a song."

What is clear to me today is that I must ignore the opinions and advice of others when they interfere with my own inner knowing. It is enough for me to know that I have a song, and by God, I intend to sing it.

35

My world has changed dramatically since I made the decision to go it alone as a self-employed writer. It is 1977, and I have spent the past year working full-time to promote *Your Erroneous Zones.*

Every three weeks or so I fly out to the West Coast to be on *The Tonight Show Starring Johnny Carson,* which has created a national audience for my book. My friend Howard Papush loves my commonsense approach and the stories I tell, and he continues to book me in the "author's spot" at the end of the 90-minute show. Generally I appear on Monday nights, with such diverse guest hosts as Bill Cosby, Bob Newhart, Vincent Price, Joan Rivers, Don Rickles, and other celebrities. The audience reactions and ratings are always up when I come on, and I feel blessed to have the opportunity for these regular appearances.

With this national exposure I'm now being beckoned by the television shows that only a few months ago were uninterested in a schoolteacher named Wayne Dyer. Recently I've been on *The Phil Donahue Show,* the *Today* show, *The Merv Griffin Show, The Mike Douglas Show,* and *Good Morning America,* among others. I've been traveling the country on a book tour financed by my publisher, and doing guest spots on locally produced shows in cities all across the United States and Canada.

I've always loved being before an audience and offering entertaining as well as compelling and educational talks, so I'm thrilled to also have many speaking engagements. I'm being paid fees beyond my wildest dreams—for a two-hour speech, I earn the equivalent of three months' salary as a university professor. My agent, Artie Pine, is booking my speeches now, and there are more requests coming in than I can manage. I travel throughout North America speaking before large audiences at churches, colleges, corporate meetings, and public seminars. As the demand for my services grows, Artie continues to raise my speaking fee. I find it hard to believe that people are willing to pay thousands of dollars to hear me say what I'd been saying for almost no pay only a few months before.

Your Erroneous Zones has now been in publication for 14 months. Each week my publisher has a display ad in *The New York Times* showing how many copies of the book are in print. From that first printing of about 6,000, it has shot up through four more printings to its present in-print total of 250,000! *Your Erroneous Zones* has become a phenomenon. It has become an international bestseller translated into several different languages to satisfy the demand for it in Europe, South America, Asia, and Australia.

On a joint conference call with Artie Pine and Paul Fargis, I am told that there are two pieces of news that are going to blow me away. The first is that *Your Erroneous Zones* will appear on *The New York Times* bestseller list on Mother's Day, May 8, 1977, as the number one best-selling book in the country. The second is equally exciting: *Your Erroneous Zones* has been put up for bid at an auction with all of the paperback publishing houses. The bidding has exceeded well over one million dollars, and Avon Books will be bringing this book out as their number one lead book for the fall of this year.

I have just been informed that I am the author of the number-one-selling book in the country, and I have also just become a millionaire as a bonus! I am over the moon with joy. I put the phone down in my little rented house on Long Island and put my head into my hands, and tears flow down my face.

I have been doing nothing but following my own vision and advancing confidently in the direction of my own dream, and endeavoring to live the life I have imagined. It is what I read on the wall of the Thoreau Lyceum in Concord, Massachusetts, when I visited and lay on the bed where Henry David Thoreau slept back in the 19th century. And this great teacher of mine, who guided me through so many roadblocks when I was back in high school, was so right. I *have* met with a success totally unexpected in common hours. I am overcome with emotion.

I call my mother in Detroit to give her the news. She receives my news with the same sort of ecstatic shock that I'm feeling. She reminds me of the poem titled "Wayne," which she wrote for me back in 1970 when I received my doctoral degree. She recites it verbatim:

A mother can but guide . . .
Then step aside—I knew
I could not say, "This is the way
that you should go."

For I could not foresee
What paths might beckon you
to unimagined heights
that I might never know.

Yet, always in my heart
I realized
That you would touch a star . . .
I'm not surprised!

She is sobbing with joy as she playfully reminds me that my book is such a huge success because she was the one who typed the manuscript before I gave it to the publisher. This beautiful woman—who sacrificed so much to get her broken family back together after being abandoned by my biological father, who worked every day of her life without complaint—is the mother of a millionaire author, who's written the most popular book in America. Before hanging up she says, "My son the doctor! I'm honestly not surprised, Wayne. You were always looking at the stars. I love you so much."

I hang up the phone and say a profound prayer of gratitude for this enormous blessing that has arrived in my life. I feel humbled by the fact that I have come from such scarce beginnings, and I pray for help in remaining unaffected in any egotistical way by all of this external bounty. I make a commitment to make certain that my two brothers and our mother will never be saddled with a mortgage payment.

Fast-forward to the summer, and *Your Erroneous Zones* is sitting atop the bestseller list in Australia, Holland, Sweden, and Norway. I agree to visit these countries to do a publicity tour.

I'm in Australia, and the paperback edition of my book is stacked high in every bookstore I visit. I'm doing an interview at a radio station when we are interrupted by an announcement that Elvis Presley has just been found dead, presumably of a drug overdose. It is August 16, 1977. I say a silent prayer for "the legend," and his family, as the station immediately begins an Elvis memorial.

During my tour, Elvis's music is everywhere, on every station. In virtually every subsequent interview, I am asked to comment on his death. I speak to the erroneous zone of addiction and am asked to read the final chapter of *Your Erroneous Zones,* which is titled "Portrait of a Person Who Has Eliminated All Erroneous Zones." During this time I begin thinking about writing a second book about getting out of victim habits that are self-sabotaging and can ultimately destroy a person.

I spend two weeks touring every major city in Australia doing an endless array of interviews for newspapers, magazines, radio, and television. It's a grueling schedule, nonstop 10 to 12 hours a day, from Perth to Adelaide, Brisbane, Melbourne, and Sydney. When I leave the country *Your Erroneous Zones* is the number one book in sales, and I have a series of invitations to return for speaking engagements in the future.

I Can See Clearly Now

What stands out most clearly to me today as I relive those glorious moments of achieving such exalted status in the publishing world is the biggest fear that I had inside of me. It concerned my ability to handle the financial uncertainty at the very beginning of my decision to leave the university and head out on my own. I loved the feeling of freedom that was so nourishing to my soul; however, my head was filled with dread over money worries.

I grew up in an era of pretty severe poverty. My parents weathered the Great Depression and money was always a very big concern. I was weaned on a shortage mentality, and placed in foster homes largely because there simply wasn't enough money to take care of the most basic of needs. My mother, who had three children by the time she was 24, worked first as a counter girl at a five-and-dime, and then as a secretary. My father, who was jailed for stealing on more than one occasion, just abandoned his fatherly responsibilities and disappeared. I grew up working from the time I was nine years of age. Money was a big issue everywhere I lived. A lack of money and fear of monetary shortages—and remembrances of being hungry and not having enough food to eat—were imprinted on my subconscious mind rather emphatically.

Consequently, heading out on my own with a family to support at the age of 36, with no guaranteed income, was a monumental thing for me. I loved the idea of being my own boss, but I dreaded the thought of not being able to provide for my family and myself. What feels much clearer to me now as I look back on this risky move is the importance of feeling the fear—acknowledging it rather than pretending it wasn't there—and then doing what my heart and soul were telling me I had to do. It was my willingness to align my body and its actions with my highest self, which could no longer handle living a lie. As I traveled the country, and then the world, doing what I knew was my Divine purpose, everything began to fall into place.

When that conference call from Artie and Paul announced my new fiscal status as a millionaire with unlimited earning capacity, I realized a very important truth. It was spelled out by Patanjali some 2,300 or so years ago. This great spiritual master offered the kind of advice that spoke to me back there in 1977. He said, "When you are inspired by some great purpose, some extraordinary project, all your thoughts break their bonds, your mind transcends limitations, your consciousness expands in every direction, and you find yourself in a new, great, and wonderful world." Then he added, "Dormant forces, faculties, and talents become alive and you discover yourself to be a greater person by far than you ever dreamed yourself to be."

I love this passage—especially the part about dormant forces. These are forces that we often think are dead and inaccessible, but he said they come alive to assist us when we are inspired by some great purpose and acting upon it. I realized I had a lot of worries and fears about money that I'd grown up with and lived with my whole life, and that they dominated much of my thinking. What Patanjali offered was true for me in a big way.

As I followed my dream—stayed *in-Spirit;* that is, *inspired*—I made more money in the first year after I gave up my employment than I had made in the previous 35 years of my life. Somehow I see it so clearly now: When we stay on purpose and steadfastly refuse to be discouraged, accepting our fears and doing it anyway, those seemingly dormant forces do come alive and show us that we are greater people than we ever dreamed ourselves to be. We discover that we are one with our Source of being, and as Jesus put it so perfectly, "With God all things are possible."

Being with God means living out one's purpose and always coming from a place of love. I see so clearly now that my resolve to follow my own innermost calling and to do it from an inner mantra of *How may I serve?* rather than *What's in it for me?* is what dissipated my worrying about financial catastrophe.

During all those years of talking to people in the media, the idea of becoming wealthy was the furthest thing from my mind. My book appearing on *The New York Times* bestseller list was a total surprise to me. The money that began to show up was truly unexpected. Abraham Maslow's self-actualization psychology had taught me to stay detached from outcome. He said it often, that self-actualizing people do what they do because they are following their heart, the call of their soul, not because of what might accrue to them. My journey was to follow what I felt so deeply inside myself. All of the largesse that appeared was a mind-blowing yet pleasant shock to me.

This is what is clear to me today: follow your heart, stay aligned with your Source of being—love—and let the universe take care of the details.

36

I've accepted an invitation to do a book publicity tour in Holland, where something unheard of has taken place. Willeke Alberti, a well-known singer/actress in the Netherlands, has apparently appeared on a national television show informing everyone watching that she's read a book that has completely turned her life around. That book is *Your Erroneous Zones,* titled in Dutch as *Niet Morgen Maar Nu,* which means, "not tomorrow, but now." Willeke has made an impassioned plea to viewers to read and apply the simple commonsense advice offered in what for her has been a life-changing book. The next day the demand for *Niet Morgen Maar Nu* is beyond anything the Dutch publisher has ever seen.

I fly to Amsterdam, where I speak with this fascinating woman who is responsible for making me an overnight sensation in Holland and Belgium. The bookstores cannot keep up with the demand for my book. I appear on talk shows, late-night entertainment shows, and a national game show; and I do interviews with a host of magazines and newspapers.

Willeke tells me that she was profoundly touched by the words in *Niet Morgen Maar Nu,* and she would be thrilled to endorse anything that I might produce in the future. I've made a friend in a country I'd never before visited, with a celebrity who speaks a language that I do not grasp, who's willing to be an ambassador for the kind of teaching I'm promoting in a book published across the ocean in America. This book is selling in the hundreds of thousands in a country that has a total population of 14 million people.

I return to the U.S. and meet with Artie Pine and Paul Fargis at T. Y. Crowell to talk about ideas for my next book. Ever since I was preempted from my radio interview in Sydney last summer, I've been thinking about the untimely death of Elvis. I want to write about something that seems to impact everyone I talk to in one way or another. I've seen in my therapy practice that even though people are able to change their self-defeating thinking patterns and correct their erroneous habitual thoughts, they still feel victimized by so many external factors that appear to them as insolvable.

I present Paul with an outline detailing fresh and even startlingly unconventional methods for getting rid of pressures and manipulations that are continually being directed at almost everyone. I want to teach people how to stop feeling victimized in all of their interactions in life—to operate from strength rather than weakness when dealing with family members, authority figures, and the demons that live inside that continually pull them away from their own well-being. It seems to me that Elvis allowed himself to be taken over by an entourage of manipulators who primarily had their own self-interests at heart. How did his life get so out of control? Why wasn't he able to resist the machinations of his handlers? Who was there to guide him away from self-sabotaging behaviors?

I want to write a book that uses the same commonsense approach that captivated so many people around the world in *Your Erroneous Zones.* I want to teach people how to avoid the victim trap that claimed the life of Elvis, and systematically acts like a creeping cancer in the lives of countless men and women. I call this proposed book *Pulling Your Own Strings.*

I receive a nice advance from my publisher that is limited due to some legalese in the original contract I signed with them. My agent, Artie Pine, unsuccessfully attempts to get the publisher to offer a substantial financial advance that goes beyond what is called for in the contract, due to the enormous and unexpected success *of Your*

Erroneous Zones. Artie is adamant and wants to put pressure on the publisher. I take a very different stand and insist that he back off and simply honor what we originally agreed to when we were thrilled to have a book contract at all only 18 months ago.

I am more than content. I don't need any more money; I now own a beautiful home in Ft. Lauderdale, Florida, where I'm a full-time resident. I'm excited about writing a second book and knowing that it will be published. I insist that Artie let go of his demand that my publisher tear up our original agreement. I want no conflicts anywhere—no hard feelings. This is not about money, and I don't want it to become an issue, not now, not ever.

As I begin writing my new book I recall reading aloud the Declaration of Independence to a civics class I was teaching at Pershing High School in Detroit. This group of high school seniors studied the Declaration of Independence one line at a time and then discussed what was being said and how it applied to them in the 1960s—almost 200 years later.

One particular line drew the most discussion:

> All experience hath shown that mankind are more disposed to suffer, while evils are sufferable, than to right themselves by abolishing the forms to which they are accustomed.

I decide before I write the first word of *Pulling Your Own Strings* that this will be the display quote at the beginning of the book, as it reveals the theme I want to address.

I write daily for three months, always focused on helping the reader to "right themselves" by choosing to not be a victim of anyone or any system, under any and all circumstances. When the hardcover edition of *Pulling Your Own Strings* appears, I'm just as thrilled as I was two years ago when I held *Your Erroneous Zones* and coddled it like a newborn child.

I am once again committed to taking this message to the world—but this time I don't have to do battle with anyone at the publishing house. Donna Gould has been assigned to me as my full-time publicist. I elect to go on a cross-country book tour, only this time I don't have to drive or be concerned about hotel reservations and keeping within a very tight budget. My airfares and hotels are all handled for me. Anything I want is given to me without question.

Pulling Your Own Strings goes immediately to the top of *The New York Times* bestseller list. I'm still making frequent appearances on *The Tonight Show,* and now I've been invited to do a taping on the daytime talk show hosted by Dinah Shore, *Dinah!*

In Los Angeles I'm greeted by the kindest, sweetest, most generous person I have ever met in all of my encounters with show-business people. Dinah asks me to do a regular weekly appearance with her on her nationally syndicated television show, suggesting that I present common victimizing situations and have actors/actresses act out various methods for dealing with these kinds of widespread scenarios. I fly out once a month, and we tape four shows on each visit to be played weekly. In the process I establish a friendship with a woman who personifies self-actualization, and that is Ms. Dinah Shore.

I watch Dinah each week displaying extraordinary kindness to everyone at the studio. The lady who empties the wastebaskets is afforded the same dignity as the starlets and well-known politicians who come to the studio. I am so impressed by this multitalented superstar who embraces everyone with love and kindness in her heart. I am honored to be on her show as a regular guest, and I am even more honored to watch and learn from someone who appears to have tamed her ego. She is my friend and a great teacher . . . I am so grateful.

I Can See Clearly Now

One of the great discoveries of my life came out of my experience in Holland with Willeke Alberti, perhaps the best-known entertainment celebrity in that beautiful country.

In the Tao Te Ching, Lao-tzu offers a paradoxical truism when he says that the great Tao (God) does nothing and leaves nothing undone. As I've contemplated this ironic statement I can see, yet not explain, the wisdom inherent in Lao-tzu's words. I could look all day and night for a millennium, and my senses could not experience God doing anything. I can't see, hear, smell, taste, or touch God, yet something is at work, leaving nothing undone—and so it is when I align myself with the great Tao and live out my dharma in that alliance.

There's nothing I can do about all of the people in Europe, Asia, South America, and everywhere else on the planet, who I'd love to have hear my self-empowering message. *But it is getting done.* I have no idea who first placed a copy of *Niet Morgen Maar Nu* in the hands of Willeke Alberti, and what it was that inspired her to speak so passionately about it on national television. I did nothing, and obviously it was supposed to happen, so nothing was left undone.

Clearly there's an invisible force in the universe that handles everything. No exceptions. This force is in me and it is in everything and everyone else alive—it connects us all. When I stay in harmony with this force, which is really pure unconditional love, it leaves nothing undone by doing nothing. The Beatles had it right when they said "Let it be."

Since that first initial visit to Holland, the beautiful Willeke Alberti has done the same thing over and over again as my books have been published in Dutch. She is a soul mate, walking the same path I walk, and it is mysteriously delightful to hold her hand as we traverse this path together, though divided geographically and linguistically as we are. Clearly this force that is within all of us works to assist each of us if we stay true to our calling. Willeke is one example of thousands of such allies who are committed to the same purpose of transforming our planet into a place of Divine love. I am but a messenger in this process. I don't own the words I write; I just allow them to come through me, and the great Tao handles all of the details.

Looking back with a clearer understanding, I can see how the evolution of *Pulling Your Own Strings* was a necessity for me. From my earliest recollections I can recall the frustration and even deep resentment over silly rules imposed upon me by people telling me that I had to do things their way, which generally meant that I was to be victimized. In my therapy practice I saw evidence of this in virtually everyone I encountered. My desire to write and speak about these kinds of everyday victim traps came from an inner awareness that *it doesn't have to be this way.* One can summon the courage to stand up to those who attempt to replace one's *knowing* what's right, with their will, or their policies, or their regulations.

I can see now that I often came from a place of ego within myself when it came to dealing with authority figures. And to be perfectly honest, I allowed my own ego to play a dominant role in my life at times in 1978, as the spotlight of stardom began to shine on me with two national bestsellers, a luminous career as a television personality, and being recognized everywhere I went.

My association with the egoless Dinah Shore helped me—I quickly saw the real truth that I was no better than anyone else. With Dinah as a model, I easily made the choice to stay humble and kind in all of my dealings with people, and toss out any supercilious attitudes that might be forming. Here I was every week with a monumental superstar—a woman who had a résumé of stardom that went on forever. Not only did she have many successful television shows, she was a movie star and popular recording artist, with over 40 albums to her credit and a long list of hit songs dating back to the year I was born. Dinah Shore was also an honorary member of the LPGA Hall of Fame and a beloved philanthropist, with far too many awards to enumerate here.

As I look back today I can see what a profound role model she was for me. She spoke highly of everyone, and never allowed her celebrity status to inflate her ego. Here I was, a newcomer to all of this prominence, and I was beginning to take on an attitude that was ego based and unworthy of a person whose mission is to serve others. This newfound stardom and recognition needed to be an irrelevant spin-off to my own mission. I can vividly recall watching this magnificent superstar of a lady treat everyone with love and respect.

I am so grateful for Dinah's presence in my life. Each week when I appeared as a guest on her television show for almost two years, I was reminded to maintain my humility, think first of others, and always come from a place of love. Throughout the years since Dinah's passing in 1994, I have recalled her loving countenance and her sensational smile, as well as her own radical sense of humility, and I'm reminded to emulate those qualities she lived so authentically.

Thank you, sweet Dinah. I was so blessed to know you. I know I was one of a legion of men in love with you from a distance. The final two lines of John Keats's famous poem "Ode on a Grecian Urn" always remind me of you.

Beauty is truth, truth beauty—that is all
Ye know on earth, and all ye need to know.

Thank you, Dinah, for providing me with a model for staying humble in the face of the many ego temptations that come with fame. Your inner beauty is my truth!

37

It is May 8, 1978, and I'm catching a train into New York City to have dinner with Artie Pine. For the past year or so I've been speaking at different venues all over the country, including businesses, colleges, public seminars, and Unity and Science of Mind churches. Artie has upped my speaking fee considerably, yet the audiences for my talks continue to grow larger.

I take great pride in speaking directly from my heart for hours at a time without the benefit of a podium or any notes whatsoever. I am somewhat of a frustrated comedian, using a great deal of my speaking time to keep the audience laughing as much as possible. This is a natural place for me to be. I love living out my own personal affirmation that I have been using for 18 years now: *I am a teacher.*

Four months ago I recited this old joke to Artie: A student asks his singing instructor, "How do I get to Carnegie Hall?" His teacher's immediate response is, "Practice, practice, practice." I told my agent how thrilling I thought it would be to speak at Carnegie Hall, to stand alone on that enormous stage where so many legends have performed and speak to a sold-out audience. I said that this was a dream of mine, but I knew it was really just a fantasy.

To my surprise, Artie told me that he had a friend who's responsible for booking talent into Carnegie Hall—if I really wanted to do this, he'd inquire about the details and the cost of renting such a prestigious venue for one evening. I once said to myself, *If I can make it here, I can make it anywhere.* Of course I want to do it! So Artie called his friend, and the arrangements were made. I'll have to pay the rental fee if the ticket sales are insufficient to cover the costs. This is the Big Apple. And this is the biggest theater in this city.

Now we are sitting at Artie's favorite restaurant, the Russian Tea Room. I am about to cross one item off of what I'll later call my "bucket list." I have rented Carnegie Hall for tonight, two days before my 38th birthday. I tell my agent that I no longer want him to put a notice in my speaking contracts that says, *No recording of Dr. Dyer's talks may be made.* I explain to him that this violates my own sense of why I do this work and travel around the world speaking. I want as many people as possible to hear these talks. This is not about my making money—it's to spread the word to as wide an audience as possible. I want people to record these messages, to reproduce my tapes, and to send their recordings everywhere.

Artie objects, feeling that it will cost me some sales of the recorded programs; after all, he is my agent and feels that it is his job to protect me financially. But he agrees to strike this provision out of my contract for Carnegie Hall, and all future speaking engagements.

We finish dinner and walk the few blocks to Carnegie Hall. I look at the marquee and see my name in lights on this stupendous edifice that has hosted so many giants in the entertainment industry. I walk through the cavernous backstage area to my dressing room and sit down feeling astonished awe. I am choked up and wondering if the enormity of this occasion will render me speechless when those curtains open and I face the audience.

I do a 20-minute silent meditation of gratitude, and walk out to gaze out at the scene before me. The main hall has enormously high ceilings, and there are balconies around this most prestigious concert stage in the U.S., which seats 2,804 people on five levels. I can't see an empty seat in the house, but the moment I begin to speak, I lose all of my jitters. I speak for two and a half hours without a break, and I am humbled by a lengthy standing ovation. There was no announcement that my lecture could not be recorded.

At the beginning of this year, I wrote these words: "I have two major goals that I intend to accomplish before the end of this year." I've completed my fantasy of speaking at Carnegie Hall, which was one of the two goals—and, as the old joke goes, I got there by practice, practice, practice. The second item for this year is to run a full marathon. Why? In part because of an experience I had a few years ago while teaching a summer-school course at Wayne State University.

A group of graduate students was in front of the class as part of an assignment, simulating a college classroom. The student taking the role of professor had his belt pulled down below his stomach, portraying an overweight professor with a protruding belly. I couldn't understand why the entire class was stifling their laughter and looking sheepishly at me. Suddenly I had the shocking awareness that this student was good-naturedly mimicking me. I realized for the very first time that I was overweight. How had this happened to me? I had a laugh with the entire class, and when I returned home I realized that this was one of the most significant moments of my life.

I made a decision on the spot that I was going to get myself into shape. I went outside with a pair of tennis shoes on my feet and tried to run around the block. I went about 500 yards and was panting and unable to catch my breath. My chest hurt, my legs ached, and I walked slowly back to my home. The next evening I did the same thing, and this time I was able to run 600 yards before collapsing in exhaustion.

I was determined to be able to run a mile within four days. On day three I made it past a half mile, and I noticed that I wasn't nearly as fatigued or winded as I had been. By the end of the fourth day I was able to jog slowly for one entire mile. I was on my way! I discovered how empowering it was to make this kind of progress—I was hooked.

I now have a running regimen that I adhere to unwaveringly. Within two months of my first day of long-distance running, I got myself up to eight miles a day. I have obsessively run every single day since that first shock at seeing myself being portrayed as an out-of-shape professor with a girth around his middle.

I did the same thing I did to get to Carnegie Hall—practice, practice, practice. For close to two years I've run eight miles a day, never even considering taking a day off. No matter where I've been in the world, I've found the hour and the place to run.

I really love this time alone. I clear my head and feel the joy that comes from having the wind in my face. I am one with nature when I run, and I am amazed at what my body is now capable of. My weight is down to a trim 170 pounds, I have very little body fat, and I feel better than I have in years, since I was on the track team in high school over 20 years ago.

I have set my intention, trained by running up to 18 miles at a time, and completing 80 or so hours of training per week. It is now October 22, and I'm signed up to run in the City of Lakes Marathon in Minneapolis, Minnesota. It is a cool October morning, and I am at the starting line to run all 26.2 miles. It is an intention in my imagination, and there is absolutely nothing that could keep me from completing this mission.

Running each day has become my life, and this marathon is to be the crowning achievement. I am unconcerned about my time, my speed, or how I stack up with the other 2,000 or so runners here today. I am totally confident that I will complete this race and accomplish that second goal I set for myself back in January.

As I run I hear people talking about the invisible wall that runners hit, somewhere around the 22-mile mark. I move on because I don't want my inner picture of myself happily and proudly crossing the finish line to be contaminated by their comments. I finish the entire 26.2-mile course in just over three and a half hours—I am ecstatic and give a silent thank-you to that student who unwittingly gave me a wake-up call when he portrayed me as an overweight professor.

I Can See Clearly Now

Looking back I see how important those two items on my bucket list were in the development of my life's work that was to follow. When I set that intention to run a complete marathon without stopping or walking, I had never run more than eight miles in my life. Yet a marathon seemed to me the pinnacle of running accomplishments.

I remembered Maslow's words: "Self-actualizers must be what they can be." He was speaking about the burning desire within to maximize one's potential as defined by oneself.

I had allowed myself to get out of shape during my mid-30s. I'd given up intense physical exercise about the time I began teaching and conducting my private therapy practice. However, I did not see myself the way other people were seeing me. The young man who was imitating me in my own classroom was one of the greatest teachers to ever cross my path. To this day I can see him cavorting about the room impersonating his teacher as a man with a fat belly. That was a quantum moment in my life.

Rather than viewing that scene as a criticism and being offended, I see that all of the participants, and especially the prancing imitator, were angels sent to guide me. They very likely saved my life. I was headed in a dangerous direction at the time: overeating greasy food, drinking beer, being sedentary, enduring a crumbling marriage, and employing a type A kind of lifestyle because I was being pulled in many different directions professionally and personally.

That young man impersonating me helped put me on a road to self-improvement in so many ways. I began a stretch of 29 years in which I ran a minimum of eight miles every day, and also ran six additional marathons. Furthermore, I began to shift my dietary habits, and my weight went down by 30 or so pounds, and stayed in the general vicinity of what I weighed when I was in high school and has remained near there to this day.

I also see so clearly today the power inherent in the idea of an intention that I was able to tap into—not a wish or a hope, but an *intention* to manifest a new concept of myself. When I decided to run a marathon, I already saw myself triumphantly crossing the finish line. As a result, I acted on the idea as if it were a completed fact. This prompted me to go out every day and challenge myself to live up to the idea I had in my imagination, since to me it was already a *fait accompli.*

The power within me that's inherent in an intention was sparked by mysterious teachers disguised as annoying impersonators—something I see now as a valuable lesson in that 1978 experience. In fact, I'm convinced that some of our greatest and most influential teachers show up in our lives disguised as people we resent or even despise. After all these years and the endless miles I've run, I'm thankful for the Divine mind that sent that student to impersonate and portray me on that day.

My performance at Carnegie Hall was another great teaching moment. I had to overcome any inner doubts about my ability to achieve my own level of greatness in the world of professional public speaking. My intention to speak on the premier stage in the country made me realize just how powerful an idea that is planted in the imagination with intent can be. I know today that everything that ever manifests into physical reality begins with a thought, and that a thought laced with intent is a virtual guarantee that it will come to pass. This was a personal challenge for me—I wanted to know that I could pull this thing off.

The conversation I had with Artie at dinner just before my appearance at Carnegie Hall, regarding permission for the audience to tape-record me, was a major turning point in my life as well. I wanted so much to live up to Maslow's definition of a self-actualized person as being someone who is detached from outcome. I did not want money to be the reason for how I conducted my life. My purpose was never about making money; it was always about teaching and reaching people on a new level. I cringed inside whenever an audience was told they could not tape my presentation. That recording by an audience member might interfere with some projected sales of my audio programs seemed entirely irrelevant to me. Making the declaration that night put me back in alignment with my soul. I want everyone to hear my message, not just those who are able to pay.

In the same manner, when Artie would tell me that copies of my books were being pirated in foreign countries and I wasn't receiving any royalties, I refused to go after these purloined editions. I want people in China, and South America, and Eastern Europe, and anywhere else where poverty is unchecked, to be able to read what I've written. They might be inspired by an author who once lived in the same kind of paralyzing scarcity but was able to transcend it.

Those two intentions that I set back on New Year's Day 1978 were the building blocks for a lifetime of writing devoted to the incredible power of intention that is everyone's birthright if they choose to change the way they look at things.

As Lao-tzu taught me many years later, "If you correct your mind, the rest of your life will fall into place." I corrected my mind and began to see myself as capable of accomplishing anything I place my attention on, and I learned that sometimes our most profound teachers show up for us wearing unexpected disguises.

38

I have been invited to participate in a weeklong conference in Vienna, Austria, sponsored and produced by the Young Presidents' Organization. YPO members are individuals who meet certain age requirements and are responsible for the full operation of a qualifying corporation or division, and they're involved with organizations throughout the world. I accept the invitation, and two days after my Carnegie Hall appearance, my wife and I fly to Vienna.

YPO has gathered a distinguished group of presenters for this conference, and I am flattered to be one of them. It is an unremunerated speaking engagement, offering a wonderful week in and around Vienna, with the opportunity to be a faculty member with an impressive group of well-known personalities—including the current Vice President of the United States, Walter Mondale.

Upon arrival I learn that I am to be on a panel addressing some 600 YPO members. When I hear who will be co-presenting with me, I'm temporarily speechless. I will be sitting next to, and considered a colleague of, Dr. Viktor Frankl. Perhaps of all the people alive today, he is the one I most admire. I think back to my days as a doctoral student, in which I took courses on *logotherapy,* a kind of therapy that Dr. Frankl created out of his experiences as a Holocaust survivor in several Nazi death camps, including Auschwitz and Dachau. Four years ago when I visited Dachau, I'd seen this hero of mine in my mind's eye during my day at the concentration camp.

I read Dr. Frankl's classic book *Man's Search for Meaning* as both a master's and doctoral student, and I made it required reading in all of the graduate-school courses I taught at St. John's University. I recall how he wrote that even in the most absurd, painful, and dehumanized situation, life has potential meaning. And he had told the world that "everything can be taken from a man but one thing: the last of human freedoms—to choose one's attitude in any given set of circumstances, to choose one's own way."

Here I am, invited to be a presenter at this prestigious conference because of the success of a couple of insignificant self-help books—and I am to share the stage with a man who was imprisoned in a series of Nazi death camps, survived to tell his story, and then wrote a classic text, which I studied and used when I taught at St. John's.

I feel so humbled, so inadequate, so unbelievably blessed to even meet this great man, let alone be considered a quasi-colleague and co-presenter to a group of young presidents here in Vienna, the hometown of this lionhearted way-shower. I feel there must be a reason for this unexpected opportunity for me to be on the same panel with Viktor Frankl. When I pick up my copy of *Your Erroneous Zones,* I note that the first words of this book were inspired by my reading of *Man's Search for Meaning:* "The essence of greatness is the ability to choose personal fulfillment in circumstances where others choose madness."

Tomorrow afternoon I'm scheduled to appear onstage with Dr. Frankl, whom I've quoted hundreds of times in my lectures. I visited the horrific death camps where the Nazis incarcerated him as a slave laborer, reminding myself that in the midst of these terrible circumstances this neurologist and psychiatrist, subjected to man's lowest inhumanity to man, was able to find beauty and meaning. I've written essays on the central idea of his logotherapy, which as he wrote, occurred in part while being shouted at and beaten by guards with the butts of their rifles: "A thought transfixed me: for the first time in my life I saw the truth as it is set into song by so many poets, proclaimed as the final wisdom by so many thinkers. The truth—that love is the ultimate and the highest goal to which man can aspire."

I meet Dr. Frankl just before I go onstage to speak to this distinguished group of corporate presidents. He is warm, very funny, and speaks with a heavy Austrian accent. I tell him how much I admire his writing and that I had been using *Man's Search for Meaning* as required reading for my graduate students. I also tell him that my two current best-selling books were inspired by him and my teachers Dr. Fritz Redl and Dr. Abraham Maslow. I am delighted to learn that he knows Dr. Redl personally, and that he was associated with Dr. Maslow before his death eight years ago. I am beyond thrilled that he's aware of the German edition of *Your Erroneous Zones,* titled *Der Wunde Punkt,* and has read it.

In response to my comments on surviving such ghastly treatment in the various death camps where he was incarcerated for almost three years, and then in his riveting address to the rapt throng of attendees, Viktor Frankl says, "When we are no longer able to change a situation, we are challenged to change ourselves." He relates being given a cup of dirty water with a floating fish head for protein as his only food for the day, and finding beauty in this repulsive offering by his captors. He emphasizes that he reminded himself to *choose to change himself.* He speaks eloquently of so many of his fellow prisoners dying, not only from the horrific hygienic conditions, but also from giving up on themselves and losing a sense of purpose or meaning.

When I speak to the audience, I am obviously feeling out of place next to this teacher who is sitting at the same conference table and has lived and demonstrated his mastery of what I have written about so amateurishly by comparison. When the session is over, I spend an hour or so talking to this remarkable man. I am so impressed by his grand sense of humor and the love that seems to emanate from him, even when he talks about the appalling treatment he received from his captors. I know that his wife perished in a concentration camp at Bergen-Belsen and his mother was killed in the gas chambers of Auschwitz. He also lost all members of his immediate family, other than his sister Stella, who escaped being in a camp because she had immigrated to Australia.

He gives me a piece of advice to apply in my own life and in all of my future writing. He speaks clearly, saying that suffering is a part of the human condition that no one escapes in their lifetime, and that it may be more despairing for some than others. However, he says, looking directly at me, "You must teach people to find meaning in their suffering, and in so doing they will be able to turn their personal tragedies into personal triumphs." This, he explains, is the essence of logotherapy. "If your clients or your readers cannot find meaning, they will ultimately perish."

I leave Vienna a changed man. I will write and speak from the perspective that Dr. Frankl offered me here at this conference, and I vow to myself to live a much more meaning-centered life. I am inspired by my contact with this great man, and purchase another copy of *Man's Search for Meaning* at the conference to reread on the plane home.

I open the book to see: "We who lived in concentration camps can remember the men who walked through the huts comforting others, giving away their last piece of bread." And then I read these words, a quote by Nietzsche that I commit to memory as I contemplate writing my next book and giving my next talk: "He who has a *why* to live for can bear with almost any *how*." I am committed to teaching and living from a place of meaning. The *how* to live will play a secondary role, while the *why* to live will be much more dominant in my work.

I Can See Clearly Now

The first time I encountered the work of Viktor Frankl was in a filmed interview that spoke to my soul. I listened with my ears, but heard with my heart. As Dr. Frankl spoke about the importance of meaning in everyone's life, I felt as if I were listening to a higher version of myself because his words echoed something deep within me. I always wanted to get beyond what appeared to me to be the petty concerns and rules created by our culture—trying to fit in and be just like everyone else.

As I watched this interview, Dr. Frankl spoke of concentration-camp inmates giving up on life and dying, unable to find any life-sustaining beauty in the most horrific of circumstances. Meaning, he said, was everything. He urged listeners to seek their own way of experiencing and trusting in an *ultimate meaning* that one may or may not call God. He noted that in the concentration camps, those who held on to a vision of the future were the ones throughout this ordeal who seemed to have a better chance for survival. Whether the vision was a significant task before them or a return to their loved ones, they were more likely to survive their suffering.

The moment I saw Dr. Frankl I felt a kind of alignment with him that I'd never felt toward any person of letters. Today, I have no doubt at all that some kind of a connection existed between us. It was no accident that some 15 years after first devouring *Man's Search for Meaning,* I was placed on the same panel with this man to whom I felt such a spiritual kinship.

When I first read the accounts of Dr. Frankl's maltreatment at Auschwitz, Dachau, and Theresienstadt in Bohemia, the suffering overwhelmed the words I was reading, and I knew I would one day visit those hideous places. In some mysterious way I felt I would meet this man who spoke so persuasively about the innate capacity humans have to transcend evil and to discover meaning, when madness screams out from every angle. I can see clearly now that I was destined to meet this man in person—something invisible and indescribable connected us. That meeting that day in Vienna in May 1978 instituted a shift in my writing and in my life.

At the time I was moving away from traditional psychology as the foundation of my own teaching and exploration. I loved the common-sense approach that permeated my first two books, and appreciated Dr. Frankl's praise for my writing succinctly and in language that anyone would understand. But the essence of *meaning* in a larger sense—exploring an ultimate meaning concerning our connection to a higher power was stirring in me.

When I met Viktor Frankl, something inside of me recognized him as if we had met before and knew each other. However it was that I was placed on that panel with one of my heroes, I can see from this perspective that the force that brought us together for one afternoon caused my life to change and my writing to start emphasizing concepts such as spirituality, higher consciousness, Divine love, and most significantly—*meaning.* I can now see clearly that I was beginning to explore the world beyond the ego.

39

It is the spring of 1980—a new decade. Both *Your Erroneous Zones* and *Pulling Your Own Strings* have been hugely successful. Both books have now been on *The New York Times* bestseller list for almost four years.

When T. Y. Crowell accepted my original manuscript in 1975 they did so with very little expectation of how well it would sell. After the phenomenal success of *Your Erroneous Zones,* my agent, Artie Pine, was disappointed when the publisher refused to renegotiate the original contract. I insisted we honor our commitment without fuss, and now the two-book deal with T. Y. Crowell has been completed.

Artie has turned to Simon & Schuster, a fixture in New York publishing. He's just called to say, "I have made a deal with a new publisher, and they're offering you an advance that's in line with what I believe you so richly deserve." When he tells me he's arranged a two-book agreement with a $1.5 million–guaranteed advance, I am thrilled. I can't even imagine being in such a fortuitous place financially. I am more than blessed.

Every day that I'm not traveling or doing publicity for *Pulling Your Own Strings* I'm writing the book that I've been imagining since the time I spent in Vienna with Viktor Frankl. This new book for Simon & Schuster will be titled *The Sky's the Limit,* and it will explain the specifics for attaining the state that Abraham Maslow called self-actualization, which I discovered 12 years ago. I still feel such a special kinship to this man who passed away on the same day that I received my doctoral degree in June 1970.

Dr. Maslow frequently said that the state of self-actualization is achieved by a very small number of people because most are stuck pursuing and satisfying the lower needs: *physiological, safety, love and belonging,* and *esteem.* He visualized those lower needs as the base of a pyramid he called "a hierarchy of needs." The apex of this pyramid he described as an exalted realm where only a few explored their sense of purpose and meaning.

I differ from Dr. Maslow dramatically on this point. I feel that self-actualization is the birthright of every person. I see it as our original nature—damaged by the de-geniusing enculturation described to me by Buckminster Fuller a few years ago. My meeting with Dr. Frankl reinforced this concept, and I know that I am not alone in this belief. The idea is quite evident in John 14:12, where Jesus proclaims that those who believe will do even greater things than he has done.

I'm writing *The Sky's the Limit* in a style similar to my two previous books, with the focus on identifying the most salient features of what Maslow called "exemplary people." I've identified 37 of these personality traits and am writing from the point of view that we can, as Viktor Frankl so brilliantly stated, change ourselves and make new choices in the face of circumstances that cannot be altered—this includes our past and our entire personal history. I am shifting away from writing about the *how-to* and into the world of *meaning*—offering readers a way to access Frankl's purpose, and the top of Maslow's hierarchy of needs and self-actualization.

My new editor at Simon & Schuster is Michael Korda, who's worked on a number of best-selling books and even written a few himself. Michael flies down to Florida, and we spend a day walking the beach and discussing the promotional plans for *The Sky's the Limit.* Then I proudly turn in this manuscript that's dominated my life for the past several months.

Michael and I speak frequently, and he tells me that the book is fine. It just needs some additional tailoring, so he's hired an outside editor to tweak the manuscript. This is a new experience for me—in the past I've done my own editing based on what was returned to me with suggestions. I trust in the process at this new publishing house, though, which is heavily invested in this book with a $1.5 million guarantee against future royalties.

The months go by and I hear nothing. I feel as if I'm back in the same boat that I was in with John Vriend a decade ago, waiting for someone else to do their job in order for my book to be completed. After six months I call Michael Korda and insist that his outside editor send me what he has completed.

Several weeks later, I finally receive a package in the mail with the first half of my manuscript reworded by this outside editor. I am in shock. I don't recognize the book that I turned in. This person has taken the liberty of deciding that my style of writing is not up to par. He's taken my ideas and simply written his own version, and basically tossed aside my original writing. His writing isn't bad; it's just not me. I don't recognize myself in any of his rewriting.

I have delivered two of the biggest-selling books of the 1970s in my own down-to-earth, commonsense style—and now I am faced with the same sort of dilemma I confronted as a college freshman, being told to write using a more literary and cultured style that's befitting the trademark of Simon & Schuster. I tell Michael that this is unacceptable, regardless of how much money they've offered me. He assures me that it will all be resolved amicably.

I wait another two months, and still no word from this phantom editor, or rather rewriter. I call Michael Korda and give him my ultimatum: I want my original manuscript returned to me. I will look over what has been rewritten, and I will do all of the final editing myself. The whole package arrives, and nothing has been done at all since I last saw my carved-up manuscript two months ago.

I go through the entire book, leaving in some of the corrections and rewrites, even though I'm not happy with the way it reads. I take the second half of the book, which the unknown editor has not even gotten to after having it for eight months, and I complete the editing process myself and turn it in. I am not totally satisfied with the final version that's going to print, but I allow it anyway because of the pressure to have it in publication by the end of the year.

I am not at all happy with myself for allowing myself to be cajoled into accepting an edited version of what I considered a masterful piece of writing. The behind-the-scenes editor hired to fix my manuscript did a fine job. However, he's included examples from his own life experience and inserted them as if I had written them. Now I have a book out that is an excellent book, but I am not 100 percent in support of it because it has the feel of someone else's writing in the first four chapters, yet it's all attributed to me. I half love this book and I half resent it. The second half and appendix are recognizable to me because they are essentially untouched, but the first half has a different flavor that is a bit repellant to me.

I poured myself body, mind, and spirit into the writing of this book, and delivered over 700 pages that I sweated over for almost a year. It needed to be cut in size, but this is the first time since college freshman English that I have an outside person telling me to write in a more acceptable literary style. I decide right here, right now, that I will never again allow this kind of rewriting to take place—not for money, not for prestige, not to please anyone else.

I Can See Clearly Now

The lesson for me in the handling of the editing of *The Sky's the Limit* is all wrapped up in one sentence: *Be wary of those who claim to know better.* I was not interested in winning any literary writing contests, nor did I care about following anyone else's style of writing. I wanted to write in simple and direct language so as to produce a book that assisted readers in achieving their highest self-actualized potential.

By allowing other voices to dictate what my book would look like as a finished product, I now know for certain that it had a contaminating effect on the energy associated with *The Sky's the Limit*. When I held the finished product in my hand, it felt very different to me than my previously published books had. All of the interviews I went on to do for this book did not have the same electrifying attention that I gave to my earlier writing.

I can see clearly now that when some of the authenticity of what I was creating was tarnished by the unwanted and unnecessary input of phantom strangers, it impacted everything about the book. My zest for promoting it was somewhat diminished, albeit at a subconscious level. When I opened the book to any of the excessively edited pages, I had a feeling of vexation waft over me like an invisible black cloud. I'd say to myself, *I didn't write it this way, and yet it has my name attached to it.*

The dedication of this book reads as follows: "To the memory of Abraham H. Maslow—the original pathfinder in the study of man's potential for greatness." This was to be my tribute to my mentor, as well as my heart's inspiration. Somehow I felt that I had let both Dr. Maslow and Dr. Frankl down by caving in to pressures that were applied to me because of the large sum of money paid to me. The idea that I should capitulate because I was highly paid stirred something distasteful within me.

I can see clearly now that this was an important lesson for me. In the 35 or so books that have been published since 1980, I have never allowed anyone else's input to trump my own. However, I have found a woman who became my personal editor as a result of my experience with *The Sky's the Limit.* Had I not had this experience of feeling discredited, I would not have had the desire to find, train, and work in harmony with my friend and editor, Joanna Pyle, for these past 33 years. Today she is like the other half of me when it comes to my writing. She knows how I think and how to do the professional work of line editing every manuscript I create. Out of that unpleasant experience I was able to attract to me a literary soul mate who takes my scribbles and makes me look like a polished writer without the need to interject what she might prefer.

This was a great lesson for me. Be wary—very wary—of those who would step into my life and decide for me what my life's work ought to look like. I look back now and realize that the energy around this book was in some mysterious way stained by the fact that I did not stay with my *I am* presence and insist upon what I knew to be true in my heart.

It is now well over 30 years since *The Sky's the Limit* was published, and it is the only book of mine that has failed to earn back the advance against royalties that was paid at the time of publication.

40

It's ten o'clock in the morning on October 15, 1982. I am in the small town of Marathon, Greece, along with 1,500 people from around the world, to run the annual Athens Classic Marathon. The race was supposed to begin at seven this morning, but because of some snafus, we're beginning at ten. This means that we'll be running through Athens, some 26.2 miles from Marathon, during the hottest part of the day. Even so, I'm confident as we begin the race that this will be my best time. This is my fifth marathon since my inaugural run four years ago.

As the run progresses a big portion of the course goes uphill, and it's getting hotter by the minute. By the 21-mile mark, I'm at a point of physical exhaustion that I've never experienced before. I'm shaking and vomiting green bile. Runners are dropping out all around me, being picked up and taken to first-aid stations in ambulances.

Because of our late arrival into Athens, we have to run on the lane markers between the lines of cars. The fumes are the worst I've ever encountered. Race officials attempt to get me into an ambulance; however, I cannot fathom the idea that I flew all the way to Greece to accomplish something I dreamed about, and won't finish.

As I lie on the side of the road in sheer exhaustion in the heat of the day, something comes over me that I can only describe as a miracle. An invisible being who comes to me in my dreams, and occasionally when I'm awake and in need of guidance, has appeared. All I can say about her is that her eyes are radiant and seem to smile at me when she speaks. This supernatural metaphysical visitor speaks directly to me now as I lie on the street. She tells me that I am strong and will finish this race, and that she will guide me all the way.

I no longer focus on what's wrong and what's upsetting me—I forget the traffic, the heat, my lost time while vomiting on the ground, the fumes. My inner companion, this amazing woman who's more than a figment of my imagination, is right there holding my hands and using her bright blue eyes to convince me that I am much more than a body that is weary. I am a spirit, and this spirit can do anything because it isn't restricted by time and space and physical form. I have five miles to go, yet I can now see myself crossing the finish line. My legs are no longer cramping, and my stomach is no longer queasy from dehydration. My energy is replenished, and I suddenly feel very strong. It is a miracle.

I enter the old Olympic stadium and do a final lap to complete the 26.2 miles. I put my hands up and in jest yell, "We conquer." Legend tells us these were the words the ancient runner Pheidippides spoke as he ran from the plains of Marathon to announce the Greek victory over the Persians, whereupon he supposedly dropped dead from exhaustion.

In that moment, with intense excitement I realize I must write about the inner feminine companion who seems to me to be responsible for my victory. Upon my return to the States I meet with Artie Pine and tell him, "I have a vision of a very wise woman who comes to me in my sleep. I want to write a story about her and what she is constantly telling me." Artie is hugely skeptical on such matters as ghostly visitors and implores me to think instead about writing a book that will capitalize on my previous topics, success as a speaker, and television appearances.

I explain to my wife that I'm drawn to write about a woman who lives in my imagination, and that I've named her "Eykis" in honor of our daughter Skye, who was born just over a year ago. By reversing the letters in our daughter's name and inserting the letter *i* for the higher self, the name Eykis appeared.

I inform Michael Korda, my editor at Simon & Schuster, that I am going to write a parable in the same vein as the fable *Jonathan Livingston Seagull,* which was written and published 12 years ago. I'm going to use my inner guide, Eykis, as the protagonist of the story. She will reside on a fictional planet that has a reality-only basis for living. This means there can be no erroneous thinking because the people on this planet are restricted in their thinking by what is, rather than what they'd like it to be.

My agent, my publisher, and almost everyone else advise me to give up this idea of writing fiction and stick with what I've been successful with so far: writing self-help books rooted in my psychological and therapeutic training. But I'm hooked on the idea of writing a fictionalized account and calling it *Gifts from Eykis.* I imagine that Eykis will visit our world, where erroneous-zone thinking is rampant, and give us the secrets to living a self-actualized life from her reality-only based worldview.

Ever since my experience running the Greek marathon, I can't shake the idea that Eykis isn't just a figment of my imagination; she is a spiritual guide who can actually speak to me and guide me in times of trouble. I rely on this invisible guidance, and I feel her presence more and more as I anticipate writing a fable based upon her teachings.

I was there on the ground in Athens. I saw people being carried away in droves. I was about to be one of those dropouts since my body had lost all of its strength. I recall the moment when Eykis's energy enveloped me and allowed me to instantaneously transcend the limitations of my devitalized and drained body. I ran the last five miles of that race with the help of someone or something that I couldn't explain, but was nevertheless very real for me. I am going to write this fable, and I will rely upon Eykis to guide me through this new enterprise.

I'm scheduled to speak in Honolulu for a national convention next month, and I make plans to spend time writing this fictionalized account on the beach at Waikiki. I gather up my writing materials, and head out to Hawaii with the firm conviction that when I return home I will have completed the first draft.

For the next two weeks in Honolulu, each day I head to a favorite spot, insert my backrest into the sand, take out my pad of paper and pen, and write. The story unfolds almost without effort. Each day of writing feels to me as if someone else is moving my pen across the page, and I just let it come. I have no outline, no idea of how this story is going to play out—I just write and write. I fill many pads of paper sitting on the beach, watching the seagulls, the children, and simply *allowing.*

After two weeks I pack up and fly over to the island of Maui. My wife joins me here for the final two weeks of my writing sojourn, and brings our daughter Skye, who is now 15 months old. I find a shady spot on the beach and, using the same backrest, continue my daily writing. In Part Three of *Gifts From Eykis,* the main character leaves her "strange but wonderful" world and comes to Earth to share her gifts with us on how to truly live from a self-actualized perspective. The story flows effortlessly, and I turn in the manuscript to Simon & Schuster. While they're not thrilled with the idea of me doing a fiction book, my publisher is extremely supportive.

Fast-forward to the release of the book in late 1983. I'm eager to tell the world about the messages contained in *Gifts from Eykis,* and I go on a campaign to have this book stocked in every bookstore I can in America and Canada. I purchase books by the thousands and mail them at my own expense. Telling the world about Eykis and her gifts becomes my full-time job. I love taking this whole project into my own hands again, just like I did with *Your Erroneous Zones* seven years ago. I'm not concerned with book sales or a position on a bestseller list. I'm having the time of my life spreading the word about something I love.

Eykis speaks to me in my imagination all the time. I feel her feminine energy around me, moving me quietly but firmly into a more spiritual approach to this life on Earth. I don't speak much about Eykis as a true guiding spirit in my life, but she is very real for me.

After purchasing tens of thousands of copies of *Gifts from Eykis* and distributing them to people all over the world, I know that I will be moving on in my writing. I see the book as a major film in the future, and I give thanks for Eykis's presence in my life. I've written and published my only fictional story, and I feel blessed beyond my ability to describe it.

While writing the final chapter of *Gifts from Eykis,* our daughter Sommer is conceived on Maui. There's not a shred of doubt within me that Eykis is real. She is moving me more and more into a spiritual realm and infusing me with her right-brained Yin energy.

I Can See Clearly Now

My experience of lying on the ground in Athens while running the marathon in 1982 was another quantum moment—a major turning point in my life. This was the first time I actually saw and felt the presence of a supernatural energy, and allowed myself to go beyond my physical self and be guided. It was as if I was no longer constrained by the limitations of my wearied body. Eykis seemed to be taking over for me in this moment of crisis. I say *crisis* because the idea of returning home knowing that I hadn't accomplished my goal of running this marathon was more than I could bear. I was living what Maslow described as being a person who must be what he can be. Quitting was not an option, yet my body was completely enervated.

I can see clearly now that there's much more to this whole idea of being human than what is measurable by our physical accomplishments. I know there's a reservoir of inner strength that can be called upon in crucial moments—and even more amazing, there's Divine guidance available to us if we are willing to believe in it and allow it to work with us.

Today I know that everything in the universe is connected to everything else by invisible spiritual strings, if you will. I know that I have spiritual guidance available to me, and that it is always there if I choose to call upon it. Eykis is a personification of this Divine guidance. She has appeared to me on numerous occasions in the years since I first put a name to my disembodied spiritual friend. I have come to trust in the availability of angelic assistance and guidance.

I recall the amazement I felt as I ran into that ancient Olympic stadium. An hour before I was so sick that I was being urged to get in an ambulance—which almost two-thirds of the runners had done because of the intense heat, uphill running, and vehicle fumes that characterized this race. Yet I had a second wind, and I was feeling stronger at the end than at any time during the race.

The writing of *Gifts from Eykis* was a magical experience for me—one of my earliest experiences with automatic writing. Every day while I sat on the beach in Honolulu and Maui, I felt the presence of this Yin energy that I call Eykis. I felt relaxed, peaceful, and confident that everything I needed to say in this parable would be there. It is what I now call "channeled writing": I was the instrument, and the words just mystically appeared on the pad of paper. My hand moved effortlessly and very fast. I can recall my hand feeling cramped because the ideas and words were coming so rapidly. Each day after writing for several hours, I'd comment to my wife that something akin to real magic was taking place with me on the beach every day.

Today I can see clearly that this was my introduction to the idea that all writing is really channeled from the world of the invisible. As Jesus said, "It's the spirit that gives life," and words on a page appearing out of nowhere are a result of the dance of creation. I know now that God writes all the books—that the words that appear on the page are not owned by anyone. I know for sure that the creative process is something that I get from a higher realm, and that Eykis symbolized for me a way to align with this energy that I call God, and when I am able to do so, I have the same "all things are possible" abilities as does the Creator.

When I was sending out copies of *Gifts from Eykis* to thousands of people throughout the country, I included a letter that said, "Eykis is being made into a movie." I didn't say, "someday"; I said it as if it were a completed fact. This was my first foray into the idea of living from the end and assuming the feeling of the wish fulfilled, and stating something in present-moment terms as if it already were a done deal. Today there is in fact a screenplay for *Gifts from Eykis,* and a director is even assigned. The idea for making this book into a film, which was only an idea at the time, is now becoming a physical reality.

Eykis showed up first in my dreams, and then in my quiet meditative moments, and finally as a guiding force in my life at a time when I needed to experience firsthand the extraordinary powers that can manifest when I feel most desperate and hopeless—if I'm willing to surrender and allow for a miracle. This is what happened during my experience in Greece in 1982. From that day on I *knew* that there's far more to my humanity than what I detect through my senses and/or scientifically verifiable data. Eykis showed up for me when I banished all doubt and allowed Divine assistance to carry me to the finish line.

41

In the summer of 1985, my life is increasingly full of sharing the responsibilities of parenting children of various ages. I am 45 years old and the father of three small girls, as well as three older children. My wife, Marcelene, and I have had three babies in the past four years; my daughter Tracy is now 18; and we have two preteenagers to raise. This is an awesome responsibility that on the one hand I think of as meeting my kids' lower-rung needs on Maslow's hierarchy—that is, to feed, clothe, and provide them a safe place to grow. But on the other hand, I'm also here to assist them in achieving their highest needs in that little compartment at the top of Maslow's pyramid called self-actualization.

I've been polling audiences at numerous speaking engagements during the past year asking, "What do you really want for your children?" The idea of writing a book about parenting behaviors specifically pointed toward raising no-limit children to become self-actualized adults has become an intriguing subject. Parenting is the place where this transformation could take place.

It seems to me that many parents are pushing their children in the opposite direction of the apex of Maslow's pyramid. So many children are taught to live by the demands of their ego—to win at all costs, to accumulate and own as much stuff as possible, to define their lives on the basis of how they stack up to others, to make as much money as possible, and to put a monetary value on everything they do. The results of these kinds of pressures on children show up in personality disorders, obesity, physical illness, anxiety and stress, and emotional instability.

My agent, Artie Pine, has just arranged a contract for two future books with another prestigious New York publishing house, William Morrow and Company. While discussing this new contract with my wife and Artie, I tell them, "I feel compelled to write an extensive book on how to raise children to become self-actualized people." I explore this idea further by describing that I've discovered that what parents say they want for their children is often at odds with how they actually raise their children.

I have thousands of responses to my inquiries in a huge file that's organized into ten categories concerning what parents say they want for their children. Out of this file I decide to create a proposed book outline. When Artie and I present it to my new publisher, they're excited and give me the go-ahead. This time I eschew the need for a large advance for my book. I don't want money to be involved as I write; I do not wish to have a repeat of my experience at Simon & Schuster.

I am totally into the writing of this new book. I decide to title it using the same inquiry I gave to thousands of attendees at my lectures during the past year or so: *What Do You Really Want for Your Children?* I am fascinated by the responses I have in my file. No one says, *I want my children to be wealthy, to be better than anyone else, to win at everything they do, to get a good job, to get the best grades, to get into the right schools, to look good to their peers.* Yet, this seems to be how they're raising their children.

I write for hours and hours every day, and I'm conscious of all that I say and do as a parent. Marcie and I have long conversations about what we truly want for our six children, and we often modify our own parenting interventions so that they more clearly reflect what we want for our kids. We're determined to put into practice the idea of raising children who feel purposeful and live at their maximum level of happiness. I watch my son and daughters as they go about their daily routines, and I am in awe of the miraculous way that they interact with each other, with us, and with their world.

I want my children to enjoy life, to value themselves, to be risk takers, to become self-reliant, to be free from stress and anxiety, to have peaceful lives, to celebrate their present moments, to experience a lifetime of wellness, to be creative, and above all to fulfill their highest needs and to feel a sense of purpose. These qualities would make them self-actualized people—and these will be the individual chapter titles for this massive writing undertaking that has completely taken over my life. I write and I watch—my children and my wife are such wonderful teachers. They fill my heart with joy and my manuscript with ideas for how to raise children to live at the top of the pyramid.

The manuscript is growing every day. I can't seem to stop writing, and once again I'm experiencing, with stunned amazement, automatic writing. Eykis is with me every day of this fabulous journey. Daily I tell my wife about what I'm writing and how fascinated I am by the way this information is coming to me. I have an angelic co-pilot who's steering this entire project from a heavenly distance. My writing has never been easier.

I have long contemplated what it would be like to have children grow up in an environment in which their total well-being was emphasized exclusively, and the demands of the ego were set completely aside. This book is dedicated to the idea that I learned from Buckminster Fuller: that we are all geniuses—it is life that de-geniuses us. My goal in writing *What Do You Really Want for Your Children?* is to explain how parents can create a life environment that doesn't de-genius children.

I recall how Dr. Maslow stressed that self-actualization is a state of awareness that's only available to a select few people who might be called geniuses. These are the people he studied: Albert Einstein, Jesus of Nazareth, Lao-tzu, and contemporary leaders in other fields as well. I am, with apologies to Dr. Maslow, taking the position that this more exalted state at the top of the hierarchy of needs isn't just available to emotionally advanced souls who happened to win the lottery when they were conceived. This peak of the pyramid is our natural birthright.

Children who are encouraged to become self-actualized, and see it modeled, will know that no one is superior to anyone else, and that these higher realms are there for all of us. It is a place where people are independent; comfortable being alone; reality-centered; and deeply accept themselves, others, and the world. As parents, what we really want for our children is to have them lead happy, fulfilled lives . . . and this is what I am totally immersed in every day.

I have been writing day and night for almost a year now. The words come fast and furious, flowing freely like water from a spigot that continues to flow because of a broken pipeline. I can't plug the leak—I've never known such intensity in my writing. It comes in the middle of the night, it comes in the afternoon, and it comes in the evening as well. I've written over 1,000 pages. I know I'll need to cut this manuscript significantly, but I will leave that to my new editor, Joanna, who is now working full-time with me.

I Can See Clearly Now

Writing about raising children to become no-limit, self-actualized adults was the natural progression for me in 1985. I was in the midst of making a portentous shift in my life, and consequently it was being reflected in my writing and speaking. I was in the early stages of a spiritual awakening. Much of this had to do with my new marriage and the continuing presence of more and more children arriving in our family—by 1989, we had five new babies who were all born in the 1980s. It was no accident that I was being directed to write about parenting as more and more parenting responsibilities were landing in my lap.

I have been a teacher on so many different levels, from elementary school through graduate school, and have always known that the best way to truly learn and understand something is to teach it. And so it was with parenting as well.

The essential lesson I wanted to convey in writing this parenting tome involved self-reliance. I've said it thousands of times, "Parents are not for leaning; they are to make leaning unnecessary." This is the message that I was always attempting to express to my clients in counseling sessions: *Learn to rely upon yourself. Take total responsibility for everything that comes into your life, and as Dr. Viktor Frankl has taught, you always have a choice in how you react to anything that life offers you.*

As my family was growing, I can see clearly now that these young Divine beings were my teachers. Yes indeed, when the student is ready, the teachers will appear! There was also the mystical aspect that I named Eykis directing the course of my life, as a man and as a professional teacher and writer.

Here's another interesting story. One of my first clients at St. John's University in my early years as a professor in the 1970s was a woman named Suzi Kaufman, the mother of a young boy named Raun who was diagnosed with infantile autism. She was also the sister-in-law of my first doctoral student advisee, Steven Kaufman.

During the course of many of our counseling sessions together, Suzi related that her young son was completely unreachable. She and her husband, Barry Neil Kaufman, spared no effort or expense in having Raun examined by autism experts around the world. The answer was always the same: "It is incurable. He is unreachable. We don't know why, and there is nothing that can be done."

So Suzi and Barry devised their own program for treating their young son. They hired students and trained them in a method they created, essentially to surround Raun with unconditional love in a contained, safe environment. For 24 hours a day, 7 days a week, for months on end, Raun was the recipient of continual loving responses.

Suzi described to me Raun's symptoms of rocking back and forth and being distant, almost as if he were in a waking coma. But after months of their own program for reaching their son, one day Raun's eyes blinked, and Barry said, "I looked at my son with new eyes." In 1976 Barry went on to write a book titled *Son-Rise,* which detailed the entire process they developed and how they were ultimately able to see Raun come back to them and leave his diagnosis of "incurable" behind. The book was made into a television movie starring James Farentino several years later.

Now fast-forward to 1985, as I'm writing on parenting. Our daughter Serena had been born in May, and within a year she had begun to exhibit some of the same symptoms that Raun had. I immediately flashed back to my sessions with Suzi and all of the things she and her husband did some 15 years earlier.

I arranged a family meeting with Marcie and all of our children, and I detailed precisely how we were going to deal with Serena, all based on what I had learned 15 years ago. We surrounded her with love: Marcie literally wore our infant next to her heart almost 24 hours a day. Serena was told over and over by her parents and siblings that she was loved—that she had nothing to fear and if she wanted to rock back and forth, then she would be the world-champion rocker as far as all of us were concerned. No judgments, no anger, only love. It worked for the Kaufmans back in the early 1970s, and it worked with our Serena in a relatively short period of time.

Again, there are no accidents anywhere. Suzi walking into my office for counseling sessions was to benefit an unborn child of mine some 15 years into the future, and she taught me exactly what to do as a parent without even knowing it.

As I finished writing *What Do You Really Want for Your Children?* I began to include many references to higher needs, spiritual awakening, and God. These topics hadn't appeared in any of my previous four books. The birth of my children, my marriage to a spiritually awake woman, and my own development as a teacher examining these spiritual principles on a daily basis were all pulling me in a new direction. I was moving toward the mystical, the mysterious—the realm of higher and higher consciousness. It's clear to me today that I was receptive to the influence of ascended masters who were inviting me to go beyond what I'd been exploring and writing about.

Seeing my baby doing what had been described to me 15 years back, and knowing precisely what to do and then successfully implementing it, gave me "the tinglies." I knew that I was being directed by a force much bigger than I. I knew that I was about to embark on a whole new adventure that had almost nothing to do with what I had written and spoken about up until that time.

All of the factors were coming together at once: The birth of so many new babies in my 40s; the felt presence of a spiritual guide that I called Eykis; a wife who modeled spiritual awareness in her mothering practices; and most significantly, an inner calling that had me talking about God, miracles, and spiritual awakening. I deliberately left these out of my earlier writing, but they were now calling me—in a way that I couldn't ignore. I didn't have it; it had me!

42

On October 9, 1987, my wife delivered our seventh child, a boy whom we have named Sands Jay Dyer. I have been on the road a lot these past two years doing both a hardcover and a paperback tour for my parenting book, *What Do You Really Want for Your Children?* I feel that my life is taking on an entirely new purpose and direction, though I'm unable to define precisely what that is.

I receive many requests to speak at church services all across the country, and have been giving a lot of speeches in humanistically oriented multidenominational churches for the past several years. It seems that the messages in my books resonate with these church memberships, and the congregations are eager to attend my seminars and talks at their Sunday-morning services. At a Unity or Religious Science church it's just as likely that a sermon is on the writing of Ralph Waldo Emerson, Abraham Lincoln, Buddha, or Lao-tzu as on the direct teachings of Jesus Christ. These Christian churches emphasize spirituality and a God-realized life, rather than the more traditional religious dogma, and people from all religious persuasions are always welcome.

I'm excited to be considered a spiritual teacher. This is new for me, since I have pretty much eschewed any specific religion. I see myself as a global person without any interest in excluding anyone. I am honored to be giving "sermon-like" talks at church services, and to be associated with the likes of Emerson, Thoreau, Leo Buscaglia, Neville, and other transcendentalist teachers. The more I speak at these spiritual gatherings, the more I want to write about personal and spiritual transformation. I feel as if I am being pulled in a new direction, and I'm not the one doing the pulling. Something way bigger than little me seems to be taking over the reins of my life.

I have now published five books, all of which have been extremely successful, and Artie Pine has some ideas about capitalizing on this commercial success by my writing two books that he's certain will be very lucrative for me and for my publisher. He suggests I write a self-help book on using my commonsense principles to be more effective at making money, and then a follow-up book telling people how to have a great sex life using the no-limit ideas I've previously written about. Thanks to Dr. Ruth Westheimer's appearances on radio and television, a new age of freer, franker talk about sex has been ushered in.

My agent and publisher both feel that we'd have runaway bestsellers if I authored books on money and sex, and all concerned would harvest a financial bonanza. As Artie tells me, "Your publisher is willing to do a two-book deal that will make you a fortune. I have given them the idea for these books. Just say the word, and I will finalize this deal for you."

I listen carefully to Artie's proposal and immediately tell him that there's no way that I am interested or willing to undertake such a proposal. I explain that the talks I've been giving in spiritual gatherings for the past year have led to my fascination with the idea that individuals are capable of achieving a kind of God-realization if they change the way they think. What I want to write is a book titled *You'll See It When You Believe It,* to contrast with the more common phrase, "I'll only believe it when I see it."

I reiterate to my agent that our beliefs as a people determine what we eventually see. I am excited by this idea of writing a spiritual guide for achieving one's own personal transformation. These ideas have been germinating within me during this period of becoming prominent as a spiritual teacher, without my consciously doing anything to bring it about.

Artie's annoyance is palpable on the phone. He asks me what the *it* is that I'm speaking about when I say "You'll see it when you believe it." I try to tell him that this is all about moving into the world of Spirit. And the *it* is anything that people place their attention on in their imagination, which will become observable in the physical realm because of the power of the mind to create anything it believes in.

I elaborate that I have seven one-word concepts that are not readily understood by the average person. A God-realized state is accessible with a clear explanation of these concepts and how they operate in life. I'll make each word/concept a chapter, with examples for turning them from fuzzy concepts to something the reader can immediately put into practice. I read the seven words to him: *Transformation, Thought, Oneness, Abundance, Detachment, Synchronicity,* and *Forgiveness.*

Then I read a statement by President John Quincy Adams that I've been carrying with me for the past year and using in most of my speeches, especially in the spiritually based church presentations:

> John Quincy Adams is well but the house in which he lives at the present time is becoming dilapidated. It's tottering on its foundations. Time and the seasons have nearly destroyed it. Its roof is pretty well worn out. Its walls are much shattered and tremble with every wind. I think John Quincy Adams will have to move out of it soon. But he himself is quite well, quite well.

Artie is beside himself in frustration with me and responds in his wonderful, New York literary-agent style, "What the hell are you talking about, Wayne? I have no idea what you want to write about. Let's just take the deal I've arranged for you. You'd be a fool to turn it down—it's more money than you've dreamed of in your life."

I say I'm sorry, but I can't let money or status or anyone else tell me what to write and speak about. I am not Dr. Ruth, and I don't want to pretend to be interested in telling people how to make money. I tell Artie that I will be writing my next book on the concept that *believing is seeing,* rather than the other way around.

William Morrow agrees to be the publisher for my next book, but they offer no advance against royalties. Both Artie and my publisher tell me over and over again that the general public is not really interested in reading books pertaining to spirituality and higher consciousness. They tell me that I'm wasting my time and effort, and there's no chance that a book with such a confusing title and amorphous concepts can succeed in the big way that my previous books performed.

I am undaunted. I know what I want to write about, and I feel the presence of something Divine whispering to me that I've made the right choice.

I Can See Clearly Now

I look back and see quite clearly that something was influencing me to make a major shift in my writing and speaking—and in my life as well. I'd written five best-selling books, all from a psychological perspective on how to live a more fulfilling and self-reliant life, yet it was so easy for me to decline an exceptionally lucrative offer to continue writing popular books in the self-help genre that would appeal to a large audience. I was turning down several million dollars of guaranteed income for something that would not have been particularly difficult for me to accomplish.

Given the circumstances I was facing in 1987, turning down such a windfall wasn't something that I would have predicted. I had a large family of seven children to provide for, including a brand-new baby boy. Four of my children were under the age of six, and I had older children who were either attending private schools or heading off to college. As I look back on my decision to turn away from that outstanding offer, though, I can still feel how easy it was for me. I didn't hesitate for a moment or ask to talk it over with anyone. My "no, thank you" came from a deep knowing within me that I couldn't go in the direction that those ego temptations were offering.

I am intrigued when I compare the index of my preceding books with the index of *You'll See It When You Believe It,* which was written between November 1987 and June 1989. In this later book, *God* has

10 citations, *spiritual* has 12, and *higher consciousness* has 17. Examining the five books I'd written previously, and my three textbooks, reveals a grand total of *one* such citation in all their indexes. That single citation is for *spiritual needs* referring to Maslow's definition of self-actualization in my parenting book. I went from a single reference to God, spiritual, and higher consciousness in all my previous books to 39 in just this one book.

What was it that was pulling me away from writing psychologically oriented books to a book rooted in spirituality, higher consciousness, and most dramatically, God? This wasn't part of any plan I had when I began writing for the general reading public.

At this crucial time in my life, there was something influencing me to stop thinking about making more money, or gaining more fame, or massaging my ego, and to instead let myself grow. I had eschewed using any spiritual or higher-consciousness terms in my earlier writing because I thought they smacked too much of religion and supernatural forces. I wanted to use the language of common sense and the idea that an individual did not need that unverifiable Divine intervention to lead to a self-actualized life.

By 1987 I was enveloped in spiritual teachings. I was reading and quoting from the Bhagavad Gita and the Tao Te Ching, as well as the New Testament. I was communicating with spiritual ministers all over the country and giving Sunday-morning lectures to huge audiences in nondenominational churches regularly. Whereas before I would not use the words *God, spiritual,* or *higher consciousness* in my writing, now I was deeply engrossed in *metaphysical* rather than purely *physical* teachings.

I had obviously gone as far as I was supposed to go with my earlier focus on rational emotive therapy and self-actualization principles. I had a foundation rooted in the material world of the corporeal; now I was being called to look much more closely at the invisible world of Spirit. I immersed myself in studying quantum physics, great philosophers, and Eastern and Western spiritual wisdom. I was drawn to attend lectures and listen to recordings on the subjects of oneness, transformation, synchronicity, and detachment—all of which became the focus of *You'll See It When You Believe It.*

Everything seemed to be moving very, very fast as I began this shift into writing about higher consciousness and spirituality. God was no longer a religious concept to me, and I was feeling closer and closer to God every day. I sensed that my days as a psychologist were essentially over, and I was thrilled to be considered a teacher of spiritual principles. I began to refuse speaking requests from businesses and schools, and began to speak almost full-time in churches throughout America and Canada. My public speaking focused on attaining God-realization and being able to create miracles in everyday life. Concepts that I once rejected and criticized were now a big part of my writing and speaking, and I knew that something was directing this new course in my life.

I put an enormous amount of effort into the creation of *You'll See It When You Believe It,* which was the first of many books that I was privileged to create in the field of spiritual nonfiction literature. I wanted to create a book that gave specific suggestions on how to tap into the invisible part of ourselves, and how to apply the same principles that govern the universe to the running of an individual life. My personal editor worked very closely with me, and I was also blessed to have a world-famous editor who had only worked on fiction books previously work on the final edit. Her name was Jeanne Bernkopf, and she was an angel sent to me to put the finishing touches on this, my inaugural book in this new field of inquiry.

I did two national book tours, and hundreds of public lectures—mostly in what were at the time called New Age churches—across the country. The audiences were so receptive that it's clear now that there was something moving me to speak and write about spiritual awakening. *You'll See It When You Believe It* contained a message about life that the general public both in the U.S. and around the world wanted to explore. My apprenticeship in the world of self-help and psychologically oriented writing and speaking was complete. I had been "pulled" to a new direction of teaching how to tap into something beyond the body/mind and truly create a heaven on earth.

Both Artie Pine and my publisher were mistaken. *You'll See It When You Believe It* proved without a doubt that there was an audience for books about God and higher awareness in a non-religious format.

The book debuted on *The New York Times* bestseller list and was well received all over the world.

I didn't know it at the time, but with the benefit of being able to look back, I see that I was living the title of that book. I saw it all come to fruition because I first believed it. Nothing could deter me from my vision—not even extraordinary financial gain. It is so clear to me now that the hand of God and a host of ascended masters were gently but persistently pulling me toward being a teacher of spiritual truth. Miracles were about to unfold in my life to help me stay aligned with this new direction.

43

It is February 14, 1989—the tenth anniversary of the day Marcelene and I met. We both lovingly and humorously recall that first meeting on Valentine's Day 1979. Someone had stuck a red Valentine heart sticker on my shirt, and the first words I spoke to my future wife were in response to her question about what was on my shirt: "I have a heart on for you."

I have accepted a multicity speaking tour of Australia that includes in the lineup John and Greg Rice, Cathy Lee Crosby, and my dear friend and colleague Og Mandino. My wife and two youngest children—Serena, three-and-a-half years old; and Sands, 18 months of age—have accompanied me on this trip. We are currently staying in the Hilton Hotel in Brisbane. I'm scheduled to appear onstage before thousands of people tomorrow, when I'll keynote a large all-day seminar open to the public.

I'm awakened by a noise. The red numbers on the digital clock next to the bed read 4:05 A.M., and I see that my wife is up and in the process of rearranging the furniture and sleeping arrangements in our room. "It's the middle of the night. What in the world are you doing? Are you awake or are you walking in your sleep?" I ask Marcelene. She is apparently sleepwalking, because she doesn't respond.

Serena is asleep next to me, and Sands, who is still a nursing baby, is in the same bed as his mother. Marcie, in a walking coma, picks up Serena and puts her in the bed with our baby and climbs next to me. She begins making advances and is thoroughly determined to make love to me. The look on her face is unlike any I've ever seen, and I am in a semiconscious state of shock/delight.

My wife has been either nursing or pregnant for the previous eight years, and consequently completely halted her menstrual cycle. She's also had one ovary removed, so conception had seemed impossible. Despite all of this, our youngest daughter, Saje, is conceived. What awoke my wife at that precise instant? What caused this behavior by a woman who is always in control? What force is operating here? Who is in charge here?

A few months later, I'm in Phoenix on a book tour for *You'll See It When You Believe It*. I'm scheduled to appear on radio station KTAR with Pat McMahon—I've visited his show on several occasions during book tours over the last decade, and he's become a good friend. It turns out that the guest on the show before me is another of my heroes.

Mother Teresa is in Phoenix to support the opening of a newly constructed homeless shelter, where she had slept the night before. Pat McMahon is an Irish Catholic, spiritual man, and he's beside himself with excitement anticipating interviewing this saintly woman. He repeatedly asks her if there's anything he can do for her: "Tell listeners about your ashram in Calcutta? Can I help you raise money for your mission? Anything? Mother Teresa, I'd like to do something for you, since you do so much for so many people."

"There is one thing you can do for me," she finally says in her broken English. "Tomorrow morning, get up at four A.M. and go out onto the streets of Phoenix. Find someone who believes that he is alone, and convince him that he's not."

I am deeply touched by her words. They confirm everything I've written about in my book about oneness, and the awareness that we are always connected to our Source of being— regardless of what our senses tell us, or what the external circumstances seem to indicate.

I am aware that the energy of the entire studio has shifted: People seem to be less hurried; the atmosphere is one of benevolence, whereas before this beautiful diminutive woman entered it was fast-paced and kinetic. I feel as if a warm shower is running inside of me, which I often call "the tinglies." And I'm not the only one who feels this way—Pat tells me that it was as if a wave of unconditional love swept over him while she sat across from him in the studio.

I can't see or touch the loving energy that everyone seemed to feel. But it is apparent to me that this devout woman, who has devoted her life to serving others and living in Christ consciousness, has all by her pint-sized self managed to dramatically impact the environment around her, and everyone in it as well.

I feel so blessed to share in this experience. It reinforces that there's far more to what we perceive to be our reality than what we experience with our senses. This is not something that can be explained, nor is it something that I believe because I'm seeing it. This is the experience that I'm referring to in the title of the book I am so proud to have had written through me. *You'll See It When You Believe It* says it all.

I Can See Clearly Now

What happened on Valentine's Day in 1989 was as momentous an occasion as any I have ever experienced. The odds against my wife getting pregnant seemed to be stacked incredibly high. That Marcie was awakened from a deep sleep and directed in her semiconscious state to participate at that instant in the dance of creation was beyond reason to me. This was the only time in our 20-plus years together that she behaved in this fashion. For me this was a confirmation that something much bigger and beyond the material world was at play.

Saje Eykis Dyer was born on November 16, 1989, and obviously she played some kind of invisible role in getting onto this physical plane of existence with me as her father and Marcie as her mother. Something beyond our explanation was at work that morning.

My youngest daughter is one of the most determined young women I've ever known—ever! That determination must have been working overtime that early morning in Brisbane. She had to tap on her mother's shoulder and somehow awaken her from a deep sleep. She had to direct her to move the furniture and rearrange her future siblings in order to activate the necessary conditions for her to get into this world from her perch in the infinite realm. This was the only moment available to Saje to come fulfill her own dharma. Any other moment, and her opening would vanish and a different someone would show up—or, more likely, no someone at all.

On Mother's Day that year, I wrote a verse to my wife titled "Brisbane," which commemorates the incredible events that transpired that morning:

Brisbane
Where God was revealed to us.

Only the two of us know the magic and awe
of that presence.

Against impossible odds . . .

Our connection to eternity further reinforced,
strengthened.

Yet the paradox always lingers . . .

We are in control/we are not in control,
doomed to make choices.

All I am certain of is our love imbedded in
forever.

The first two lines say it all. This was the moment when God's presence was truly revealed to Marcie and me.

I can see clearly today that I was involved in a Divine intervention as I watched my wife move about the room in a somnambulant state, directed by a force that I had never witnessed up close and personal before. This was a turning point for me. My future writing would emanate from this firsthand knowing of the sacred that I witnessed in the conception and subsequent birth of our daughter Saje. I knew from that moment on that there truly are no accidents in this world. We think we are in control, but as Lao-tzu once observed, "We are all doing nothing, we're just being done." And Jesus also said, "It's the spirit that gives life." The spirit was at work in that Brisbane hotel room back in 1989.

Every time I look carefully at Saje, I think back to the invisible spirit that was speeding up the process of getting here, as I said, against impossible odds—and then I remember "With God, all things are possible." When I observe her indefatigable persistence and unwavering determination, I recall how that must have been at play in a gigantic way as she manipulated events in order to ensure her incarnation. I have always thanked God for the beautiful spirit that is my daughter. But I am even more thankful for being allowed to be a participant in something that I can only call "real magic," which was to be the title of the next book I would write three years into the future. I had now left the world of psychology behind in my writing permanently.

I can see clearly now that a person who achieves a level of God-realization is able to impact everyone they encounter simply by their presence in the same room. It's been said that when Jesus entered a village, just his presence and nothing more would elevate the consciousness of everyone in the village.

This was the same phenomenon I observed in May 1989 when Mother Teresa walked into that studio, and everyone seemed to feel the impact of her saintly presence. This is not Psychology 101; it is advanced spirituality and Divine love in action. I decided right then and there that this was something that I would aspire to for the rest of my life. By observing how this woman affected the world around her, I was given a role model for how I would like to impact others as well.

It reminded me of the way Dinah Shore's loving presence seemed to elevate everyone around her. With Mother Teresa, there was the element of a spiritual impact as well. This saintly woman's presence seemed to make everyone around her want to be more Christlike—

to be less judgmental, to overlook and forgive any shortcoming, to literally feel closer to God because of the pheromones of love she emitted by her very presence.

Years later, on the morning of September 6, 1997, I was about to address a large gathering of people in Sydney when I was handed a note informing me that Mother Teresa had passed away the night before. I told the audience of my experience in Phoenix with this future saint, and remarked that it was just like her to slip away unnoticed at a time when the entire world's attention was focused on the funeral for Princess Diana in England.

Mother Teresa lived her life beyond the ego. She didn't want any credit or attention given to her—she was all about service to others, especially to the disadvantaged. She once commented that every day she saw Jesus Christ in all of his distressing disguises. This is how she lived. And this is how she died—at a time when all of the fanfare and attention would be elsewhere.

This woman's Divine, saintly presence invigorated and enhanced not only the energy of the immediate surroundings, but everyone who was in her presence as well. I remember thinking that I could become like this if I were I able to live and be only a fraction of the goodness and godliness that Mother Teresa represented. She was definitely a miracle worker, and I was so inspired by her to become more like her. I knew I would have to undergo a radical transformation in my way of living, particularly in taming my ego and putting more of the focus of my life's work on the realm beyond the physical.

I can clearly see that my brief encounter with Mother Teresa, just as I was about to launch a national book tour for *You'll See It When You Believe It,* pushed me to look into the world of the miraculous and examine the possibilities of real magic. The kind of magic that I saw take place when this woman walked into a studio, and made everything and everyone feel aligned with God.

44

I am on a new mission in my life in the fall of 1991. I've been reading a great deal about spiritual masters, ancient and contemporary, who are capable of performing what are called "miracles" of all descriptions—stunning feats such as raising the dead, instant healing from crippling deformities, acts of alchemy, telepathic communication, astounding manifestations, and synchronicities. I believe so strongly that if any one person can perform this type of magic, then everyone can. This is what I want to explore.

Henry Miller said, "Don't look for miracles. *You* are the miracle." I can't get this idea out of my mind. I am going to write about the notion of teaching people how to maximize their own highest potential for achieving what have come to be called miracles. I too am about to participate in my own stunning feat and undergo a radical transformation.

I watch the world-famous illusionist David Copperfield perform astonishing acts of magic in Las Vegas. As I sit there enjoying the show, the idea comes to me that I have been immersed in something that doesn't involve smoke, mirrors, and trickery to fool the audience. There *is* real magic, and I've been on the periphery of this phenomenon for the past couple of years. I return to my hotel room and stay up all night writing an outline for a book on how to create miracles in everyday life. I am going to call it *Real Magic,* and I can't wait to get started on it.

One of my spiritual mentors is Nisargadatta Maharaj of India, who passed away a decade ago. As I prepare to write my new book back home in Florida, I'm drawn to read and reread this advice that he gave to a devotee: "If you desire to reach your highest potential and fulfill the dharma for which you incarnated, you will need to live a life of sobriety." Gradually I realize the sentence is speaking to me about me, and that I must make a choice.

I have been running a minimum of eight miles every single day for almost 15 years now. It is as normal for me to run several hours in a day as it is to brush my teeth before going to bed. Sitting at my desk now, I try to remember a day in which I have not had a few beers to drink in the evening after my run. I mentally go back ten years, and I know that it is even longer than a decade. It hits me hard that almost 15 years have passed in which I've consumed alcohol every single day, no exceptions. It is a habit, and my life revolves around this habit. I allow a recent scene to replay in my imagination.

Last week I made my wife and all six of our children pack up and leave a restaurant because it had temporarily had its liquor license suspended. My need for a couple of beers became the reason to inconvenience seven other people. I am ashamed that I have allowed this habit to become such a dominant force in my life, and that it has moved into something of a daily obsession for 15 years now.

I hear the words of Nisargadatta ringing loudly in my ears. If I want to reach my highest potential and fulfill my life's mission, I need to live a life of sobriety.

I tell myself, "I *am* sober . . . I never get drunk . . . I always stop after two or three beers . . . I really don't have a problem." But I know I'm fooling myself. That's over 5,000 consecutive days of putting alcohol into my body. Hokekyó Sho once said in his Sanskrit text, "After the third cup, the wine drinks the man." I wonder what he would say about 5,000 consecutive days of three beers. I think hard. Indeed, the beer is drinking me.

I make a decision on the spot. I make an agreement with God, my highest self, that I will not drink a beer tonight. I will practice the total sobriety that Nisargadatta recommended to one of his devotees in Bombay back in the 1970s—which also happens to be when I began this daily habit of beer drinking. Perhaps he was talking to me.

I never met Nisargadatta, but I studied his work *I Am That* in depth. Whenever I read the transcripts of his dialogues with his students and devotees, it always seemed as if he was speaking to me. This is another of those quantum moments—I can actually see him with me now as I replay my crass behavior in the restaurant, where I conducted myself in such a boorish and inconsiderate way toward my wife and children. I ask for guidance and support in my new endeavor. I tell no one about what I'm undertaking.

Tonight passes, and I am surprised by how easy this is. I feel the hand of a guiding spirit at work here. I'm not doing this just because I don't want to disappoint myself, my family, or anyone else. I no longer wish to disappoint God—my highest self, the individualized expression of God, which is pure love. I came from perfect health and well-being, and I intend to stay aligned with this and keep alcohol out of my body, because alcohol destroys brain cells and therefore is destructive to my well-being. I have a *senior partner* in this undertaking and I feel confident, blessed, and truly inspired to change this habit—one day at a time—and love every minute of it.

I write furiously, and my new publisher, HarperCollins, is thrilled with the manuscript. Every day I become increasingly aware that deep within all of us is a unified field of limitless possibilities. I ask myself, *Who am I to undertake such a task as to speak about miracles?* Then I stop with the doubt, and just listen and allow myself to be directed as Spirit seems to be calling me.

My opening words in *Real Magic* are an observation by St. Francis of Assisi, a saint I've known about superficially and considered one of the greatest examples of miracle making: "I have been all things unholy; if God can work through me, he can work through anyone." These words reflect both the humility and confidence I feel about this venerable subject of real magic.

Skipping ahead to the fall of 1992, I've completed a full year alcohol-free. I know in my heart that this decision, prompted by my long-departed guru Nisargadatta Maharaj, put me on this new path.

I give thanks to God, St. Francis, and Nisargadatta for the beautiful book with the rainbow on the cover titled *Real Magic,* which I hold in my hand. I am blessed.

I Can See Clearly Now

Well over two decades have passed since I heard Nisargadatta Maharaj speak those words on the necessity of complete sobriety in order to fulfill a man's destiny. Today I can say that those words I heard back in 1991 were among the most momentous I ever encountered. I have never once been tempted to go back on my commitment to sobriety since that extraordinary quantum moment.

I can see clearly now as I look at my decision to break a 15-year habit of daily consumption of beer that it was my awareness of no longer wanting to displease or disappoint my highest self, which is in total alignment with the Source of all being. I can see clearly now that breaking self-sabotaging habits is not difficult when I invest myself in my highest God-realized self.

I knew back then that I had "promises to keep, and miles to go before I sleep," as Robert Frost wrote so succinctly in his famous poem "Stopping by Woods on a Snowy Evening." Yet I also knew that if my habit of daily alcohol consumption continued, it would not allow me to fulfill the promises I made when I came into this world of spirit. It was the promise that I made to my creator, to that infinite intelligence of well-being from which I originated and would ultimately return to, that I fully intended to keep.

Once the decision was made—with the assistance of contemplating what my future, and my brain particularly, would look like when I was no longer destroying brain cells with my alcohol consumption—real magic actually began to appear in my life.

I received a phone call from Michael Jackson inviting my entire family of ten to spend five days with him at his Neverland Ranch in California. During three hours alone with Michael on a mountaintop, all he wanted to know from me was, is there truly such a thing as real magic? And how can we access it?

I met and teamed up with Deepak Chopra, and we went on to lecture together all over the world, including in England, Greece, and Australia; and at the Sphinx and Great Pyramids in Cairo, Egypt. We were both open to the idea of being able to not only become miracle workers ourselves, but to teach others how to tap into their own unique and unlimited potential for greatness.

I can see clearly now that all of these real-magic experiences came from the singular quantum moment in which a great enlightened spirit spoke to me and set the wheels in motion for me to make a huge decision that would impact me for the rest of my life. Giving up my daily beer-drinking habit seemed an impossibility for me one day, and an easy-to-carry-out directive from my most respected teacher the next.

I look back now on the shame I felt at having been so inconsiderate toward my family, in the name of an ego-based craving for a substance that was destroying my capacity to reach a more evolved and enlightened state, and I can see that a Divine force was at work.

I know full well the Buddhist homily that says when the student is ready, the teacher will appear. The teachers were there all the time. I had read and reread Nisargadatta umpteen times before. Yet that day, because of the alignment of my own self-repudiation—along with my desire to write about miracles from my contact with Mother Teresa, the words of my long-dead guru, and my intention to be a better person—I, the student, was ready.

I maintained that readiness by systematically abolishing so many unhealthy and decidedly non-spiritual habits I had acquired, and replacing them with a reverence for serving others and attempting to live a God-realized life as a teacher. No longer a teacher of just psychological principles for a self-actualized life, but a teacher who was and is being guided by a host of ascended masters to attempt to teach others how to find the sacred in themselves and in everyone they encounter.

My decision to leave alcohol behind was one of the most far-reaching things I have ever done, and it all came about because I was told that I could no longer destroy a few brain cells each day and hope to fulfill the dharma I had signed up for. I look back on the events of that day in 1991, and all of the shame and disappointment I was feeling, as among the greatest gifts I've ever been granted. I was actually able to glimpse into the future and see myself as either a sober spiritual teacher, or a man addicted to a self-limiting, brain-destroying habit. The implementation of my new vision was, and still is, essentially effortless.

45

It is the spring of 1994, and I've been touring the country promoting both the hardcover and paperback editions of *Real Magic.* My publisher is asking about a follow-up book, and I think back to a very special day almost ten years ago when Ken Keyes, Jr., and his wife, Penny, came to visit. Their car pulled up in front of our home in Boca Raton, Florida, and I watched a young woman pick up the man who was in the passenger seat and carry him into our house. I then spent one of the most memorable evenings of my life.

I had been an admirer of Ken Keyes, Jr., for well over a decade. I read and reread his classic book published in 1972 titled *Handbook to Higher Consciousness,* never realizing that he was a quadriplegic. It turns out that Ken had been paralyzed for almost 40 years of his life, due to the fact that he contracted polio in 1946 shortly after his discharge from the military at the conclusion of WWII. He'd only ever mentioned it in a very early book, in which he wrote, "My reality is that I am far too busy and involved in my life activities to have time to concern myself with self-consciousness in the wheelchair department. Today I view my so-called handicap as another gift my life has offered me."

During the '80s I read and lectured about his then-recently published book *The Hundredth Monkey,* which I distributed to my audiences for several months. The book details how higher consciousness can be implemented to prevent a nuclear war; it focuses on the idea that all humans are connected on a spiritual level, and every thought we have individually impacts every other individual because of this interconnectedness.

Ken and Penny were as excited to meet me as I was to have them in my home. My books had graced bestseller lists for almost a decade and my many appearances on national television had brought a great deal of recognition my way. Ken's book had been very important to me and to many others on a spiritual path; however, it had not yet reached the kind of large audience that I believed it warranted.

As Ken, Penny, Marcelene, and I sat around the kitchen table, he returned often to discussing the area of higher awareness. He said to me, "I encourage you to explore the world of higher consciousness. You have a big voice, and the entire planet will listen if you write about it." We spent a great deal of time speaking about the possibilities of transforming our world through the implementation of spiritual principles. This area of writing was relatively new for me, since I'd only recently departed from an exclusively psychological perspective.

After Penny and Ken drove away, I took some notes on what we discussed. I detailed four keys to higher awareness that came out of our intense and inspiring conversation that evening. I made a mental note to incorporate these four keys in my lectures, and maybe one day write about them. They were: *banish the doubt, cultivate the witness, shut down the inner dialogue,* and *free the higher self from the ego.* I spent the next decade making these ideas the centerpiece of my presentations.

I think back to that gloriously stimulating evening I spent with Ken Keyes, Jr., and his wife, Penny, some ten years ago as I consider what my follow-up book is to be. I have been talking about the ability we all possess to create real magic in our lives, and now I am preoccupied with the idea of writing about the sacredness that is everyone's very essence.

We are all sacred—pieces of God—and it's not so much about creating miracles for me any longer; it's about recognizing God within us. Living beyond the ego, which is really the false self. We all come from God, therefore we must be sacred—a piece of what we come from. Unfortunately, so many people reverse the letters in *sacred* and are living *scared.* I write an outline and present it to my editors at HarperCollins. They are very excited about this book that I'm calling *Your Sacred Self.*

It has been three years since I've been in a writing mode. I am most content when I'm able to sit at my writing table and write without interruption. My family is now living in a new beautiful home that my wife and I designed and built in Boca Raton, Florida. We have five daughters and a son living with us, from ages 5 through 18. So, I awake every morning at approximately three o'clock and go to my local office where I can be in a peaceful environment without interruption.

The words seem to come effortlessly as I fill page after page. I learn that my friend and spiritual teacher Ken Keyes is now in kidney failure, and I keep his photo as well as the *Handbook to Higher Consciousness* within view as I allow *Your Sacred Self* to come through me. I write a chapter on each of the four keys to higher awareness that Ken and I discussed in depth a decade ago in my kitchen.

I'm almost obsessed with discovering ways we can overcome that huge hurdle, which is our ego, to know our sacred selves. I write extensively on the specifics of moving from an ego-based identity with its focus on competition, fear, and outward appearances; to higher awareness such as peace, truth, love, and purity. Each chapter on transcending our ego seems to flow from my pen onto the pages that I write every morning while Marcie and all of our children are sound asleep a few miles away.

I conclude *Your Sacred Self* with an essay titled "Toward an Egoless World" that's inspired by that glorious day I spent with Ken Keyes, Jr., and our discussion of the hundredth-monkey phenomenon. This was his vision, what motivated him to encourage me to become a spokesperson for higher consciousness. I give thanks to Ken, who passed on December 20 of kidney failure, and end with a quotation from another of my spiritual teachers, Nisargadatta Maharaj: "My stand is clear; produce to distribute, feed before you eat, give before you take, think of others before you think of yourself. Only a selfless society based on sharing can be stable and happy. This is the only practical solution. If you do not want it, then—fight."

I say a silent prayer of thanksgiving for the presence of these two enlightened souls in my life.

I Can See Clearly Now

I remember so well the day that Ken and Penny arrived at my home, and know it was a Divine appointment. The energy of that one evening together in our home stayed with me for a decade, inspiring me to write *Your Sacred Self.* It was during that evening together that I came face-to-face with a man who was living what he had written about in his *Handbook to Higher Consciousness* a dozen years earlier. But more than what we talked about that night, which was to become the impetus for a major in-depth book on discovering one's sacredness, was what I noticed in these two soulful people.

Ken Keyes, Jr., was trapped in a body that was dysfunctional in many ways. His paralysis developed into quadriplegia and was sufficiently severe that he was unable to turn himself over in bed, and he required aides for bodily care for over four decades. Yet what was most revealing to me that night was that this man, who had written a classic book on higher consciousness, did it by paying no attention whatsoever to his physical body. He not only knew that we are all spiritual beings having a human experience, he was living it, because his body was essentially inoperable.

I can see clearly today the importance of the inner world in contrast to the outer. The inner is invisible, formless, and has no concern with the data that is revealed to us via the senses. It is in this inner meditative realm where I access a great deal of my own creative energy.

I write and speak often of the *I am* presence within each of us, and how to live a spiritually directed life by ignoring the illusion of our corporeal selves. "That which is real is that which never changes" is a statement I've made thousands of times. That *I* that is the ghost in the machine is real; the machine itself is constantly changing, and therefore not real. But I haven't had to test this principle. Ken Keyes, Jr., lived and taught from the only place where he was whole, and that is his inner *I am* presence. He never complained; he just went within and offered a handbook on how to attain spiritual fulfillment regardless of our circumstances in the physical world.

I had to see Ken and Penny up close and personal. The image of this woman picking up the man she married and doing so from a place of pure unconditional love is seared into my memory permanently. And the image of this man sitting there with his hands unusable and his legs dangling helplessly, and talking to me about the importance of my writing about what he was living, burns brightly on my own inner screen.

Benjamin Franklin once observed, "While we may not be able to control all that happens to us, we can control what happens inside us." No one personified the truth of this better than my friend and colleague Ken Keyes, Jr. His presence in my life inspired me to not only write a book on one's sacred self, but to work even harder on taming my own ego.

I remember talking to my friend Elisabeth Kübler-Ross about Ken and his impact on my writing. She told me something that later appeared in her book *Death: The Final Stage of Growth*:

> The most beautiful people we have known are those who have known defeat, known suffering, known struggle, known loss, and have found their way out of the depths. These persons have an appreciation, a sensitivity, and an understanding of life that fills them with compassion, gentleness, and a deep loving concern. Beautiful people do not just happen.

She was describing Ken with these words.

I can see clearly that the surprise Divine appointment that day with Ken Keyes was to impact me and my writing in a very big way. I love you, Ken. Thank you for the inspiration. You truly are one of those beautiful people Elisabeth spoke of.

46

On the day after Christmas 1995, I read an article in the newspaper about Kaye O'Bara, a woman who's been a 24/7 caretaker for her daughter, Edwarda, for the past 25 years.

Edwarda slipped into a diabetic coma on January 3, 1970, when she was 16 years old. Her very last words were: "Promise you won't leave me, will you, Mommy?" Kaye O'Bara, holding her daughter's hand, said, "Of course not. I would never leave you, darling, I promise. And a promise is a promise!"

Kaye's promise to her teenage daughter has involved a kind of self-sacrifice that few people are ever called to undertake: Edwarda needs to be fed every 2 hours, 24 hours a day. In addition, her blood has to be checked and tested every four hours, and she has to be given an insulin injection six times a day. Kaye has not slept in a bed for the past quarter of a century, as she has cared for her daughter around the clock.

The story in the newspaper captures my very soul, and I am compelled to assemble the rest of the family to hear it. I tell them, "I want each of you to come into the kitchen and listen to this story I am going to read to you. I want us as a family to do something for this woman and her daughter."

My family is in tears as they hear about the ordeal of the O'Bara family and the sacrifices that are being made by this saintly woman who lives only 40 or 50 miles from our home in South Florida. Kaye O'Bara, who has sacrificed all of her personal concerns in the name of service to her daughter, is a living example of God-realization. It feels to me much like I remember feeling when I encountered the amazing energy that Mother Teresa projected six years ago in the radio station in Phoenix.

I write a brief letter to Kaye telling her that she is my hero, and send along with it a copy of *Real Magic,* since this book explores the idea of being able to create miracles in everyday life. I put my letter and book into a package with a donation and a card signed by my children and my wife, and send everything off to Kaye in Miami, along with a silent prayer for her and her now 41-year-old daughter.

In January I leave for the west coast of Florida. I plan to write a new book on manifesting, and will commute home on the weekends. I keep Kaye and her daughter in my prayers, but my focus is on my writing. I am engrossed in this idea of manifestation and feel as if I am somehow channeling information along with the spiritual principles for being able to attract into our lives all that we desire.

After a long day of writing and researching, I turn on the television to watch the evening news. Deborah Norville, who's interviewed me several times in the past few years, is announcing that her show *Inside Edition* will be featuring a story about a woman who has been taking care of her comatose daughter for 26-plus years. When the show comes on, there's Kaye O'Bara reading to Edwarda from *Real Magic,* which I had sent to her less than two weeks ago! I watch amazed as I hear Kaye reading the first words of Chapter One to her daughter: "This is a book about miracles."

I am in awe of the synchronicity at work here. I am watching television, something I rarely do, a show that I've never seen, and there is Kaye reading to her daughter from a book I sent because I was so profoundly touched by this woman's unconditional love. To top it off, the title of the chapter I'm writing in my new book, *Manifest Your Destiny,* is called, "Connecting to the Divine Source with Unconditional Love."

I make a decision to contact Kaye when I return home from my writing sojourn. When I get back to Boca Raton, I see a thank-you letter from Kaye O'Bara on the top of my mountain of mail. I immediately call her and make arrangements to visit the following day with my wife.

When Marcelene and I arrive at Kaye's modest home, we are greeted by a woman who is full of life, totally committed to serving her comatose daughter, and devoid of self-pity. Both Marcie and I feel as if we are in a sacred space when we enter Edwarda's room. I hold Edwarda's hand and somehow I feel as if she can hear me speaking to her. After an hour passes I say out loud that we are about to leave, and a small tear appears and she seems agitated and restless. When I tell her that we'll be back, Edwarda almost instantly seems more peaceful, as if she knows we are there in the room with her.

I feel such a strong connection to both of these women. I know that Edwarda is connecting with me in some way that I cannot explain. I have been writing about sacred spaces, real magic, and now the spiritual principles involved in manifestation. I know that it is not an accident that I am here in this sacred space where unconditional love has been omnipresent for the past quarter of a century.

I make it a habit to visit the O'Bara home whenever I can, and learn of the enormous financial burden this family has been under, the extraordinary expenses involved in Kaye fulfilling her promise to Edwarda to never leave her. I keep asking myself what I can do to help these beautiful people who are living from a place of higher consciousness, while I merely write about it. I know my wife and I have been sent to help these people. There are no accidents in this universe and certainly this is not an exception.

After several weeks my son Sands, who is nine, comes running out of his bedroom one morning after his shower. In a somewhat hysterical fashion, he announces, "Mom, Dad, I just saw Edwarda in the shower. She was awake and smiling at me. Honest, it was her, and I ran out as fast as I could!" Sands is hysterical. He, along with all of our children, has been to Edwarda's home and observed Marcie and me interact with her in her comatose state.

When I tell Kaye what my little boy has seen, she says that she can feel when Edwarda leaves her body. Edwarda has appeared as more than an apparition with others around the world as well. I'm skeptical, but I remember that Jesus said that all things are possible to those who believe, which leaves nothing out. I remind myself that when I enter Edwarda's bedroom and speak with her I always feel a sense of tranquility and the slight fragrance of roses.

I make a decision that I want to help alleviate the financial burden that hovers above Kaye at all times, and I want to tell her incredible story to the world. I feel that it will help others reach into their hearts and extend compassion and love in their own lives wherever and whenever possible. I'm going to put my writing on hold and tell the story of Edwarda and her mother's devotion to her, and donate the profits and royalties to Kaye. This will be the first time in my life that I can turn all of my writing energy into something that will benefit another human being without bringing any financial remuneration to myself. I have been given a gift from a woman who has been in a coma for over 26 years. I am blessed.

My wife and I are alone with Edwarda in her room several times each week as I prepare myself to write this amazing story for publication. Though Edwarda is in a comatose state, we always sense a higher presence in the room. I never leave the visitation without the sense that she is fully aware of my presence.

Furthermore, the more I learn about what Edwarda was like before the onset of her coma 25 years earlier, the more I believe that she is an extremely spiritual person. She was kind to everyone, never judged, and had only loving things to say even to those who were often on the opposite side of her value system. Her sister describes her as a child of peace, and she radiated that peace outward to all she encountered.

When I ask her mother of what use is Edwarda's life as she lies motionless and without words, Kaye replies, "Truly she gives meaning to all of our lives. You might think I'm crazy, but I believe she is doing the work of the Lord."

I conduct many hours of interviews with Kaye, and her saintly doctor who has worked tirelessly and without pay. I gather up all of the medical records, my tape recordings of our interviews, and devote every working moment to writing the almost unbelievable story of a mother's unconditional love and what it can teach us.

A Promise Is a Promise will be published by Hay House. I ask Marcelene to include a chapter on a mother's point of view, since she is a devoted mother of seven children herself.

I Can See Clearly Now

The presence of Kaye and Edwarda O'Bara in my life was another of the great gifts bestowed upon me. As I look back at all that transpired in order to facilitate this new relationship, I can see there were so many synchronistic events that occurred in order to bring this gift to me. This was the work of a higher power coordinating the entire undertaking.

I had been writing books that focused on spirituality, miracle-making, and connecting to the sacred that is inherent in all beings. Yet it is one thing to write books about higher consciousness and spirituality; it is quite another thing to actually live it, day in and day out. Edwarda and Kaye were hugely instrumental in my moving from being able to write about spirituality and God-realization to being able to practice and live those teachings.

Kaye O'Bara's selfless demonstration of unconditional loving service to her daughter for over one-quarter of a century—eschewing any and all personal concerns, and sacrificing even the simplest of pleasures such as sleeping in a bed or buying anything for herself—is demonstrative of God-realization in action. It was time for me to begin to live out what I had heretofore only paid lip service to in my writing and speaking.

Here are some of Marcelene's words from *A Promise Is a Promise:*

> When Wayne heard of their financial situation, he said to me, so matter-of-factly, "I'm going to write a book about Kaye and Edwarda. All of the profits will go to Kaye. What do you think of that?" I looked into the blue eyes of this dear, kind man, and I saw his resolve. I have personally seen him evolve over the years into

that spiritual teacher we all love, and I saw this as his greatest act of serving yet. He would not only write this book, he would promote it worldwide and take nothing from it.

I see clearly that Edwarda and Kaye were on my life path to offer me the opportunity to live as God lives—to align myself with the pure energy of giving without asking anything in return. This is how God works. This is how the great ascended masters lived and worked. Asking only, *How may I serve?* rather than, *What's in it for me?*

Some of the most fulfilling months of my life were spent writing *A Promise Is a Promise.* The "coincidences" that occurred are certainly of a higher order. Starting with me reading the news story about this unconditional love, their living near where I lived, seeing Kaye reading *Real Magic* to her daughter on national television, going to their home, and so many other so-called coincidences were all part of the promise of a great Source of love called God, beckoning me toward living from a place of service to others. I am grateful every day to Kaye and Edwarda O'Bara for that precious gift.

Before Kaye died, she'd tell me that I was an angel sent to her by God to help her through the travail that defined her life. I told her many times it was the reverse—that she and Edwarda were angels sent to my life to teach me firsthand the meaning of the words from one of my favorite poets, Rabindranath Tagore:

I slept and dreamt that life was joy.
I awoke and saw that life was service.
I acted and behold, service was joy.

47

It is January 1997, and I have just put the finishing touches on *Manifest Your Destiny.* I have been intrigued by this idea of manifestation ever since I began writing and speaking from a spiritual perspective more than eight years ago. It comes from my fascination with the deeds of Jesus, who was reported to have had the capacity to turn five loaves of bread and two fish into a banquet that fed 5,000 people by looking to the heavens and commanding that food appear.

I have heard of ascended masters alive today who are able to manifest the sacred ash called *vibhuti* and other material objects from their thoughts without the benefit of smoke and mirrors. Deep within me I know that all of us are Divine because we come from the Divine. And I also know that when we fully align ourselves with our original nature, we are one with the creative Source of the universe, and we therefore gain all of the same powers as the creator. The ability to instantaneously manifest from our thoughts is rare because so few humans have ever been successful at ignoring the demands and temptations of the false self that is the ego.

I've been writing on the specific principles for being able to reduce the time lag between having a thought and having that thought manifest as a physical reality. These principles have come directly to me in the past two years or so from my daily practice of *Japa meditation,* which I do twice daily as a result of this letter from Shri Guruji:

> *Dear Wayne,*
>
> *The purpose of this meditation is to end the suffering of human beings through the manifestation of their desires. Before I developed and offered the technique I prayed with Siva and Nandi. I would never allow it to be misused, that is the reason I chose you.*

This spiritual teacher from India selected me to learn the ancient Japa technique for meditating for manifestation that was originally conceived by the father of meditation, Patanjali, over 2,000 years ago.

The word *Japa* literally translates to "saying the name of God repeatedly." I am enthralled with this technique, which just showed up in my mailbox with a recording and instructions on how to practice it. The package came from a distinguished spiritual teacher from India who goes by several names, including Guruji, Dattatreya Siva Baba, and Dr. Pillai. He is a scholar mystic who has taught Indian studies at the University of Pittsburgh, when he's not traveling the world teaching while doing this Japa mediation.

Two years ago, when Shri Guruji's letter and instructions arrived at my home, I began a serious practice to prepare myself to teach Japa at my public-speaking events around the world. I contacted my publisher and arranged to create a CD called *Meditations for Manifesting,* demonstrating this ancient Japa technique. People all over the world were enthralled by the real magic inherent in this practice.

By repeating the sound of the name of God as an inner mantra and placing attention on what one wants to attract into one's life, these Divine sounds act as a vehicle for bringing it into physical manifestation. As Guruji reminded me in his letter and subsequent discussions we had in person, the beginning of everything is God, so in order to begin something, we need the sound of God's name. In the Book of John, the opening lines say, "In the beginning was the word, and the word was with God, and the word was God."

I look at the manuscript I've written, which includes a chapter on "Meditating to the Sound of Creation," and feel awed by being able to use this Japa technique to create an entire book with nine principles specifically delineated in the proper order. I had no outline—no idea what the second, third, or ninth principles would be as I wrote the first one. I totally trusted in the power of the Divine name that I used as an inner mantra while writing *Manifest Your Destiny.* And I have been able to manifest nine spiritual principles and write a complete chapter on each one almost effortlessly.

I've read the sutras of Patanjali and applied this ancient wisdom in all areas of my life. Meditation is now a regular part of my daily life, and I spend time mastering the Japa technique. I use it in a wide variety of ways, and find small miracles showing up when I use these Divine sounds. I'm able to eliminate fatigue and any kind of sickness symptoms by doing Japa regularly, and by continually chanting God's name I find that I can participate directly in the act of creating and manifesting.

My gratitude is enormous for Shri Guruji placing his faith in me, knowing that I would never allow this ancient technique for manifesting by using the sound that is in the name of God to be misused or sullied in any way. I am uncertain why he chose me to be the teacher of Japa, but it feels as if it were in some way orchestrated by God Himself. I treat this as a sacred assignment. My head swims in blissful ecstasy, and I have a sense that I am bridging the gap between the world of the physical and the Divine, from whence all physical particles come.

I gaze at my completed manuscript of *Manifest Your Destiny* and wonder how all nine of these principles could have been transmitted so gracefully. I take out my pen, and I write my dedication: "Shri Guruji, thank you for the inspiration to explore the world of manifesting. Namaste."

This is indeed the calling of Spirit into my life. I feel not only aligned with this great teacher who has chosen me for such a resplendent assignment, but I also feel aligned with Patanjali and, yes, with the creative Source of all—the one Divine mind—with God. "And the word was God," I say over and over several times a day.

In addition to being a teacher, I am now a confirmed meditator as well.

I Can See Clearly Now

Something indefinable was at work in 1995 when Shri Guruji, now known as Dattatreya Siva Baba, was motivated to write to me and send audiotapes and instructions for me to learn Japa and become a teacher of this practice. That spontaneous decision of Guruji inspired me to learn and ultimately teach the Japa meditations through my CD titled *Meditations for Manifesting.* It also prompted me to channel and write a book on manifesting two years later, and then to write my own book on meditation, titled *Getting in the Gap*, some eight years after receiving Guruji's letter.

This beautifully spiritual man from India was one of the most influential people to cross my path. Before Guruji I dabbled in meditative practices, but I had never considered it as a discipline. Once I began the art of Japa meditation and saw the amazing results that were showing up, I decided to make meditating a part of my everyday life, in both the morning and evening.

While writing *Manifest Your Destiny* I'd repeat the sound *AH* and place my attention on receiving guidance for each of the nine principles in this book. Following long sessions of repeating this sound and visualizing myself receiving what I needed, I saw my pen moving across the pages effortlessly, as if it were in the hand of an invisible force.

In my lectures I explained the theory and history behind this provocative meditation practice and then asked audiences to chant the sound of God—*aum*—while placing their individual attention on what they would like to manifest into their lives. The results were astonishing. I included many of those results in the body of my book *Getting in the Gap.*

It's pretty clear to me that this sublime being was sent to me so that I might get on with the next stage of my own personal dharma. A meditation practice was vital for me, yet I wasn't anywhere close to adopting one until Guruji decided to make me the recipient of this spiritual awareness. Somehow he knew that I would take this Japa practice seriously and incorporate it into my lectures and media appearances.

It turns out that Guruji had prayed to two of his holiest of saints, Siva and Nandi, asking for guidance on who should be the person in the West to introduce this 2,000-year-old meditation method to a global audience. I feel honored to have been chosen for such a venerable undertaking.

Two years after I'd begun to teach Japa, I met this spiritual man face-to-face. I was invited to a home in Los Angeles following a lecture I gave to a large seminar gathering and was told that Guruji would like to meet me. I waited in a private room for 30 or so minutes, and then this great guru walked into the room, all dressed in white, and sat across from me. Neither one of us spoke a word for close to an hour. We were both speechless, yet the love between us is what he has come to describe as Grace Light on his website:

> Grace Light is the light of God. It is invisible to the human eyes but visible to sages, prophets, messiahs, angels and other high beings. Grace Light has incredible intelligence and energy to know and do everything. It is the almighty power of God. Once it is transmitted, Grace Light will do its work in a miraculous way. It will transform the body, mind and soul.

I felt this Grace Light that Guruji describes as we sat there in silence in our very first meeting. After a long silent period, a tear left my eye and crept down my cheek. We embraced and said thank you to each other. There were very few words spoken, but I felt that we had communicated with each other via what I quoted above. I left that home in Los Angeles and had the realization that all of this had somehow been prearranged by a celestial force that I would always be grateful for.

Something inside this man knew that he was instructed to contact me and get me started on a path of going within. Japa has been a godsend for me and the millions of people who have taken up this practice as a result of my speaking and writing about it publicly. I can see clearly now what Lao-tzu meant by, "You are not doing anything, you are just being done."

I didn't know it at the time, but I was about to make a shift in the work that I was sent here to do, and the practice of Japa and my meeting with Guruji were absolutely essential for me as this new course in my life was about to unfold. A much wider audience was awaiting me. I obviously needed to have a procedure at hand that would bring me instantaneous inner peace and a true knowing that "all things are possible."

Thank you! Thank you! Thank you, Guruji, for being willing to bring this phenomenal teaching to me and trusting me to never, ever abuse it in any way.

48

It is the spring of 1998, and I've spent the better part of the past year writing a book of essays based on the wisdom of 60 of the most profoundly influential teachers that have graced my life. I am calling this compendium *Wisdom of the Ages,* and I can imagine future English and philosophy teachers using it as a way to bring these stimulating ideas into the lives of young people.

Being a teacher first and foremost, I warmly recall a particular high school class that I taught in the 1960s. I have always felt very strongly that poetry, philosophy, and spiritual literature do not have to be dry—they should come alive, especially for young, inquisitive minds. My students in that class learned to apply ancient wisdom to their contemporary lives by studying some of our greatest masters. Almost 40 years later I am still teaching the wisdom to be found in great essays. As I consider writing my essays on these teachings, I ask myself, *What do our ancestral scholars, whom we consider the wisest and most spiritually advanced, have to say to us today?*

Included in this compendium of 60 essays that will provide readers the opportunity to receive guidance from our great scholarly forebears, and to recognize their own potential for greatness, are Jesus, Buddha, William Blake, Emily Dickinson, Walt Whitman, Mahatma Gandhi, Rabindranath Tagore, Paramahansa Yogananda, and Mother

Teresa. These ancestors of ours were not just pedantic types, writing for professional recognition; they wrote from a place of passion with a desire to raise the human spirit to a higher place beyond the piddling concerns of the ego.

It's been a gratifying year—like being back in college studying the great masters who lived before us, without being concerned about writing a term paper or taking an examination for a passing grade on a transcript. I also envision bringing these ancient words of wisdom to a much larger audience, and as a result impacting the consciousness of our country and our world.

A letter appears in my mail one day from Niki Vettel, who introduces herself as having been an executive producer of several PBS pledge specials. She writes, "I would like to know if you might be interested in creating a program for PBS based upon two of your most recent books. I would love to work with you in creating such a program, and I would love to produce it as well."

I'm fascinated by her letter and follow-up telephone inquiry about my interest in creating a program to be aired nationally as a fund-raiser for the Public Broadcasting Service. Just a few days earlier I received a letter from fellow author Leo Buscaglia encouraging me to bring my message of spirituality and higher consciousness to television audiences.

The outcome of my communication with Niki is that we arrange to record two special programs, one based on my recent book *Manifest Your Destiny,* and a second program on this new book, *Wisdom of the Ages.* There appears to me to be a calling to bring this all about—Leo's and Niki's unsolicited letters, and my subsequent conversation with Niki, alongside my desire to impact more and more people in a spiritually enlightening way. I know that only one in ten people buy books, but virtually everyone watches TV in their homes. I am excited by the prospect of bringing these messages of higher awareness to a whole new audience.

As we approach the production deadline, Niki nervously asks if she could talk to me about something. It turns out that she's concerned we might not have enough money in place to get the specials together by the deadline we've been given, and she wonders if I would be willing to do what's called a "bridge loan," in which I would put up the money now and be reimbursed later. I believe in my ability to make this show a success for PBS and all involved, and agree to help provide the financial underwriting myself if necessary. The project is under way!

We record my first Public Television pledge show at the Boca Raton Resort and Club where an audience is gathered for the taping. I record the first show, *How to Get What You Really, Really, Really, Really Want;* take a one-hour break; and then record *Improve Your Life Using the Wisdom of the Ages.* My 16-year-old daughter, Skye, sings a beautiful a cappella version of the classic spiritual song "Amazing Grace" for the second program.

Several weeks after completing the taping of both shows, and while they're being prepared for broadcast, I receive a notification that my colleague Dr. Leo Buscaglia has passed away on June 12. He was a pathfinder and a way-shower for how to give compelling, entertaining, and provocative television lectures. I vow to myself that I will do all that I can to live up to the faith that Leo had in me when he encouraged me to not only support his favorite cause, public broadcasting, but to reach a much wider audience through television.

I am reminded of the commitment I made more than 20 years ago to my first book for general audiences—*Your Erroneous Zones*—I'm in the same place. I decide that I will visit every PBS station in the country that will have me. I'll become a spokesman, not only for my own work, but for the cause of public television as well. I love the programming on PBS—my children were all raised on *Sesame Street,* the fabulous PBS children's program. I love the fact that violence is nonexistent on PBS daily broadcasts, and that they're commercial free—it feels like a perfect fit.

I'm geared up to go back on the road again and bring these lectures to America's attention. I see the potential for transformation here, and I am grateful for the opportunity to have my messages of spirituality brought to the living rooms of people in every state in the union.

I Can See Clearly Now

That query from Niki Vettel in early 1998 was a major turning point in my personal and professional life. It launched me into an entirely new way of reaching large numbers of people. During my first meeting with Niki, I reminisced about my fascination with Bishop Fulton Sheen when I was a young boy. While all of my friends who had television sets watched the comedy of *The Milton Berle Show,* I sat transfixed listening attentively to Bishop Sheen speak directly to me about the power of my own mind to create the kind of life I want for myself.

I so loved his Tuesday-night show—it was a well-constructed, entertaining, and informative lecture that held the attention of viewers in their homes back when television was in its infancy. I was confident that I could do likewise and make it work for all concerned—and that I'd have celestial assistance as well!

I recalled Milton Berle's comment when he discovered that the popular bishop had earned an Emmy Award, while Berle had been overlooked for his popular comedy show. Berle quipped, "He's got better writers, Matthew, Mark, Luke, and John." Perhaps I could enlist these same writers in my presentations as well.

I took on this new adventure with the same fervor and commitment that inspired me to take to the road 22 years earlier when *Your Erroneous Zones* was published. With the completion of the first two shows, I began making personal fund-raising appearances at local PBS stations on a regular basis. It was quite clear to Niki and me that when I was able to come to a local studio and talk to the audiences during the pledge breaks, the dollars raised for supporting public broadcasting increased dramatically. I had visions of doing precisely what I did back in the '70s and early '80s with the publication of each book I wrote—I'd assume total responsibility for all aspects related to the success of these shows.

The number one priority for the executives at PBS was fund-raising. If the show made money through viewers calling in and contributing, the show would air, again and again. My number one goal was raising the consciousness of people throughout the world.

A larger viewing audience meant more people inspired to support PBS financially. Both PBS and I could reach our highest callings and objectives.

Within weeks of the release of the first two shows I earned back the costs related to putting the show together. Within a year we were in contract talks with PBS to do two more shows, which were scheduled to record in Concord, Massachusetts—the home of two of my most hallowed and beloved spiritual mentors, Ralph Waldo Emerson and Henry David Thoreau.

Niki Vettel; my friend Reid Tracy, who is the CEO of my new publisher, Hay House; and I were now a team. During every single pledge period I was out on the road going from station to station, frequently at my own expense, just as in the days a quarter of a century earlier when I was traveling all across the country because it was the only way to reach everyone at that time. There's a flame of intense desire when it comes to fulfilling the wishes that are burning within me. No one else can do it for me, and I can find no acceptable excuses for participating in a project that flounders.

I was told by many of the executives in New York and Washington that the kind of programming associated with my presentations was not predictive of economic success. I had been told and shown the statistics on the large number of shows that failed dismally. They would be produced and then aired, and with a few notable exceptions—such as Leo Buscaglia (fondly known as Dr. Love)—they were pushed to the wayside after one or two airings.

I used to watch Leo on TV in the pledge breaks, and I wanted to jump through the screen in my home and hug this man. His *enthusiasm,* which in the original Greek translates to "the God within," was his secret. I knew I could communicate my ideas with passion and enthusiasm as well. I knew that people would watch and support their local PBS station if I could make this material come alive within them—to tap into the viewers' internal God, if you will.

I devised a plan for breaking down the financial hardship of contributing, and made arrangements with Reid at Hay House to offer a stupendous array of thank-you gifts for a contributor of a dollar a day for public broadcasting in America. As I look back now on my transition from writer/speaker to television personality in public broadcasting I can see more clearly than ever that it is that inner burning desire that was carrying me through this transformation. I had nothing at all on my unwilling-to-do list in order to make my future dream a present fact.

Over the next ten years, I made over 200 personal fund-raising appearances at virtually every single PBS station in the country. A visit meant spending four hours on television while the shows aired and then pitching the PBS mission and offering a profusion of thank-you gifts, comprised of the books and audio and video recordings associated with the program. I was indefatigable in my energy, and was reaching millions of people who might not otherwise have been exposed to these ideas of higher consciousness. And with each new book, Reid and Niki and I got together to design a new program, with a whole new set of thank-you gifts, and I'd head out to make more appearances on local stations, many of which I'd visited 10 or 12 times previously.

Looking back at the ten PBS specials that bear my name and my evolving message, I'm proud to say that I've been privileged to often be referred to as "Mr. PBS." The amount of money raised for public broadcasting in America isn't measured in thousands, hundreds of thousands, or millions of dollars—but in *hundreds of millions* of dollars. I feel that I was called to this work, and was being prepared to do so when I was that young boy sitting in front of our little black-and-white television set watching Bishop Fulton J. Sheen on *Life Is Worth Living.* My fascination back then created something within me that excitedly murmured, *I could do this. I know I could.* Those inner promptings are the work of angelic forces that have always been there, inviting me to pursue wider and more far-reaching vistas.

Leo Buscaglia was one of the angels, as was Niki Vettel. Her decision to write to me and encourage me to put together a trial program, and her tireless energy in producing all ten of these specials for PBS, was also directed by invisible celestial energy. When I read Niki's first letter about the possibility of appearing on my own PBS show, I thought, *I knew this was coming—I knew this was my destiny.* Both my wife and my agent heard me say at the time that this was something

I'd been aware of since my youth, when television as an entertainment medium was in its infancy.

I can see so clearly now that my inner affirmation at age 19 of *I am a teacher* meant far more than one classroom in one school. I had a message of self-empowerment and spiritual ascendancy to bring to the world. Bishop Fulton Sheen, Leo Buscaglia, Niki Vettel, and Reid Tracy were all angelic instigators accompanying me in bringing to fruition this vision that I've had since I first watched television.

Clearer now than they may have been then are the two mental lists that I carried with me. On one list is everything I am *willing* to do to make my future dream a present fact. On the second list is everything I am *unwilling* to do—that list is always blank. When the first two shows were brought to me, Niki asked if I would be willing to fly to Fresno, California, which involved three flights each way, and essentially pay my own expenses to be in the studio for the first program. Because of my two mental lists, I agreed wholeheartedly. That visit became the first of over 200 station visits bringing the message that's so close to my heart into the homes of America.

We all have a destiny, a dharma to fulfill, and there are endless opportunities, people, and circumstances that surface throughout our lives to illuminate our path. The incidents and the people create tiny sparks that cause us to recognize, *This is for me—this is important; this is why I'm here.* Those sparks are signals to pay attention and be astonished and know that those little sparks are being ignited by the same Divine Source that is responsible for all of creation.

I have always been eager to say yes to life in the belief that when I trust in myself, I am trusting in the very wisdom that created me. That inner spark is God talking to me, and I simply refuse to ignore it. I know that if I feel it and it ignites something in me, then the igniting process is the invisible, the Source, the very essence of all creation—and I trust it to the max. This is what launched my public broadcasting career, not some lucky break or inexplicable coincidence. It was saying yes to those thoughts that burned inside of me, and refusing to let them be extinguished until they were fulfilled.

49

In October 2000, I agree to take a small group of people to the city of Assisi in Italy. This is the birthplace of St. Francis, a man who has become a vital force in my life over the past several years. I have been working on a new book, *There's a Spiritual Solution to Every Problem,* based upon the famous Prayer of St. Francis, and I have come back to Assisi to put the finishing touches on the manuscript.

I feel drawn to this place and want to do some writing here because I feel that St. Francis is directing not only my writing, but all aspects of my life. The words and ideas for this new book have been so accessible, and I have felt a Divine kind of extremely peaceful energy since I decided that this was going to be my next writing project.

In the early morning I go for long walks alone in the countryside, away from all of the tourists who also seek to be close to this man of God who lived here some 800 years ago and left so many lasting impressions. I have read of the miracles that were attributed to the man born Francesco di Pietro di Bernardone, and I wish to be in nature and meditate in the energy of this well-preserved, Divine city. I feel this energy with me, as it seems to have been for the past year while I have been writing every day.

When I was considering accepting the offer to be a guide and lecturer accompanying a small group of people on a tour of Assisi, the decision was made when I heard myself say to my wife, "Let's go back to Assisi and do a meditation together in the Portiuncula Chapel that we visited six years ago."

Marcie and I had first visited this city in 1994 with three of our children, and since that time we'd both spoken of our desire to return and do a meditation together in the small chapel called Portiuncula, a sacred space of welcome for those seeking peace of mind, body, and spirit. It is situated now inside the Basilica of Saint Mary of the Angels, surrounded by modern architecture, with beautiful frescoes on all of the walls and domes. The chapel commemorates the amazing life of this little man who touched the lives of so many people—it was here that Francesco understood his vocation clearly, and with Divine inspiration founded the Franciscan Order. This is where he lived and died.

In the corridor of our home leading to our children's bedrooms hangs a beautifully framed image of the Prayer of St. Francis that was handed to me by a woman at one of my public lectures. She designed and created this portrayal and told me as she handed it to me that the message of this prayer would be very important for me. At least once a day for the past decade I've read it. Long ago it was completely committed to memory:

Lord, make me an instrument of your peace.
Where there is hatred, let me sow love;
where there is injury, pardon;
where there is doubt, faith;
where there is despair, hope;
where there is darkness, light;
and where there is sadness, joy.

O Divine Master, grant that I may not so much seek
to be consoled, as to console;
to be understood, as to understand;
to be loved, as to love.
For it is in giving that we receive;
it is in pardoning that we are pardoned,
and it is in dying that we are born to Eternal Life.
Amen.

Every time I recite or read it, I say to myself, *This is not a prayer; it is a technology. It is about being an alchemist and converting hatred to love, doubt to faith, despair to hope, and sadness to joy.* In recent months it has truly come alive for me, because each of the final seven chapters of the book I am now completing are titled by the first seven lines of this prayer. I feel as if St. Francis has been next to me encouraging me to write in modern language what he was teaching back in the 12th and 13th centuries.

Marcie and I enter the Portiuncula and sit across the aisle from each other, able to hold hands while we meditate. Something very strange is happening. We both feel it. A cloud of tinglies envelops us. I can hardly breathe, the feeling is so overwhelming. My skin breaks out in gooseflesh as if energy is running through my entire body. As we leave this holy place we both look at each other unable to even talk. We are both touched at the soul level.

The next day we visit San Damiano to see the home where St. Clare lived and preached as a devoted Franciscan, living out her vow of chastity and poverty. I am walking up the winding staircase to the third level when a young man named John Graybill II, who has braces on his legs due to his muscular dystrophy, informs me that he's unable to continue the upward climb. The staircase is too narrow, and he can't extend his leg far enough to either side in order to make the next upward step. He is a member of our tour group and asks me what to do, as he can't walk up and he cannot retreat.

I tell him to put his arms around my neck—I will carry him on my back. I simply forget that I've been told that my quarter of a century of daily running and tennis has created enough deterioration that I will soon be a candidate for a knee replacement. I don't think about my knee, with bone on bone, or that I forgot to put on the small brace that I use for support.

I take three or four steps upward with John on my back, cradling his arms over my shoulders, and I suddenly feel my knee growing weaker and weaker. I am about to collapse with the weight of John and his braces on my body. I panic. There's a single long line of people behind me. I start to go down with John on top of me, and suddenly I see an apparition of Francesco. He looks directly at me and says nothing. He holds out both of his hands and motions them upward, signaling for me to stand up. I right myself, and suddenly I am exploding with high energy. I start to walk up with John on my back, and then I move into a trot on the stone circular stairway. I begin to run with unabated energy. My knee feels as if it's never been stronger!

I reach the top, where my wife and most of the rest of the tour group are waiting to visit the small reproduced bedroom of St. Clare, the founder of the Poor Clare Sisters. With a startled expression on her face, Marcie asks, "What happened?" I tell her that I just experienced a genuine miracle. I saw St. Francis and he motioned me upward.

She says, "But everyone else is all out of breath, and you're running with John on your back, and you forgot to put on your knee brace this morning." I tell her I can't explain it. I am fully energized, my leg feels healed. I ask everyone around me to please excuse me.

I walk over to the edge of the balcony on the third level of this ancient edifice, put my hands together, and look out to see if I can once again gaze on the apparition of St. Francis. Only a few weeks back I was carried off of a tennis court because my right knee had given out, and I was told the news that I'd probably need a knee replacement. Now it feels stronger than ever! As I say a silent prayer of gratitude, a woman named Patricia Eagan snaps a picture of me leaning over the balcony giving thanks to St. Francis. I take my wife's hand and walk effortlessly down the winding staircase after saying a prayer in St. Clare's humble abode here in San Damiano. We go for a long walk in the countryside, and I am walking without any pain in my knee for the first time in years.

Bliss has overwhelmed me, and I feel very humbled by this second visit to Assisi. I have been reading and contemplating the Prayer of St. Francis for almost a decade. Now he's come into my life and shown himself to me for just a few seconds.

Later, sitting in my hotel room, I put the final finishing touches on *There's a Spiritual Solution to Every Problem.* I know that the spirit of this man from Assisi, who lived almost 800 years ago right here in this beautiful village in Italy, is guiding and directing my life in a way that defies description. I feel so profoundly loved, so blessed to have partaken of this miraculous experience.

I Can See Clearly Now

Ever since I made the shift to focusing on teaching spirituality and higher consciousness, Francesco di Pietro di Bernardone, aka St. Francis of Assisi, has been a major force in my life. This saintly man has had a unique place in my heart for some time. I think it began when I hung the gift of the beautifully framed print of the Prayer of St. Francis on the wall of our home. As the days and years passed after hanging it there, I must have recited the prayer thousands of times. I believe that Francesco played some kind of a Divine role in placing that framed prayer in my hands back in the early 1980s.

I have watched every film ever made about St. Francis, and I have a small library of books written about him. In a past-life regression some years ago I saw myself living as, or with, St. Francis. When I came out of that hypnotic state I had such a clear vision about how to handle an ongoing crisis in my life that it was all resolved within minutes of my coming back to the present moment.

I find this all very fascinating as I look back on Francesco's influence in my life. I wasn't raised in a Catholic tradition, but somehow I'm incredibly drawn to the story of this man's life and his profound devotion to his belief, along with his spiritual connection to Jesus, which brought him the stigmata in the final years of his life. Something was putting enormous pressure on me to go to Assisi and experience it firsthand. It was an internal knowing that this man and his life story were somehow mystically tied in with my own.

I've always been touched by St. Francis's ability to commune peacefully and lovingly with the animals, especially the birds who fearlessly gathered near him. I loved his compassion for everyone, including those he personally feared, such as the lepers whom he befriended. I can see clearly now that Francesco lived up to what Patanjali offered in his yoga sutras a thousand or more years before the birth of the saint. "When you are steadfast," Patanjali said—meaning you never, ever slip, "in your abstention of thoughts of harm directed toward others, all living creatures will cease to feel enmity in your presence." Francesco was of such purity that even wild animals were tamed by his steadfastness. He was pure Christ consciousness, and everything I read about him made me want to be like him in as many ways as I could summon.

Looking back at that moment when my knee healed at the castle in San Damiano, I can see much more clearly how and why this came about. For a long period of time I let my ego explain it away, saying to myself that this happened to me because I was a well-known spiritual teacher who loved Francesco and this healing was a gift to me. I know better now.

The ascended masters come to us with guidance and help, not because of our prayers for their intervention, or our prominence—they come to us when they can recognize themselves in us. That moment occurred when I put my ego aside, spontaneously offering assistance to a frail man in need, without thoughts of any problems this might present for me. I acted in the way an ascended master such as St. Francis would act. He recognized himself, a being of unconditional love, in me at that moment, and he manifested. In his presence, the injury in my knee was pardoned. As his prayer says, "Where there is injury, pardon." I learned a huge lesson from that day in San Damiano—miracles happen when we think and act as God does. I now see clearly that this means serving without hesitation, ignoring the demands of the ego, and asking for nothing in return.

The following year the newly published *There's a Spiritual Solution to Every Problem* was available to the public with Patricia Eagan's photo, after that miraculous moment, on the cover. With tearful appreciation for all the wisdom it contained for living a spiritually enlightened life, I held the book I'd written partially in Assisi, based on the illuminating teachings of the man who grew up there and became a living saint before his death in 1226.

I decided to do a massive book-promotion tour to share Francesco's teachings and help raise the consciousness of our troubled world. I flew out to San Diego to begin the eight-week tour that was scheduled to start in September. The PBS show based upon the teachings of the Prayer of St. Francis that I'd recorded in Concord, Massachusetts, would air simultaneously with my national tour.

Following a full day of scheduled interviews on San Diego media, I awoke to a phone call from my daughter Tracy, who told me to turn on the TV. Our country was being attacked, and the World Trade Center buildings in New York were on fire and in danger of collapsing.

It was 6:15 A.M. A copy of *USA Today* for September 11, 2001, was on the carpet inside my hotel room door. Amidst the chaos shown on the television, I opened the newspaper, and there was an ad for my just-published book covering 80 percent of the page. In bold print the heading announced *There's a Spiritual Solution to Every Problem.* I thought of the irony that an almost full-page ad in a national newspaper would appear on this day when we appeared to be ensconced in a very big problem that affected everyone—not just in our country, but on our entire planet.

I look back with a knowing that the ad appearing on that day, proclaiming that there is a spiritual solution to every problem, was not an accident. There *are* no accidents, no coincidences—we have to work together to come up with a spiritual solution to the hatred that fosters such mean-spirited, evil actions. Man's inhumanity to man will only be solved when we take up the mantle of the life and teaching of St. Francis of Assisi. I can see clearly now that those inexplicable feelings of connection to this man were and are the expressions of a Divine Source that seeks to be known in our world now.

I inhale and exhale gratitude for my healed knee every day when I do yoga, or swim in the ocean, or go for long walks. I smile as the visage of Francesco crosses my inner screen, and I imagine him there holding out his arms and beckoning me to rise. And I can see clearly now that what happened to me individually is being offered through me to the world.

50

It is the spring of 2003. I am 62 years old and going through my very first bout of extended deep sadness. I sleep for long periods of time, can't seem to get myself motivated to do much of anything, and have lost at least 25 pounds. I don't feel like eating, and I have to force myself to get outside and continue my daily running practice. People close to me often ask if I have some sort of illness that I don't want to talk about. I know I am in a state of depression.

Two years ago I suffered a mild heart attack. An angiogram revealed that I had a 99 percent blockage in one artery leading into my heart that may have been a part of my physical anatomy since birth. My heart's strong, and damage is minimal. A stent was inserted in the blocked artery, and I was back to my normal exercise and work routine quite quickly.

Today I have a healthy heart according to all of the medical exams—however, it is indeed very much broken otherwise. My wife and I separated almost two years ago. She is involved in a relationship with a man she loves very much, and I am essentially in a state of shock.

I never imagined that at the age of 62 I would be experiencing the emotional effects of a separation. I've been down this road before, and I thought it was all in the past at this stage of my life. Marcelene and I have seven beautiful children, and we both love them very dearly. There is no fault to assign here. I take full responsibility for my role in the breakup of this marriage. It's just that I can't seem to bring myself out of this funk. Medical-doctor friends urge me to take antidepressants. When my family physician writes me a prescription for one of these drugs, I tear it to pieces after reading the potential side effects of this kind of pill therapy.

Several of my children are concerned about my health and try to help in their conversations with me. They've often suggested lovingly, "You seem so depressed . . . maybe you should try writing to bring you some peace of mind." I am deeply grateful for their concern, and at the same time Marcie and I are doing everything we can to keep the children out of this separation anxiety that we both feel.

A year or so ago I came across some words while reading Carlos Castaneda's book *The Power of Silence* that struck a chord deep within me. I had the statement copied and laminated on a card so that I could carry it with me. The moment I read these words I knew the direction my writing would take, yet this separation and semi-breakup of our family has kept me from even thinking about taking on such a gigantic project as planning and writing an entire book.

Today I remove the laminated card from my shirt pocket and read Castaneda's words softly to myself: "In the universe there is an unmeasurable, indescribable force which sorcerers call *intent,* and absolutely everything that exists in the entire cosmos is attached to *intent* by a connecting link." I am enthralled by this idea of intention not being something that we do, but rather an energy that we are connected to.

I put the card back in my front pocket, feeling the impact of these words. We are all connected to an indescribable, invisible field called intent—all I have to do to heal myself is cleanse myself of the numbness that I feel, and my connecting link to this great Source called intent will be once again whole.

I begin to see that I have been wallowing in my ego, and I'm filled with deep sadness because I retreated to an ordinary level of consciousness. I temporarily lost my connection to God—to the field Castaneda is calling intent. I have an epiphany right on the spot. I am going to take the advice of my children and begin doing what I love the most—that is, writing. I will cleanse my own connecting link to intent, and I will write a book that will help millions of others to do the same.

I had thought of intention as something that I do—an attitude of determination and indomitable will. But I suddenly recognize that is the ego's definition, needing to take credit for making big-time changes in one's life. Now I am thinking of intent as a field, to which I'm always connected albeit with a seriously corroded link. I call Reid Tracy at Hay House and tell him that I am going to be writing a book on the power of intention, based on the ideas that are on a laminated card that I have been constantly carrying with me.

I spend the better part of the next year writing every day; in the process, I come out of the sadness that enveloped me the past two years. I find that my state of despondency over my new marital status of "separated" is changing the complexion of my writing. I have more compassion for myself as a result of actively doing what makes me feel purposeful, which is writing. This compassion is reflected in what I write, and my writing is flowing in a way that is entirely new to me.

I have a small frame on my desk that I look at each day as I begin to write. It says:

Good morning,
This is God.
I will be handling
All of your
Problems today.
I will not need
Your help, so have
A miraculous day.

I feel that the presence of God—the field of intent, if you will—is doing the writing here. I realize that the pain of my separation from my wife is actually making me a more tender and empathetic writer. I notice that my public lectures are a bit softer, laced more with kindness and love rather than being witty and maybe even a tad hard-hearted. My broken heart is healing; my relationship to Marcie and her new love has improved significantly.

Fast-forward to the following spring. Three years have passed since the shock of the separation, and my newest book, *The Power of Intention,* is about to be released. I have contacted Niki Vettel, and she is going to be the executive producer of my new PBS special to be filmed at Emerson College in Boston.

When I hold *The Power of Intention* in my hand, I have the paradoxical awareness that it was my own deep grief that allowed me to write from a new place of compassion and empathy. I consider that I truly needed to go to the lowest point in my life in order to advance to the next stage of my own Divine mission. No accidents here, I realize. I needed this jolt in order to understand and write this highly spiritual book on learning how to co-create one's own life.

Intention is not something *I* have done, even in the writing of this book. It is a joint effort with the creative Source of all, which the great sorcerers call intent. I know that intention is not something that I do because of a rigid determination to bring it about; it is what happens when I clean corroding elements from the connecting link to the field of intent. That is when intention starts to kick in. I know as I hold this book in my hands that God writes all the books, and builds all the bridges, and delivers all the speeches. I can become a corrosion-free link to the Source of all—the field from which all things are intended.

I Can See Clearly Now

At the time my wife and I separated—after over 20 years of togetherness, and in the process of raising seven children together—I thought my world had come to an end. Despite all of my training and life experience, and my many books on self-empowerment, the emotional impact of our separation left me feeling anything but empowered. And yet as I look at the significance of this event from a distance, I can see clearly that this traumatic episode shifted me upward into becoming a more compassionate and spiritually aware person. Virtually all spiritual advances that we make in our lives are preceded by some kind of a fall. That fall of living in the middle of melancholy forced me to figure out a way to climb out and reach higher.

I look back on our separation (which still continues today, even though we have never filed for a final divorce) as a gift. A gift for which I express my gratitude every day. Marcie and I are closer now than we ever have been. All of our children feel the love that both of us have for each and every one of them. We spend time together as a family frequently, and there is nothing but respect and love for each other.

The book that I wrote while I was feeling so despondent over our separation was by far the most well-received book I had written since *Your Erroneous Zones* was published 28 years earlier. I have received more mail and have had more people tell me how much *The Power of Intention* influenced and changed their lives for the better than I have for any of the 41 books that I have authored since 1971. People say to me, "There is something about the way you described intention that really spoke to me. It truly changed my life."

I wrote this book from a place of almost radical humility, and compassion virtually oozed onto every page. My own fall forced me to climb upward and write from a far more God-realized place—a place where I could have genuine empathy for everyone wanting their connecting link to the Divine Source of all to be cleansed of all the corrosion that keeps them living at ordinary levels of consciousness.

The PBS show that I recorded as a pledge special for *The Power of Intention* was the most successful show in raising funds for PBS that I have ever done. The ideas in this lecture, which were taken from my book, seemed to resonate with audiences all across the country. The show was aired thousands of times, frequently in prime time. It is clear that the desolation and depression that I was going through as I wrote impacted millions of people in a positive way. Had I not had the opportunity to go through this gloom and write my way out of it, this book could never have come about.

I have come to understand that I should always strive to be in a state of gratitude, not simply for the niceties that show up, but also for the things that appear to be so devastating. A hard lesson, but one that I apply regularly now, ever since I saw the enormous spiritual advances I was able to make over what I thought at the time was the end of my happiness.

On the day that I decided I was going to write a book based on a little quote from the teachings of Carlos Castaneda, which I had been carrying with me in my pocket for well over a year, I received a letter from my spiritual teacher and guru, Shri Guruji. The man who was responsible for teaching me the Japa meditation a decade earlier heard about my separation and subsequent despondency, and he sent me a letter with one sentence, which is taped to the wall of my sacred writing space to this day. It says, "Dear Wayne: The sun is shining behind the clouds."

This was the spark that made me stop engaging in my pity party and get on with my own dharma. The clouds represent any and all of the so-called problems that are omnipresent in all of our lives. The sun behind the clouds is God—the field of intention, the Divine mind. All I needed to do was clear away those clouds, and there shining brightly, I could now see clearly my Source of being. And the words of my friend the late Elisabeth Kübler-Ross ring true to me as I write today: "Should you shield the canyons from the windstorms, you would never see the beauty of the carvings."

The saddest, most difficult time of my life ultimately allowed me to write a powerful book and produce a spectacularly impactful PBS special, both of which touched the lives of millions of people. That storm in my life was responsible for many spiritual advances being carved out, and it steered my life in a new direction on many fronts that extend way beyond my public persona.

As I look back, I am in a profound state of gratitude for all of the storms of my life, especially for that Category Five hurricane that showed up to keep me on the path of teaching and living Divine love and higher awareness.

51

I have just finished giving a lecture in New York City before several thousand people at an Omega Institute seminar on April 3, 2005. I'm standing outside the hotel ballroom surrounded by people seeking autographs and photo opportunities. I look up, and my eyes catch an incredibly striking African woman at the back of the circle of people around me. I am immediately taken by the fact that she seems to radiate such a highly spiritual energy, it's almost angelic.

As the crowd of people begins to thin out, I approach this woman and ask her, "Where are you from?" In very broken English she replies, "I am from Rwanda."

The night before in my hotel room I had watched the film *Hotel Rwanda.* I ask her if she is familiar with what transpired in that African nation in 1994. Her friend who is helping her with the language responds, "Yes, Dr. Dyer. She was there. She was locked in a bathroom for 90 days with seven other women, and the story of how she survived that holocaust is one of the most inspiring stories of courage and faith that anyone has ever heard. Ever."

I ask the Rwandan woman to write down her name and exchange e-mail addresses with my daughter Skye, who is standing next to me. I want to know more about this fascinating individual whose radiant, almost celestial energy captured me the very first moment I laid eyes on her. A week passes and I ask Skye to please send her an e-mail asking her to call me in Maui, where I'm putting the finishing touches on a new book titled *Inspiration*.

I still don't know this striking woman's name, but something inside of me has taken over and replaced all logic. I have an instantaneous knowing that we are going to work together on the same mission. I feel a strong need to call Reid Tracy and tell him, "I have just met a remarkable woman who has an astounding story that must be told. I want you to publish her as-yet-unwritten book, and I will put her in my next PBS special to introduce her to the world." Reid tells me that he would be happy to publish her story and will find someone to work with her since English is her third language.

I finally receive an e-mail from Skye telling me that she has located the lady from Rwanda. I pick up the phone, and Immaculée Ilibagiza and I speak for the next several hours. And she relates to me the most astonishing story of survival I have ever heard.

It is estimated that more than one million men, women, and children were slaughtered with machetes in this tiny country that's about the size of the state of Maryland. The Hutu and Tutsi tribes had lived side by side in the once-peaceful country, but a conflict erupted when the president of Rwanda was killed and the Hutus declared a "final solution" for the Tutsis.

Immaculée hid in a cramped bathroom with seven other women for 90 consecutive days. During that dark nightmare of unabated killing, her weight dropped to 65 pounds, and her parents and two of her brothers were all slaughtered mercilessly. Yet she managed to stay alive.

The very first moment we met, I knew in an absolute flash of insight that I was in the presence of a uniquely Divine woman. Our long conversations have given me a whole new perspective on the power of faith, and I know that Immaculée has a message for all of humankind. Her story has to be told, and something deep within me is pushing me to make this happen. I ask her to title the book *Left to Tell,* and tell her that I'd consider it an honor to write the Foreword to her book when it is complete.

I commit to doing everything I possibly can to bring this heroic woman's story to the world. I contact Niki Vettel and inform her that I want to introduce Immaculée to the American public on my PBS show on inspiration, which is to be recorded in November in San Francisco. I ask Immaculée to keep her schedule clear for the next two to three years because I want her to speak at each of my public lectures.

The more details I hear of Immaculée's ordeal in the 1994 Rwandan holocaust, the more I begin to believe that I am talking to a person who has achieved an extraordinary level of enlightened, higher awareness. When she converses at a dinner table, all who are present are almost magnetically drawn to her. There is something more than charisma at work here. Immaculée not only speaks about unconditional love, she radiates it with everyone—even toward the Hutus who were responsible for the horrific murders of her entire family in Rwanda. She lives at an elevated level of spiritual consciousness, and I am blessed to be able to do all that I can to bring this extraordinary woman and her story to the world.

It is now October 1, and I will be recording a new PBS show 40 days from now. Immaculée is working every day on her book, and she is very nervous about speaking on television for the first time because of her language considerations.

I have been immersed in the unbelievable challenges she underwent in her determination to survive—when only a tiny handful of Tutsis survived the 100-day bloodbath that left so many corpses littering the countryside of that formerly bucolic country in central Africa.

Immaculée is a devout Catholic. While only inches away from being hacked to death, she used her faith in Jesus to stay alive; in fact, she says she truly discovered God in the midst of a demonstration of man's abominable inhumanity to man.

I am inspired to challenge myself in a minor way, just to gain a tiny appreciation of the struggle that Immaculée experienced. Jesus, whom both Immaculée and I love unconditionally, spent 40 days in the desert at the beginning of his public ministry. This was a time of testing and preparation for him. Today, I'll be taking my first Bikram yoga class—90 minutes of intense yoga practice in a room that is a desert-hot 110 degrees. It pales in significance to what Jesus and Immaculée experienced, but I am 65 years old and choose to test and prepare myself as well. I am committed to doing 40 consecutive days of this practice. The word *yoga* means "union." That is, union with God, our creative Source of being. The word *inspiration* means "in-Spirit." A way of experiencing union with our spiritual Source and to stay in-Spirit. It all seems to make perfect sense to me.

When I take Immaculée to the Bikram yoga class, she jokingly tells me that it was harder than living in the tiny bathroom with seven other women. Yet on November 10 I complete my 40th consecutive hot yoga class—and I am a committed yogi. I will practice this ancient spiritual custom for the rest of my life. My 40 consecutive days leave me feeling as if I can accomplish anything.

Well into my three-hour television program for PBS, I bring Immaculée onto the stage. Even though her language is a bit of a barrier, she completely mesmerizes the audience and receives a standing ovation. Everyone who sees her has the same reaction that I had the very first moment my eyes met hers just seven months ago. I am so proud to have her share the stage and the spotlight with me. I can write about inspiration all day, but this woman with her unconditionally loving and forgiving countenance is a living, breathing example of what it means to live in-Spirit.

Fast-forward to Monday, March 6, 2006. The new PBS pledge special, *Inspiration: Your Ultimate Calling,* has played in prime time in virtually every city in America that has a public television station. The show is scheduled to air several thousand times this month alone. Immaculée is a huge hit across the country—her story of faith and survival leaves no one untouched.

I am on the phone with her now as she stares at her computer screen to see that the two top-selling books in the country are *Inspiration* and *Left to Tell.* The following week, Immaculée Ilibagiza is a *New York Times* best-selling author. I am beyond elated. I am honored to have had this Divine being show up in my life and teach me the unfathomable power of faith and Divine love in person.

I Can See Clearly Now

Immaculée traveled with me to every speaking engagement for over two and a half years, and wherever we went, audiences fell in love with her. As I look back on the impact she's had on me, I immediately see images of both Mother Teresa and Viktor Frankl. She has the same impact on audiences that Mother Teresa did: Somehow the room gets softer when Immaculée speaks. She has the same quality of being able to make everyone feel more at peace, almost as if she radiates outward a kind of angel mist that envelops everyone who comes into contact with her.

Viktor Frankl was also a holocaust survivor, and his determination to survive the Nazi extermination camps was fueled by his obsessive desire to tell the story to the world. It was in Dr. Frankl's honor that I asked Immaculée to title her book *Left to Tell.* The very fact that a Tutsi woman was able to survive that 100-day machete rampage against any and all members of her tribe was a miracle in and of itself. She truly felt that it was her duty to tell every detail of her harrowing ordeal.

Immaculée's presence in my life at that time was another of those events orchestrated by a Divine power. There was an indefinable spiritual connection that existed between us from the very first moment our eyes met. Divine intervention was working so that Immaculée "happened" to be in that hotel on that day and was curious enough to stay and watch a book signing by an author she'd never heard of. I have never before or since been so possessed to act on an inner feeling. I *had* to locate her. I *had* to help her get published. I *had* to put her on my TV show. I *had* to have her travel with me so the world could see a true miracle—a saint in my eyes.

What I can see clearly now is that Immaculée was directed into my life to have me see, up close and personal, a living, breathing example of what we all can accomplish when we go within and surrender to a Divine Source. She became one with God during her confinement in that bathroom. She knew that God was with her, as she actually saw a cross of light bar her and her companions from certain death—and angels of love and compassion seemed to emerge out of nowhere the more she intensified her communion with Him. While hiding in the bathroom Immaculée was aware of the rampage of murder taking place in her country against her fellow Tutsis because she could hear radio broadcasts outside of her bathroom window. Yet in the midst of this hideous outrage, she was able to forgive her tormentors and even send them love.

Immaculée brought a whole new sense of the possibilities of miracles occurring when a person is 100 percent aligned with his or her Source of being. My almost obsessive desire to find her, help her get her story out, write the Foreword for her book, have her on the PBS special, and take her with me for over two years of speaking engagements had to be coming from a Divine Source. She's also totally responsible for motivating me to take up the practice of yoga, which I desperately needed, and which I still do regularly as a component of my own spiritual practice.

Left to Tell is one of the best-selling books that Hay House has ever published, and Immaculée's message of hope, unconditional love, forgiveness, and pure faith continues to impact millions of people all over the world.

Hanging on my wall is this brief note:

> *Dearest Wayne:*
>
> *You are the most beautiful being in the whole world! I love you with all my heart. I can only pray that God gives back a thousand times the blessings and joy you give. If you only know how blessed I feel to know you. (I had to write this in case I don't get serious enough to express these feelings.)*

I treasure this note, and all I can say is I could have written it myself and directed it to the beautiful soul who was *left to tell*—right back atcha, Immaculée.

52

It is May 11, 2005—the day after my 65th birthday. This is the traditional age at which I am supposed to retire and spend my remaining days sitting in an idyllic setting listening to the birds and contemplating my navel. My work is now supposed to be complete. Yet I cannot even ponder the concept of retirement! Retire to what? Retire *from* what?

I am feeling a strong inner push to make a significant change in my life, which I've never felt before. When I look around at the mountain of stuff that I've accumulated, I feel oddly that all of this stuff really owns me. It's an empty feeling, and I feel trapped by it. If I choose to move, how am I going to get all of this stuff from here to where I want to go? I sit down in the blue leather chair where I've spent countless hours meditating over the past several years, and I ask for guidance.

I have a calling to do something very big—something that will challenge me more than I have ever been challenged before. I continuously think of Immaculée, who attributes her survival to her faith—her conscious contact with God—and of how she endured physical and emotional hardships beyond what anyone could imagine. I know that I'm not being called to suffer, as was Immaculée's fate, but I am feeling an irrepressible sense that it is now time for me to make a huge change in my life.

I have been staying in and out of Florida for the past four years and am still separated from my wife. I am not happy or healthy staying so close, and I know that it is time for me to begin writing again. Sitting in my blue chair meditating, I note a familiar figure repeatedly moving across my inner screen that triggers thoughts of having just reread the Tao Te Ching, 81 short verses offering spiritual awakening to those who study and live by its teachings.

The 2,500-year-old spiritual text was given to me by my friend Stuart Wilde more than a decade ago. But the Tao has been coming up for me a lot lately, I realize. I just completed reading the book *A Million Little Pieces* by James Frey, and the Tao Te Ching is all over it. While in Las Vegas on a speaking engagement I joined friends at the Tao Restaurant, where the entire décor, and even the menu, is a Taoist theme. I also remember Stuart telling me how much wisdom is in that little book, and how he encouraged me to study it in depth, frequently telling me that this was the wisest book ever written.

Now I see an old man who is Asian in appearance, informing me that I am being called to begin living by the teachings of the Tao Te Ching, and that this will return some of my lost health and happiness. I come out of my deep meditation, and I have a certainty about what I must do.

I recall how my wild and crazy mentor and friend Stuart once told me how he had left everything he owned behind just by closing the door and walking away from it. For years I thought of the paradox inherent in such a scene. Leaving everything seems so final, and besides there is such an attachment to a lifetime of accumulated stuff. On the other hand, there is such freedom in having nothing to hold one back—to move ahead unencumbered, to be as free as those birds I'm supposed to listen to now that I am of retirement age. I feel as if I am being directed to make this move to shed everything.

I pick up the phone and call my personal assistant, Maya, who has worked for and with me for over a quarter of a century. I tell her to drive over to my garden apartment, which has served as my office and writing space for almost three decades. As she walks up the sidewalk, I hand her the key and say, "I want you to get rid of everything I own, and then I want you to put this place up for sale."

Maya is in shock. She tells me there must be 20,000 books in there. What should she do with all of the furniture? My clothes? My shoes? My framed mementos on the walls? The photographs? The mountain of old tax records and personal papers? I tell her, "Here is the key; I am done here. I'll tell my children that they have first choice on everything in there. The rest you are to dispose of. Give it all away."

She tries to talk sense into me, but I am adamant. I am letting go of all my attachments and heading to my writing space on Maui. I am being called to do something on the Tao Te Ching. I'm not sure what, but I know I am being told to let go, and let God.

I walk away from everything. Maya is in charge of all of my stuff, and I am feeling an unbelievably strong sense of relief and just plain awe. I remember how I felt when Stuart told me how he had left everything behind—there was an excitement in the pit of my stomach, and here I am doing precisely the same thing.

At different times during the transition I think about things I might really want. *I don't even have a copy of my doctoral dissertation. Oh well, I've never once looked at it in 35 years. What about my favorite pants and shoes and all of the great shirts?* Maya has given them all away to a group of people who live under an overpass in a homeless enclave. I remember what I have taught in so many of my books and lectures: We come from *no-where* to *now-here* with nothing. We leave *now-here* for *no-where* with nothing. No-where, now-here; it's all the same. It's just a question of spacing.

On Maui I read and study the Tao Te Ching every day. It is a book filled with paradox. *Do less. Achieve more. Think small and accomplish big things. The Tao does nothing and leaves nothing undone. We are all doing nothing; rather, we are being done. God is everywhere. God is nowhere.* I know in some mysterious way I have been called by Lao-tzu, the author of the Tao, to bring the messages of the Tao Te Ching to a 21st-century audience.

I talk to Reid at Hay House and inform him that I am going to write individual essays on how to apply the wisdom of each of the 81 verses of the Tao Te Ching. But before I can write these essays, I must invest myself in each one of the verses. I explain my plan to Reid, and he gives me an enthusiastic go-ahead.

I will read the Tao Te Ching verse one, on day one. Then I will meditate on it, toss it around in my mind for four days, and consult with Lao-tzu. I have several portraits of him around my writing space: In one he's clad in a simple robe, in another he stands with a staff, and in a third he is astride an ox. But the most telling image I have of him is the one I see when I close my eyes in meditation. After contemplating and pondering the meaning in verse one, I will awaken on the fifth day and write an essay on how to apply the wisdom of that verse.

I intend to do this four-and-a-half-day ritual for each of the 81 verses; devoting the entire year of 2006 to this project. This is what I feel so called to do. All of the omens that have come to me concerning Lao-tzu and the Tao are directing me to this exciting task. I will not only write about the Tao Te Ching, I'll become a Taoist myself and ask Lao-tzu in my meditations what I should say in each of the 81 verses. I will call the book *Change Your Thoughts—Change Your Life.*

I am on a Taoist mission. I have left everything I was attached to in order to engage myself in this herculean task at the age where everyone tells me I should be slowing down and enjoying myself. I am truly overjoyed with anticipation. I know that the great wisdom of Lao-tzu is not outdated in the least, simply because it was written 2,500 years ago. The word *Tao* is the Chinese version of the word *God*—the invisible, nameless energy that's responsible for all of life.

I receive a book from a person who knows I am undertaking this project, called *Jesus and Lao Tzu: The Parallel Sayings,* edited by Martin Aronson. On one side of the page are the words of Jesus, who walked on Earth long after Lao-tzu; and on the other side of the page are the words of Lao-tzu, expressing the same ideas using slightly different words. This is ancient truth, Divine wisdom, and I am now about to begin a new and exciting chapter in my life. I am not just a teacher, but a student *and* teacher of ancient wisdom, with a 2,500-year-old invisible mentor as my guide.

I contact Niki Vettel and inform her of my new project, and ask her to check with the executives at PBS. I can envision doing a pledge show that brings the teachings of the Tao Te Ching to the living rooms of America in prime time. This is a calling that could impact millions of people and initiate a transformational shift in our collective consciousness.

Niki makes arrangements with the set decorator for the film *Memoirs of a Geisha,* and they allow us to use this magnificent set for my new special. The show, titled *Change Your Thoughts—Change Your Life,* becomes an instant hit. The great teachings of Lao-tzu in the Tao Te Ching are broadcast in prime time into the homes of millions of people wherever PBS is being aired—which is every major and minor market in America. And the book containing the verses and the essays goes on to top *The New York Times* bestseller list.

I Can See Clearly Now

I can recall with crystal clarity the quantum moment when I came out of that deep meditation in my blue leather chair at my office the day after my 65th birthday. Something I had been thinking about in a vague sort of nonaction way became my absolute reality. The fear of making such a drastic change and letting go of so many attachments to so much stuff was gone in a moment that Zen Buddhists often refer to as *satori,* a word that means "seeing instantly into one's true nature." All doubt was removed and replaced with a certainty about what the next steps in my life were to be.

When I handed Maya the key to my apartment and all of its contents, I spoke from an internal knowing, almost as if I was being directed to overcome all of my resistance and do what is associated with the recovery movement: *Let go and let God.* It was so clear that what I had to do was let go of the strong pull of the ego and allow Spirit, or the invisible Tao, to do what it knows how to do perfectly.

I can see clearly now that my year of immersion in the Tao Te Ching was something that I absolutely had to experience firsthand, before I could get on with the work I was destined to do. That year of living the Tao and then writing an interpretive action-oriented essay on how to apply this infinite wisdom was without a doubt the most critical and substantial year of my entire life.

I look back with much more clarity now with the benefit of 20/20 hindsight, and I can see that many Tao-centered omens were being directed my way by the universal one mind. Time after time when a Tao reference would surface in a book, on television, in a movie, in a restaurant, or during a phone conversation, I would stop and have a momentary internal aha—*I know the Tao is showing up, over and over; I wonder what this means?*

I was reading the book *The Alchemist* by Paulo Coelho, and he would refer over and over to what he called *omens,* which are clues from our invisible Source of being to pay attention. Rather than think of it as a continuous running coincidence, he said to listen and let yourself be guided—and most important, banish fear. When Stuart Wilde told me about the time he was instructed to walk out of his home in London and leave everything behind, that story left an indelible impression on me. I knew the day would come when I too would be called upon to undertake such a momentous journey. That image of leaving everything behind and moving forward with absolute trust never left me.

Somehow the combination of reaching the age of 65, which symbolizes the end of a material world passage, and the continuous presence of omens related to the Tao—along with that powerful meditation—all coalesced to imprint on my inner screen a knowing that I had to act. Living the Tao Te Ching for a year was like having a complete body, mind, and spirit makeover. The word *Tao* is the hidden force that brings the 10,000 things into being—the closest synonym there is for God. Lao-tzu teaches that we gain awareness of love or Tao-nature through the loss of emphasis on the physical conditions of our lives.

Over and over I read and interpreted and applied what Lao-tzu was teaching. It is all about letting go of our attachments to this physical plane. As I would read and then write, I found myself giving more and more of my stuff away. It was not at all a surprise to me that I was originally inspired to come to Maui and immerse myself in the Tao Te Ching by an almost uncontrollable desire to release my attachments to all that I had accumulated in the previous two or three decades. It was that quantum moment in my life that initiated a project that was to bring the wisdom of the Tao to untold millions of people all over the world.

I experienced a kind of automatic writing when I went to write the brief essays on how to do the Tao now. In the years that have passed since *Change Your Thoughts—Change Your Life* was first released, I have received letters from many Taoist scholars around the world, particularly in China, telling me how well these essays align with their vision of what the Tao Te Ching is teaching. I can see clearly now that it was my own destiny to not just write a book on the wisdom of the Tao as it applies to our contemporary world, but to make the shift myself to a more Tao-centered way of being.

I found myself behaving in far less ego-directed ways, in fact practicing a kind of selfless humility inspired by the words of Lao-tzu. I was living softer and with a kind of detached contentment that was not a character trait associated with me in pre-Tao times. I found myself listening more and speaking less, and I noticed nature's inherent wisdom so much more. I began to see that all of my attachments to objects, status, my culture, and even those close to me were keeping me from being free in the great way of the Tao. I was feeling freer, and people were noticing it everywhere I went.

I can see clearly now that my sudden satori quantum moment on May 11, 2005, was to have a far-reaching effect, and that it didn't happen for me personally, as my ego would like to believe. As the Tao teacher states in Verse 57: "If you want to be a great leader, you must learn to follow the Tao. Stop trying to control. Let go of fixed plans and concepts, and the world will govern itself." As I let go more and more, I noticed the truth of this passage.

I am certain that this satori moment the day after my 65th birthday —when I was urged to let go of everything and come to Maui to study, live, and write about the great wisdom of the Tao—was orchestrated by a Divine intelligence that I listen to and trust in a way that I once didn't grasp. I can see with great clarity that the last line of Verse 40 was at work in that quantum moment: "Being is born of nonbeing."

The TV show that went into so many homes and the book interpreting the great Tao Te Ching that was read by so many people are all now *beings* born of *non-being*. It was non-being that touched my soul that May day in 2005 and allowed a whole new me, and a whole new teaching, to be born into being. I see more and more clearly, and I am more and more in awe.

53

PBS is airing my television special during their pledge drives in the spring of 2008, which means that millions of people in the U.S. and Canada are taking in the wisdom of Lao-tzu from the 2,500-year-old Tao Te Ching. I'm not ready to begin the rigorous undertaking of either writing a new book or creating another television special in the immediate future, as writing *Change Your Thoughts—Change Your Life* was a formidable task. I literally lived each of those Tao verses while writing the 81 essays interpreting the words of my ancient mentor Lao-tzu, before taking on the task of condensing them into a format for a television audience. I am weary but stimulated by all that this grand project has brought to my life.

Reid Tracy, the CEO of Hay House, asks me, "Would you be interested in doing a dramatic film based upon the work you have produced, and do you think you can play a starring role in the movie with no acting experience?"

I tell him I am interested—the idea of doing a film is something that has long resided in the recesses of my imagination. And I do have some acting experience, portraying Julius Caesar in a play at Marquette Elementary School when I was 13 years old.

Reid has been communicating with a brilliant young man named Michael Goorjian, who's been both a professional actor and film director; in fact, he recently directed Kirk Douglas in a movie. Michael has read a screenplay written by Kristen Lazarian in which there are three intertwined stories of an overachieving businessman, a mother of two seeking her own expression in the world, and a director trying to make a name for himself. In the film these three come together at Asilomar, a retreat center in Northern California, where Wayne Dyer is doing a series of interviews on a forthcoming book. I am to play myself in this drama, which shouldn't be too great a stretch since I've been doing precisely that for 68 years now.

My only reluctance to take on such a project stems from the fact that I've viewed a considerable number of films based on spiritually oriented books, and I've always come away disappointed. They have seemed a bit amateurish—in part because the author attempts to assume the role of a professional actor. Often the script seems weak, the acting unpolished, and the entire film an embarrassment.

I express to both Reid and Michael that I do not wish to be associated with a clumsy-looking final product. I will only undertake this project if everything and everyone associated with it is of the highest professional caliber. I insist that all of the actors and technicians be top-level talent. If I am going to be in a movie based upon the spiritual principles of higher consciousness that I've been writing and speaking about for the past several decades, then the final project has to reflect a proficiency that matches the elevated ideals of higher consciousness and God-realization.

I make it clear from the onset that I'm willing to do whatever is asked of me in order to create a movie that will survive the test of time and potentially make a huge impact on everyone who sees it. This means it needs be of such high quality that it will set a standard for future filmmakers who opt to create a dramatic presentation of spiritually based writing. The people financing and directing this project agree.

I love the script, and after extensive talks with the filmmaking team I'm convinced the movie will be a finished product that I can promote with pride and enthusiasm. I feel honored to have so many highly skilled and competent people to work with on this project as I head out to California to learn about moviemaking, acting, and film editing. I'm in my late 60s, about to once again take the road less traveled and immerse myself in a brand-new vocational endeavor that may be a means to reach people who aren't readers.

Recently I'd read that approximately 10 percent of the American population buys 95 percent of all the books, and virtually 90 percent of the adult population never buys a book at all. By contrast, almost 100 percent of the population goes to the movies, or watches them at home. These alarming-to-me statistics suggest that my time writing and producing books on self-development and spirituality means that I've been unable to reach almost 90 out of every 100 adults in America. The idea of positively impacting a large percentage of the population who are untouched by my life's work is an exciting prospect for me.

It is my desire to get ten million people to view this film, called *The Shift.* This number represents approximately 3.14 percent of the population of the U.S. and Canada. I remember the number 3.1416 from my days struggling through algebra and geometry—it is called *pi* (π). I recall hearing that when that percentage of a population is exposed to a new or a radical idea, it represents something in physics called a *phase transition,* and it triggers a message to the remaining members of that population to begin to shift and align with those who are in that newly aligned critical mass.

In quantum-physics experiments, when a given number of electrons within an atom are lined up in a specific way, and the critical mass is reached, the other untouched electrons begin to automatically line up with those in the experimental grouping. I love this idea: Get a large number of people in a population to shift their awareness to a more God-realized place, and regardless of any other external forces—such as political issues, economic status, unemployment figures, educational practices, weather patterns, wars, conflicts, and on and on—the entire population will ultimately be brought into a more spiritual alignment. When enough of us begin to choose higher awareness, we will reach that critical mass.

I have always felt that big-time radical changes will not come about because of the efforts of political leaders to make changes in the system, but because enough individuals within the system opt to shift their own consciousness. This is what will impact the entire collective consciousness, independent of what anyone might attempt to impose upon the majority.

I love this idea of shifting. The major focus of this movie will be about shifting from *ego,* with its attendant emphasis on ambition and acquisitions, to *meaning,* wherein the primary inner desire is serving others and creating a world where God-realization is a universal reality rather than the hopeless ideal of a few highly evolved spiritual dreamers.

Portia de Rossi will be playing one of the movie's lead characters. A few months back Portia and her fiancée, Ellen DeGeneres, asked me to officiate at their wedding, which is scheduled for August 15, right smack in the middle of our filming schedule. I agree happily, excited to be the one who pronounces them a legally married couple.

I arrive at Asilomar to spend the next several weeks deeply absorbed in this fascinating new world of moviemaking. I meet with the entire production team, including Portia and the rest of the actors. Everyone associated with the making of this movie is 100 percent on board with the objectives that are stated clearly and emphatically by Michael Goorjian and me at our initial meeting. I am a bit intimidated by the prospect of being in a movie with these experienced actors and the directing crew. I keep reminding myself that I'm only playing myself—but it is still acting.

It is the day before shooting is to begin, and Michael arranges to give me my one and only acting lesson. We spend two hours together walking through an imaginary scene. At the end of the session I feel confident that I can make this happen at a higher level. As the shoot begins, however, I become exasperated with the endless reshoots that are required for a variety of reasons. The shadows were too dark, the soundman picked up the chirp of a bird overhead, the director wants to have a safety reshoot, and on and on they go. This is very different from anything I've done before.

When I speak to live audiences, I simply walk onstage and wing it for the next several hours, speaking from my heart and telling stories that punctuate a point that I want to make. If I cough, I cough and move on. If I stumble a bit, I regroup and move on. If there is a microphone failure, or a disturbance of any kind, it is corrected and we move on. Not so here on the set of this movie. Although it is tedious, it is also exhilarating, and I am enthralled by how much time, energy, expertise, and love go into the process of filmmaking.

On the third day of shooting I make my own shift—a quantum moment for me. For the past two days I'd been trying to memorize my lines and appear natural, but it all felt very contrived and artificial to me. I'd been doing as I'd been directed, and encouraged by the actors in the film, but I didn't feel the same way I do when I'm onstage or in a television interview just being myself.

So Michael says to me, "Wayne, forget the script, forget the lines you're memorizing—just speak to the other people in the scenes as if you were talking to them in a similar real-life situation. Whatever you say will be exactly what we want for the finished product."

I let go, and like I've been doing for so many years, I let God. I turn it over to a higher aspect of myself—to the God within that knows exactly how to be—and I sail through the remainder of the filming.

On August 14, halfway through filming, Portia has completed all of her scenes. I fly down to Los Angeles to perform my first wedding ceremony, writing a heartfelt letter to Ellen and Portia that I will read to them. On August 15, with paparazzi soaring overhead in helicopters, the immediate family gathers in the couple's basement, with all of the windows covered to dissuade any errant photographer from crashing this very private wedding party. I officially bring these two incredibly special people together as a legally married couple.

The next morning I fly back to Asilomar and resume a daily schedule of 12 to 14 hours of shooting. Early in September we have a final gathering with all of the filming now completed. My work is done for now, and the big job of editing and putting everything into a finished product begins for the director and his editing crew. I am so appreciative of all of the dedicated people who have worked so many hours to bring this to fruition. I am very excited about this film that addresses the message of transcending the call of the ego and urges viewers, through the medium of a series of intertwined dramatic stories, to find their own purpose.

A few months later, I have the opportunity to review the many edits for the film. It is now a finished product titled *From Ambition to Meaning,* and a cross-country tour is planned to introduce the movie to audiences in New York City, Chicago, and Los Angeles.

I travel to these three movie premieres with the executive producer, Reid Tracy; the director, Michael Goorjian; and a special soulmate companion, Tiffany Saia. We are all riding in a rented bus when I have an epiphany concerning the title of our movie. I say that I love the movie, and am thrilled by the audience reactions and the standing ovations. What bothers me is the title—if I were doing it over, I'd change the title because it sounds too much like a documentary or a live lecture. I'd title it *The Shift,* which is a theme that's repeated throughout the movie. Reid comments that it will be costly to do so, but he's willing to incur the additional expense to give it this new title, which everyone agrees is more indicative of the content of the film.

It is now March 2009, and I have added a new moniker to my résumé—movie star. Is this a miracle or what?

I Can See Clearly Now

As I look back at all of the events that had to coalesce in order for me to become the driving force behind this movie project, I can see clearly that there was some kind of a Divine hand working to transform it from an idea into physical reality. Ever since I was a young boy I've known that the "crazy" ideas circulating in my mind were destined for larger and larger audiences. Whether it be speaking or writing, there has always been an internal awareness that I'm to share this with as many people as possible.

This entire project seemed to be given a silent blessing by a celestial force that was watching over all of us. The Asilomar Conference Grounds and State Beach are located on 107 acres of ecologically diverse beachfront land on the Monterey peninsula in Pacific Grove, California. Over 90 film crew members gathered at this breathtakingly gorgeous "refuge by the sea," which is what the word *Asilomar* means in Spanish. Large numbers of visitors attend many diverse functions throughout the year here, and this is particularly true in the summer months when we converged on the grounds with big trucks, lighting, sound equipment, and the vast array of technicians and support personnel that are required for making a film of this caliber. Every day in every way everything seemed to fall into place for us.

At the time of our shooting there was a large conference of spiritually inclined people associated with Unity and Religious Science churches across America. I was spotted by some of the attendees and asked if I'd give a keynote address, since their featured speaker was forced to cancel her scheduled lecture. When I was introduced to the audience, they were happily surprised that I could offer them a free lecture—with Ellen DeGeneres and Portia de Rossi seated in the front row as honored celebrity guests to boot. When we needed extras for many of the scenes in the movie, those who had been at that lecture in the beginning of the shoot were only too happy to oblige.

When we needed cloud cover, it magically appeared. When we needed the clouds to disperse, they seemed to obey some invisible executive director and accommodate our needs. These kinds of mini-miracles were constantly being observed, and commented upon, by everyone associated with the making of *The Shift.*

I can see clearly now that the making of this film was a Divinely ordained appointment. I had been lecturing about the quantum notions of critical mass, phase transition, and the hundredth-monkey effect for decades. Now it was all happening on a different scale. From a distance I can see the truth in the idea that when I follow my excitement, I align myself with who *I am* as an infinite being. The excitement or feeling of inner bliss that arises when I contemplate what I truly know I must do is God-realization. When I stay in that state of following my bliss, everything I undertake is not only going to be effortless, but even more significantly, I will be fully supported by the universe as well.

The idea of creating a full-length dramatic film that could help people shift from the selfish demands of the ego to a more spiritually meaningful life piqued my excitement in a very big way. Moreover, the thought of reaching all of those folks who never read books and creating a critical mass where this shift could happen globally was a thrilling thought that I do not have words to describe. When I'm following my excitement with integrity, I know I truly am on the path I'm meant to be on in this lifetime.

Doing this film at the age of 68 was not just a new undertaking to fill up time or attract fans. Because it triggered that sense of excitement, it was a message to me from my Divine Source of being, saying, "You must do this. Your highest self is demanding it. It cannot be ignored." I see clearly now that my excitement is the signpost—it is me.

Once I had this idea firmly planted in my imagination and felt the excitement, I knew I would be fully supported by the universal Divine mind from which I was originally intended. I discovered that when I follow my excitement, it is akin to turning the entire project over to God and watching the endless flow of synchronistic miracles unfold perfectly. The entire business of making this film flowed effortlessly because it was all turned over to a higher power that matched up within me and everyone involved. We were listening to our highest selves, which are identifiable because our excitement is being triggered and acted upon.

As I look back at the way *The Shift* has been accepted and reviewed, I see more and more clearly how the universe supports the ideas presented in the film. It has aired many times on national television and received many glowing reviews. It has found a life of its own and continues to make a mark on audiences all over the world since it has been translated into dozens of foreign languages. My original enthusiasm envisioned ten million people viewing *The Shift* and beginning a phase transition to a more spiritually awake planet—I can see clearly now that this is under way, and I am truly being fully supported in this vision.

I look back at the day that Ellen and Portia asked me if I would be willing to be the person to marry them. As they sincerely made their plea to me, I was reminded of many of the stories I've related here in this book: the images of Rhoda, my Jewish classmate in grade school; Ray Dudley, my best friend in the Navy, being punished for the color of his skin; the Guamanian civilians who were denied privileges because of their ethnicity; and so many, many more that I have not delineated in the pages of this book. I have so frequently been called to stand up for causes, long before they become accepted by the masses.

I responded to Ellen and Portia enthusiastically that I would be honored to serve in this capacity at their upcoming marriage. I was thrilled and honored beyond measure to perform the wedding ceremony for these two beautiful people, who opted to tell the world that they were in love and wanted to be treated with the same respect and rights as any other two people, independent of their sexual orientation.

I have never been able to comprehend unequal treatment for any of God's children. I know for certain that I am here to learn and teach a fundamental truth that has been a part of my own life experience since I first showed up here on planet Earth in 1940. We must all work toward being steadfast in our abstention of thoughts of harm directed toward ourselves and all others, and simply refuse to have any judgment, criticism, or condemnation toward anyone or any part of God's creation. I can see clearly now that this is a part of *The Shift* that is inherent in the movie.

It is no accident that Portia—who starred in this film, along with many other superb and stellar actors—joined this movie set to help our entire world shift to a more Divinely loving awareness. She did so by standing up publicly and marrying the woman she loved, who happens to be one of the most nonjudgmental, noncritical, world-renowned celebrities I have ever had the privilege of calling my friend. This is what the movie is about. This is what Ellen and Portia are all about.

Helping make this shift on our planet is what has truly defined my life. This was one of the great quantum-moment honors for me, and it couldn't have come at a more propitious time, right smack-dab in the middle of making a film to be titled *The Shift.*

54

After several months of filming, I have returned to my writing space in Maui in the fall of 2008. I'm working on a theme for a new book on eliminating the propensity for excuse-making, and I've compiled a list of the most commonly used excuses that I believe keep people from living at their highest level of self-actualization. I've heard these excuses for a lifetime, and have even frequently employed them myself when I've temporarily taken the path of blame rather than self-responsibility.

I am also reading a very stimulating self-published book titled *The Biology of Belief* by Dr. Bruce Lipton, a prominent cell biologist. I note with interest that he writes, "I came to the conclusion that we are not victims of our genes, but masters of our fates . . . the primacy of DNA in controlling life is not a scientific truth."

I am listening to an interview on CNN, and I hear the person being interviewed explain why he conducted himself in the fashion that he did. Quite matter-of-factly, he says, "I couldn't help myself from acting the way I did; after all, it's in my DNA, and everyone knows that no one can change their genetic makeup. It's what we are born with."

I know I've expressed a similar sentiment myself in the mistaken belief that our genes are what comprise our very humanity, and obviously they cannot be changed by our mind or any amount of willpower. I grew up in the age of genetic determinism, and until now I have never considered that I may have been programmed to rely upon one gigantic excuse when all others fade away.

After reading *The Biology of Belief,* I encourage Reid Tracy at Hay House to publish this extraordinary book. I tell him I want to make it a part of my next PBS special and present it to the public as one of the gifts offered in return for a donation to their local public broadcasting station, and he agrees.

I am intrigued by the idea that our beliefs can literally change our genes, and Dr. Lipton gives a great deal of scientific evidence to support this revolutionary idea. If our entire genetic blueprint can be changed by altering the way we process life, then all of the other petty excuses we employ can also be eradicated. What if we were raised to truly believe in my oft-quoted maxim offered by Jesus, "With God, all things are possible"? And that no excuses are ever necessary?

I have compiled a list of the most common excuses that I have heard over the years as a therapist, lecturer, media personality, and parent of eight children. In addition, I have created an *Excuses Begone!* paradigm that consists of seven questions I've used with clients to help them see that all of these excuses that are so frequently employed are really a way to avoid responsibility and shift to a blame mentality. I have received an okay from the powers that be at PBS to record a three-hour pledge show introducing this paradigm for use in everyday life. I know it works—I've seen people shift out of a lifetime of habitual patterns when they use this paradigm seriously, and I've put it to work in my own life to eradicate patterns of excuses that I have used since I was a little boy.

Ridding oneself of the 18 typical excuses—such as *It will be difficult, It's going to be risky, I don't deserve it, I can't afford it, I'm not smart enough,* or *I'm too scared*—that everyone uses to explain their inability to get things done the way they would ideally like to do them can be a life-altering experience when using the *Excuses Begone!* paradigm regularly. It is the area of overcoming the really big excuses that keep people stuck in place for life that I find most challenging. I feel deep within me that lifelong self-defeating habits can be eliminated, and I am excited by the idea of teaching others how this can be readily accomplished.

Science is now informing the world that our most-cherished beliefs, such as the supremacy of our genetic makeup and the existence of long-held memes embedded firmly in the subconscious mind, are amenable to change. I write about how to change self-defeating thinking habits, and I apply them to my own life as well. I recall the experiment of a blister forming on a woman's arm because of the strength of her belief, as well as how I was able to heal myself of a diagnosis of a pilonidal cyst by using my mind. Now in *The Biology of Belief* I've read about how the power of the mind can be trained to overcome not only genetic predispositions, but memes and mind viruses that have been cemented into our subconscious from the time of our infancy.

I challenge myself to be rid of any and all excuses, and see myself transformed by using this new awareness on many of my lifelong habitual tendencies. I write furiously and with renewed excitement on this new book *Excuses Begone!*—though it seems also to be writing itself. I act as a conduit and simply allow this material to come through me.

I go on to take the *Excuses Begone!* paradigm on the road with me to seminars that I conduct all over the world. I bring people up onstage and guide them through the paradigm and watch in amazement as old habits begin to fade away in front of thousands of people. An angry man with a short fuse makes a commitment to remember his Source of being, which is eternal gentleness. A woman gives up smoking on the spot and makes it a public pronouncement. A shy young lady in her 30s changes her subconscious programming and commits to a life of assertiveness and non-victimhood. A woman suffering with an eating disorder for over 20 years, who looks as if she is a refugee from a death camp, allows me to guide her through the paradigm, commits to eating a healthy meal, and decides to let her long-held excuses be gone on the spot. She is no longer a person with an eating disorder.

Skip ahead to June 2009, and the three-hour pledge show on *Excuses Begone!* airs across the country in every major market. Millions of people in the U.S. and Canada see my presentation of this material on how to change anything about themselves that is not in harmony with who they'd like to be, regardless of how deeply embedded these behaviors, habits, or even illnesses have been. The response is overwhelming. The book goes to the top of *The New York Times* bestseller list, as does Dr. Bruce Lipton's *The Biology of Belief.*

I am giving lectures all over the world on how to apply the material in the *Excuses Begone!* paradigm, when I am presented with a totally unexpected gift from the universe—an opportunity to abandon all excuses in dealing with a situation that I never, ever expected or thought possible.

I Can See Clearly Now

Three days after the national premiere of my PBS special, on Thursday, June 4, 2009, I was in Dr. Kepler's office in Kihei, Maui. Some blood tests taken during a routine physical exam revealed that I have chronic lymphocytic leukemia (CLL), a blood and bone marrow disease. I was informed that CLL is believed to be incurable and predicted to slowly get worse.

As I look back at my first reaction to the diagnosis of leukemia, I was in a state of shock. I was being told that my life would have to undergo a serious shift: I would begin to incur night sweats, frequent bruising, elevated white blood cell counts, and fatigue, among other things. I would have to meet with an oncologist, and perhaps prepare myself for possible chemotherapy and bone marrow transplants. My life was being redesigned for me by a team of well-meaning medical people, and I was being handed a whole host of excuses that I'd be able to use to explain my deteriorating health, my lack of energy, and my inability to carry on and do the work of empowering people and helping to transform the planet into a more God-realized habitat.

On the same day that I received the CLL diagnostic report, I met a woman who was a nurse-practitioner and was wanting to enlist my support in her alternative-medicine practice. She was using some of my more recent books, particularly *The Power of Intention,* with her patients and had come to Maui to see if I could be of assistance to her. When I told her that that very morning I received the news of my leukemia, she decided to reach out to serve me.

I can see clearly now that there was no accident in our meeting, on that very day that I was walking around in shock. Pam McDonald became my health practitioner, helping me redesign my eating habits so that I was getting the proper nutritional balance to assist the healing of my body. Pam wrote a very important book titled *The Perfect Gene Diet,* for which I later wrote the Foreword, and she presented her research and work to many of my seminar attendees for a couple of subsequent years. This was indeed a Divine appointment.

I had spent more than a full year writing daily, creating a book that was designed to help people overcome their most intransigent excuses. I was writing about being able to overcome any genetic predispositions and to reprogram the subconscious mind to surmount the most embedded early childhood programming by eliminating any and all excuses. Now I was being forced to apply this same teaching to my own diagnosis of leukemia. I said at the very beginning of *Excuses Begone!:* "Hence, the title of this book is really a statement to yourself, as well as to that system of explanations you've created. It is my intention that *all* excuses be . . . gone!"

A quotation from Gandhi that has always stuck with me is: "My life is my message." And so it has been with me—everything I've ever written about has come out of my own life experiences. Learning to overcome difficulties; rising above the ordinary; taking on unpopular causes; challenging authority; transcending abandonment; surmounting addictions, relationship struggles, and parenting issues . . . all of it was what I was being presented with by a supreme Source.

For the first few months I allowed myself to buy into the protocol for how to deal with a body that has a blood and bone marrow cancer: I started to have serious night sweats, I noticed more strange bruising, and I became more easily fatigued. I gave up my yoga practice for almost an entire year, and I changed my normally busy and exciting life to one of caution and even subconscious fear. And I read all of the literature being sent to me on CLL, and sort of adopted the *it's incurable and will worsen* messages that are so rampant in the medical literature.

I was out there speaking on television about having no excuses for living an extraordinary life; I was promoting a book written with the intention of teaching others to expunge any and all excuses, big or small; and still I was somewhat unconsciously adopting my own excuses, rather than seeing this leukemia diagnosis as a gift to hammer home the truth of what I'd been researching and writing for the previous two years.

I had accepted that I could literally change genetic information. I had endorsed the idea that I could undo early programming. I was teaching these radical ideas in my writing, in a multitude of public lectures, and on millions of television screens. But for a brief moment or two, I forgot that I was instantaneously put into another big excuse factory called, *I've got a serious disease.* I can see now that a truth doesn't really become fastened to our consciousness until we experience it directly. All of my research, writing, lecturing, and pontificating meant nothing in terms of really understanding the message of living an excuse-free life. This leukemia was a gift, and just like everything else in my life, it showed up precisely on time.

By the end of 2009, and throughout all of 2010 and beyond, I began to use this gift that was handed to me, in a way that was both beneficial to myself and to those who were making themselves available to my teachings. I worked the *Excuses Begone!* paradigm on myself and worked it into my writing and speaking as well.

I asked myself the seven questions, and these were my brief answers to myself:

1. Is the Cancer Excuse True? I can never be 100 percent certain the leukemia has to slow me down or get worse. Thus, the excuse may or may not be true. So I decide not to believe something that is just as likely to be false as to be true.

2. Where Did the Excuse Come From? From the endless messages about cancer that flood the medical literature. From a portion of the medical community who make a living off of cancer. From the Internet. From things I've heard, and so forth. But the excuse did not come from me or my Source of being, which is eternal well-being and Divine love.

3. What's the Payoff for Using This Excuse? If I use the "I'm sick" excuse, I can take the easy way out: I can avoid dealing with my own inner capacity for well-being and healing; I can blame the food, the air, my parents, the water, and the fact that we all are forced to live in a carcinogenic world. I can get a lot of sympathy and, of course, I can be right, which is the gigantic payoff of the ego.

4. What Would My Life Look Like If I Couldn't Use These Excuses? (This was the most helpful to me.) If I were incapable of believing that I had to be in any way incapacitated because of this diagnosis, I would be forced to think thoughts such as, *I am as strong as I need to be to do anything I choose. I have the inner capacity and the connection to God to heal anything. I am a vigorous person who possesses all the liveliness and vitality to accomplish anything I set my mind to.*

5. Can I Create a Rational Reason to Change? *Yes.* Emphatically. My choice to live a life without an "I'm sick" excuse makes sense to me —it is doable, it will allow me to feel good, and it will allow me to stay connected to God. And with God, all things are possible.

6. Can I Access Universal Cooperation in Shedding This Excuse? Yes, a million times, *yes.*

7. How Do I Continuously Reinforce This New Way of Being? Create a knowing within that banishes all doubt. Live from my highest self and respect my eternal divinity, have regular conversations with my habitual subconscious mind—and stop myself when I am about to haul out the leukemia excuse, and substitute a conscious response that is fully aligned with my commitment to live a healthy life. Practice more meditation and reduce the noise level of my life. Spend more time in the ocean and in nature. Make my connection to my Source of being my number one relationship in life. Work the paradigm regularly.

From this perspective of seeing more clearly, it is patently obvious to me now that my writing and lecturing on living an *Excuses Begone!* life came at the exact moment when God said to me, "Here is an opportunity for you to really bring this message home. Now practice what I've revealed to you on yourself, and continue with your commitment to serve others in a spectacular way."

55

It is the spring of 2011, and I have lived with my diagnosis of leukemia for almost two years. I have been a patient of two oncologists and getting my blood tested for my white blood count on a regular basis. I've been following the eating protocol outlined and monitored by my friend Pam McDonald, who is a practicing nurse-practitioner and an expert on alternative medicine. I have stayed away from Bikram hot yoga for the past year on the advice of my medical doctors. I've been practicing the *Excuses Begone!* paradigm on a daily basis, and I've included my diagnosis of leukemia in my lectures as an example of how I'm dealing with this situation in my body. *ABC World News* picked up on this story and aired a national segment on my leukemia diagnosis that ran on the day after Thanksgiving last year.

I hear from Dr. Rayna Piskova, an eye surgeon who has a practice in Madera, California. She tells me, "I am making a second trip to Brazil to see John of God. I would very much like you to come as well, I can't emphasize enough how important I feel this is for you."

A man who goes by the name John of God has been treating people for over 40 years in Abadiania, Brazil. Millions of people from all over the world have come to this small village to receive treatment from this simple man whose surgeries are done by entities who enter his body.

I know about John of God and the miraculous healing stories that have emanated out of the Casa de Dom Inacio because eight years ago my wife, Marcelene, visited there twice and was asked to assist at one of his healing sessions.

I have long thought that I would love to visit there and experience firsthand this unique individual and the miracles I've read about. He makes one thing very clear: "I do not cure anybody, God heals, and in His infinite goodness permits the entities to heal and console my brothers. I am merely an instrument in God's Divine hands." While many are skeptical of this miracle man of Brazil, I have come to a place in my life where I have a mind that is open to everything.

I plan to join Rayna on her trip, but decide not to because of my looming writing deadlines. Yet she is on a mission for my healing and makes intricate arrangements for me to have a remote healing experience. She tells me that she is almost possessed, so certain is she of my need to experience the Divine healing offered only by this one man in the tiny town of Abadania. Via FedEx, she forwards blessed herbs and blessed water along with instructions for me. She instructs me to take the herbs, dress all in white, and have my photo taken from four different angles for John of God to see.

After e-mailing the photos, I'm told that the surgery is to be conducted on the evening of April 21, 2011—which happens to be the date of my mother's 95th birthday. I go to bed as instructed at ten o'clock Wednesday night, sleep in all white clothing, drink the blessed water, and meditate peacefully.

In the morning I awake to a phone call from Rayna, who's also having surgery simultaneously with John of God in Abadiania. She informs me that I need to go back to bed and sleep for the next 24 hours, and treat this remote healing the same way as if I'd just had my gallbladder removed by a local surgeon. I hear Rayna's pleadings to me—however, I do not listen. I feel fine and have no memory of anything taking place during the night. I decide that I am going to go for my normal 90-minute walk, and perhaps the entities were unable to locate me for any kind of healing because John of God was in Brazil with a seven-hour time differential. I walk out the door but get no more than 500 yards before I collapse!

I need the assistance of two of my children to get back to my bedroom. They help me back into bed and that is where I stay, sleeping for the next 24 hours—just as Rayna had instructed. I am fatigued and feel exceptionally weak. As the days pass I take on flulike symptoms, cough up phlegm, and am only able to eat a bit of soup. This is my condition for a full week. No exercise, no swimming, no walking—simply detoxing from something invisible that I do not understand.

Rayna tells me by telephone that on Thursday, April 28, precisely one week from the remote surgery, I am to go through another remote procedure called the removal of the sutures. There are no sutures, of course, and there wouldn't be any for a healing of a blood cancer. Wednesday night, April 27, at 11:00 P.M. (6:00 A.M. on April 28 in Brazil) I take my designated blessed herbs and drink the water blessed by John of God, and I go to bed clothed in white. I am weak and a bit emaciated from not having eaten any solid food and being quite sick for the past week. I awaken the next morning feeling very different than I have ever felt before.

The first thing I discover is that my brand-new wristwatch has stopped functioning. This is strange because this is a precision instrument that's guaranteed not to malfunction or ever lose time. I walk out of the bedroom to greet my son and daughter and am overwhelmed by feeling profound unconditional love for both of them. I reach out to hug them both and tell them how much I truly love them. Sands and Serena ask me, "Dad, have you been doing drugs? You have no pupils in your eyes, and your left eye appears to be scratched."

I feel like I am pure love. My plants are pure love. The ocean is calling me to come swim in this liquid love potion. My children look like angels to me. I feel strong, hungry, and totally blissed out. I have no idea what took place in my bedroom last night; all I know for certain is that the world and everyone in it feels very different from anything I have ever experienced before.

I am in a state of ecstasy every day now since my "suture removal" experience several days ago. An annoying piece of litigation disappears, and all I feel for this seeming adversary is love. I walk and swim with renewed energy, a heightened sense of empowerment that I have never felt before in my entire life—and especially since the leukemia diagnosis almost two years ago.

A little over a week passes, and it is May 10, 2011—my 71st birthday. I am in San Francisco to finish filming a movie titled *My Greatest Teacher,* which is about how I found my father's grave site in Biloxi, Mississippi, and was able to communicate with and forgive him. I am in my hotel suite, sitting on the bed meditating in the early morning hours. Suddenly I'm overcome by a very strong sensation that I need to be an instrument of an outpouring of unconditional love.

I take a wad of $50 bills and head out of the St. Francis Hotel, and spend the better part of my birthday passing out love and money to homeless people. I give passionate hugs and listen attentively to men with no teeth who are as grubby as you can imagine. I reach out to little ladies who are inspecting trash containers in Union Square for the possibility of a prize in the form of an empty soda can or a discarded plastic water bottle. I don't notice the filth; I see only the unfolding of God in these vacant eyes. And I am so in love with everyone I touch.

I pass out all of the money and return to my hotel room and sit on my bed sobbing in gratitude for what I have been able to experience today. This is the most memorable birthday in my 71 years.

Twenty days have passed since the removal of the invisible sutures, and it's now May 18. I am sitting in my meditation chair and hear a distinct inner voice say to me, *Do not go for a walk today. You can now do yoga.* I am visibly shocked. I have avoided my hot yoga practice under the advice of several medical experts for almost a year. I immediately get up and drive to the yoga studio on Maui I once went to regularly, and I complete the 90-minute session, doing both sets on each and every asana. I'm a bit rusty, but thrilled to my inner core at being able to do what I love so much—90 minutes of intense exercise.

I am living my excitement and imbued with the energy of Divine love.

I Can See Clearly Now

In the last chapter I examined briefly the sixth question in the *Excuses Begone!* paradigm: *Can I access universal cooperation in shedding old habits?* As I reexamine the miraculous events that led to my healing with John of God and the entities that work through him, I can now see clearly a seminal truth. When we shift our energies to live from our original nature, and practice the four cardinal virtues outlined by Lao-tzu, which include: *(1) reverence for all life, (2) natural sincerity, (3) gentleness,* and *(4) supportiveness,* we align with our one Source of being and receive universal cooperation. These four virtues aren't external dogma—they are part of our original nature.

I can see clearly now that my experience with John of God and the miraculous results that followed these strange happenings were all a function of my shifting to a more God-realized place in my life. The familiar message from the New Testament is, "With God, all things are possible." That leaves nothing out, including healing an incurable disease.

Dr. Rayna Piskova's insistence that I have an encounter with the entities via John of God was indeed a Divine intervention. It was connected to my adherence to the four cardinal virtues when I made the shift to living more and more from an *Excuses Begone!* perspective. I can see quite clearly that the presence of this leukemia was an opportunity for me to be able to teach, via my own example, how to live from a place of no excuses and Divine love. I know that Rayna's persistence in having me go through this experience was inspired by a force bigger than both of us. I know this to be true, because Rayna has confided to me that it was impossible for her to shake or even ignore this burning desire of hers to have me experience these healing entities firsthand.

Five months after my remote healing experience and the vitality I recaptured from the remote spiritual surgery, I was invited to the Omega Institute in Rhinebeck, New York, to attend a four-day gathering where John of God was appearing in person. Some 1,500 people a day, dressed only in white, filed past him, and the entities performed various kinds of spiritual surgeries.

I was placed in the line with all the others, without any special priorities of any kind. As I stopped in front of this man of God from Brazil, I was only one individual in a long line of people. He looked up at me and said in Portuguese, "You are well," three words that flooded me with tears of gratitude and deep emotion. Later, I sat in what's called "the current room" at the invitation of John of God, and drank in the loving energy that permeated the entire conference center.

Debbie Ford, an old friend and colleague, was in the cabin next to me at Omega. She was there to have spiritual surgery for a debilitating and rare cancer that she'd lived with for many years. Several times each day after her intervention with the entities I went to her cabin to talk with her about my amazing healing experience. As weak as she was, I saw in her eyes a sense that something truly miraculous was taking place, and I was so happy that we had decided to make this trip. (Even though she ultimately succumbed to the disease in 2013, I felt as if this beautiful soul were being healed on some level as well.)

The morning after I heard the words from the entities through John of God, I was invited to address the entire contingent of people in a huge tent. Looking out at a sea of white I told them of my experience and what I had been told the day before, and I rededicated myself to sharing this gift and helping more people move into a God-realized place where they can engage the one Divine mind to send universal cooperation their way.

I have long held the belief taught in *A Course in Miracles* that there are really only two emotions—*fear* and *love.* When we are in fear, there is no room for love; when we're in love, there is no room for fear. As I look back with a clearer sense at the experience I had the morning after the suture removal, it is patently obvious to me that those Divine healing entities placed a kind of enchanting love inside my consciousness, and by doing so there was no more room for fear. Never before had I known the feeling of love for everyone and everything that so drenched my entire being. Just the word *leukemia* is so loaded with foreboding that I must have internalized some of the disquietude associated with the idea of having cancer cells streaming through my blood.

The first day after my suture-removal experience I went to my refrigerator for an alcohol-free beer, which I've done every day for some time. Although I quit drinking alcohol many years before, I still enjoyed the taste of nonalcoholic beer—but on this day, something told me that this was not what I should be consuming. I left behind an old habit in that moment and haven't been tempted to put that drink into my body again. The remote healing experience led me to seek healthy ways to love and care for myself, and for some still-unknown reason, that alcohol-free beer no longer resonated with me as a healthy habit. I now know for certain that this experience was orchestrated by a force much larger than me.

I have always affirmed that *I am a teacher,* and this experience, along with so many other wondrous events, was given to me to use as an example to serve and support others. I no longer say, "I have leukemia," which I said routinely during the earlier days of my diagnosis. Instead, I begin each day with the statement that the entities spoke to me as I stood before John of God: "I am well. In fact, I am in perfect health."

I have learned to use these two words *I am* with great reverence. This is the name of God as revealed to Moses in Exodus 3:14. I do not use anything external to myself to define who I am or what I am doing. I do not determine my state of health on the basis of what a number says on a medical printout. Therefore, I have eschewed looking at those kinds of reports. I feel strong, I eat healthy, I exercise daily, and I have a meditation practice that allows me to stay in conscious contact with God.

What I see most clearly today is that I have Divine assistance, which I believe is true for everyone. By removing fear, I've allowed Divine love to fill my inner awareness. And this love, which I have felt so personally and so powerfully since that April day when I experienced the full impact of the remote surgery, has been my healing.

I need look nowhere else for validation of my affirmations: *I am well, I am in perfect health.* I can see clearly now that it is my own *I am* presence that is truly who I am and determines my state of health. My job is to live each day in a state of gratitude for this *I am* presence. I am here to also teach all who will listen that they too have this invisible

Divine *I am* presence—it is their very essence—and they must trust in it and stay in an exalted state of appreciation for it every day.

The Sufis tell us that when we walk in the garden and step on a thorn, we must always remember to say thank you. For the thorn of leukemia that brought me closer to my own *I am* presence, and to the one Divine all-knowing mind of God, I offer a heartfelt thank you, thank you, thank you!

56

I'm reading a small book that's creating the kind of epiphany awareness that happened 40 years ago when I first read Dr. Albert Ellis's book *A Guide to Rational Living.* Throughout this book's 27 short chapters I keep feeling that it's telling me, *There's something of great importance here for you—pay attention and take notes.* For example, I love these words from the very last chapter: "In all creation, in all eternity, in all the realms of your infinite being the most wonderful fact is that which is stressed in the first chapter of this book, you are God, you are the I Am, that I Am."

The book is *The Power of Awareness* by Neville Goddard, who wrote ten books under the pen name Neville. It is like a magnet in my possession—I read, then sit and ponder every few sentences, then I write myself a few notes. I try to put it down, but it continues to call me to pick it up again. I have had this experience on many occasions in my life, and when it happens I know that there is a force operating telling me that this is a part of my life plan, a dharma that I cannot ignore.

By November 2010, I've listened to many of Neville's lectures and finished four complete readings of *The Power of Awareness.* I order eight copies of the book as Christmas gifts for each of my children, encouraging them to explore this radical idea that "imagining creates reality." I ask them to let me know how they feel about the book after they've read it, and I give them one of Neville's most impactful quotes: "Assume you are already that which you seek and your assumption, though false, if sustained, will harden into fact." Each of them responds with the same sentiment, which essentially is, "Thanks, Dad, I tried to read it, and I had to reread it over and over and then it just lost me. Too deep—too confusing."

For me, the words of Neville Goddard retain their power to electrify, as he asserts with complete ease that our thoughts create the world, and they do so in the most literal sense. I feel almost compelled to make his teachings more accessible and understandable to the contemporary world. I decide to write a book titled *Wishes Fulfilled* and create a ninth PBS pledge special to introduce the empowering ideas that he has sparked in me. I feel that these could lead to, and perhaps initiate, a quickening of the shift in collective consciousness.

It has been my own path to take somewhat abstract and often overly complicated ideas and make them available in a simplified and understandable fashion. I feel this is what Dr. Maslow conveyed to me at his death—to introduce the average person to the hidden powers of self-actualization that are dormant within each of us. Neville passed away on October 1, 1972, just as I was beginning my writing career; now, some 40 years after his passing, his many lectures and books are awakening a sleeping inquisitor within me. I have written 40 books up to this point, and the ideas that Neville offers are stirring inside of me like a cyclone that needs to be expressed.

I begin a thorough reading of the New Testament, paying particular attention to the words of Jesus, who offers up the Divine wisdom that we are all God. Our highest self is God; it is our pure essence. We come from God and we are God—we just have to overcome the many mind viruses and religious teachings that want us to believe this is nonsense and blasphemy.

Next I immerse myself in *The "I Am" Discourses* by Ascended Master Saint Germain and feel the excitement roaring through me as I have the realization that the two words *I am* are the name of God as reported in Exodus, and that every time I say those words I am referring to the name of God.

I read *The Power of Awareness* for the fifth time in less than six months. I am eager to put these powerful teachings to work in my own life, so I retreat to my sacred writing space on Maui every day and melt into them. I am seeing that the greatest gift I've ever been given is the gift of my imagination. By affixing into my imagination an *I am* God-realized statement, I and all of humankind could achieve any goal. This only requires *assuming the feeling now of the wish already fulfilled.* I declare to myself that *I am well, I am in perfect health,* and the universe responds by sending me the energy that matches up with my *I am* statement that is firmly lodged in my imagination.

I am living in ecstatic awareness. My hand moves across the empty pages and fills them from I know not where or how. I am being used as an instrument. The chapters continue to flow, and I love this feeling of almost automatic writing. I write about what I consider to be the five most salient teachings of Neville's work; the work of Uell S. Andersen; and the channeled teachings of Saint Germain.

Meanwhile, miracles are happening every day. I speak to my producer Niki Vettel, and we have the full blessing and permission of the powers that be at PBS to create a three-hour special. This will air throughout the country for the next several years, giving millions of people the opportunity to discover what I am so excited to share. I refuse to allow fear of potential criticism from those who take a different view of God to cause me to hold anything back. I study the words of Jesus and his many *I am* pronouncements. I pull no punches in the actual video filming for this ninth PBS special.

March 2012 arrives with the new pledge special, *Wishes Fulfilled,* airing in virtually every television market in the United States and Canada. Over $18 million is raised for public broadcasting in the U.S., bringing the grand total raised to over $200 million since 1998, when I began this journey of visiting almost every PBS station during pledge week.

The book *Wishes Fulfilled* jumps to the top of *The New York Times* bestseller list, and I receive a ton of mail from millions of people who tell me of the many miracles they've seen take place in their lives by applying the spiritual messages of my book.

I say a silent prayer of gratitude for Neville's brilliance. He took Psalm 82:6, "You are Gods," as the literal truth of man's condition. I pored through all of Neville's teachings—particularly those on the power of awareness, and studied the words of Jesus, and *The "I Am" Discourses*, and made every effort to keep all of these Divine messages simple, understandable, and applicable in the now. I observe with great pride and personal excitement the enormous positive response to these teachings—the awareness that God is not an external concept but rather an awareness within. That knowing we are merged with God—beyond ego—the manifestation of our desires is not only probable, it is guaranteed.

I am so blessed and so proud to have had the inner push to read, reread, study, and put into practice the words of this articulate and charismatic teacher. Neville captures the sheer logic of creative mind principles as perhaps no other figure of his era. His work came to me in these past two years with an insistence that I pay attention, study it carefully, and make it available to as wide an audience as possible. These *Wishes Fulfilled* teachings carry with them the power to make heaven on earth a reality.

I Can See Clearly Now

I've often cited the Buddhist proverb "When the student is ready, the teacher will appear." Although it is not always evident at the time, all of our experiences in this life, even those that are painful, have a true and necessary purpose in our soul's journey. Today I can see quite clearly that Neville's teachings impacted me at a time that seems to have been exquisitely attuned to my degree of readiness as a student and teacher of the principles of higher consciousness and spirituality.

In the earliest days of my writing, as I've indicated previously, I never mentioned the words *God, spirituality,* or *higher consciousness.* This was because I was writing from the place of my own readiness. The teachers I needed during that time were helping me get my message of motivation and self-development to audiences. As my level of readiness was elevated, so too was the spiritual awareness of the teachers who appeared.

As I look back I can see that my entire career was beginning when I was that young boy in an orphanage. I can see the shift happening throughout all of my years in high school, in the military, as an inquisitive college student, as a young schoolteacher, as a university professor, and throughout over four decades as a writer of many books and a lecturer to millions of people all over the world. From a distance, I look at it all and can see the patterns from my earliest days until now as a septuagenarian. It has been a long-term journey, and the overall motif is clearly visible to me now. I was unable to see, at the time of every position I was in, how each step led to a higher step on the ladder toward God-realization.

I shifted from never using or even considering the words *God, higher consciousness,* or *spirituality* to slowly introducing these ideas on rare occasions in my writing and speaking. I gradually shifted to a place where I was open to considering the significance of writing about a relationship to God, and discovering that the next step was being more like God. From Neville Goddard and Saint Germain in *The "I Am" Discourses,* I learned the infinite wisdom of living from the highest self—*that is, as a piece of God.* Wow, what a journey!

With the benefit of 20/20 hindsight, I notice that 15 years before writing *Wishes Fulfilled,* I wrote a book titled *Manifest Your Destiny.* This was my degree of readiness at that time. I was in the early stages of my transition from being a writer based in psychology and motivation to being a student and teacher of spirituality and higher consciousness. Back in 1996 I was putting the focus on getting what you want, emphasizing that when you learn the principles of manifestation, you will be able to do so using the nine important components of the process of manifestation. Each of these nine principles of manifesting were and remain essential to living a life in which one is able to attract all that one wants. Fifteen years later, I gradually shifted into the areas of God-consciousness.

The kind of manifestation I explore in *Wishes Fulfilled* is based on my own inquiries into the works of *The "I Am" Discourses* and particularly the teachings of Neville Goddard. It is not about getting what you want through practicing specific principles. The theme of *Wishes Fulfilled* is that spirituality is not about manifesting *what you want,* it is about manifesting *what you are.* I know now that all of my wants for things come from a consciousness of lack. I can see clearly now that I am already whole and complete, and that the process of manifestation is about becoming all that I was intended to be—reclaiming my divinity, my connection to my Source. Living a life of God-realization is what true manifestation is.

Dwelling day by day in thoughts of peace and love toward every creature is the path of awareness that leads to abounding peace. This is what I was to add to my original book on manifesting written 15 years earlier. By thinking and acting like the creative Source, I transcend the ego's desire for more and more physical stuff, and I come to understand that I do not manifest what I want. I manifest who I am. By staying aligned with the Tao, or God, or the Divine mind, I gain all the power of the creative Source of the universe. It is my highest self. It is God—and when I live this way, *I am.*

I can also see clearly now that my fascination with the teachings of Neville and *The "I Am" Discourses* was being handled for me by a force that wanted me to understand that it is only by being aligned with God-consciousness that one can attract spiritual guidance from those who have left this earthly domain. By eschewing judgment, criticism, condemnation, and all thoughts of harm, the angels of higher awareness recognize themselves in a person who is wired together in pure love, and the universe will conspire to open those doors to abundance and supreme happiness that have remained tightly shut. I see clearly now that the more a person lives a life of Divine love, the more guidance is received from nonphysical Sources.

The message here is clear to me now. In the highest vision of the soul, a waking angel stirs, so use your imagination in such a way as to keep it fully aligned with Divine love. It's not that these powerful teachings, which became the backdrop for *Wishes Fulfilled* in 2012, were unknown or unavailable to me 15 or even 5 years earlier—it is always a question of readiness. I became more open to the ideas of spiritual guidance being there for me, and to the idea that God was not an external concept but deep within me and everyone who has ever lived.

The creator planted a fragment of itself within humanity, a spark of its *I am* nature that can grow into the fire of realization that *at my very basic essence, I am God.* As my own personal readiness shifted to accepting what I previously considered a radical concept, the teachers I was ready for began to show up with astonishing alacrity. What was once obscure and dismissed by me at an earlier stage of my life became sensible and intensely exciting. Nurtured by my excitement, this evolved through me into the book and PBS special titled *Wishes Fulfilled.*

At the airing of my ninth PBS special on national television, based on the teachings of Neville and *The "I Am" Discourses,* I was able to bring Anita Moorjani onstage to tell the amazing story of her near-death experience and subsequent amazing healing from end-stage lymphoma. Anita's story came to me at the same time that I was becoming more ready to receive these mind-bending teachings. This teacher arrived in my life when I was able to help her publish her book, *Dying to Be Me,* and I was privileged to write the Foreword.

Anita discovered firsthand that she was not separate from God, and that she was healed from the ravages of a debilitating cancer that had proceeded so far that she was given only a few hours to live. No one who had been at this end-stage of cancer had ever survived, yet Anita came back—cancer-free—to teach others what she learned during her near-death, unconscious comatose state. Her story has touched the lives of millions of people and the book became an instant *New York Times* bestseller. She now travels the world sharing with audiences what she learned and knows for certain: All we have to do is to treasure our own magnificence and know in our hearts that we are always committed to God—and with God, truly all things are possible.

I can see clearly now all of the circumstances that had to fall into place, in order that I might know about Anita's phenomenal experience on "the other side." My unquenchable desire to locate her in Hong Kong, help her tell her story, see to it that her book was published, and then bring her to America to appear on my PBS special was all choreographed by a higher power. Millions of people were able to shift in their own development as a result of Anita's book and

PBS appearance. They needed to see and hear from someone who had experienced the power within all of us and reinforce the idea that we are all God.

I am in awe of the exquisite synchronicities that were at play here. Indeed when we students are ready, the teachers and the teachings just magically appear.

57

It is the middle of June 2011, and I am back in Assisi. Several months back I arranged with Reid Tracy, my close friend and the CEO of Hay House, my exclusive publisher for the past 12 years, to promote this trip we're calling *Experiencing the Miraculous.* The itinerary has us flying into the sacred places of Assisi, Lourdes, and Medjugorje via private plane. In each of these three locations, where verifiable miracles have occurred, I will give a two-hour lecture. One hundred sixty-two people, the maximum number of seats on our chartered jet, have signed up for this once-in-a lifetime trip.

This is my third visit to the home of the saint who has been so instrumental in my spiritual evolution over the past 20 years, and I knew when I was planning this spiritual odyssey that I had to come back here. It is my vision to actually live the ideals that defined the life of St. Francis of Assisi, who has been such an enormous force in my life over the past several decades.

When I check into the hotel, I am offered a brown robe to use, designed in the same fashion as the monks of the Franciscan Order wear (and as St. Francis wore himself when he founded this spiritual order over 800 years ago). I put on the robe and walk through the grounds of the hotel here in this village in central Italy, and I am in a state of semi-awe at being back where I encountered those miracles of healing in the 1990s. I touch my knee in remembrance and offer a silent prayer of gratitude to the man whose visage I observed when he asked me to rise with John Graybill hanging on my back, and gave me a healing that's kept me from even considering knee-replacement surgery.

The next day our group (which includes three of my children) visits the many holy places that are a testament to the influence that one person can have on the world's population, more than eight centuries after his passing in 1226. Francesco's life was one in which he had a deep connection to Jesus Christ. He was convinced that living a life of Christ consciousness could literally bring forgiveness, love, faith, hope, light, and joy to a world in which people are willing to let go of revenge, hatred, doubt, despair, darkness, and sadness.

I am deeply touched to receive permission to give a lecture the following evening at a very special venue that has never before been available for such an event: the Church of San Pietro, a Benedictine abbey that was founded in the tenth century. We are also given permission to bring in one video camera to record this lecture. Surely, Francesco is playing a role in allowing me to give a lecture and have it filmed here.

The date of my lecture happens to be the summer solstice: Tuesday, June 21. That evening we are greeted by a Franciscan monk as everyone quietly enters the church. He smiles approvingly as I speak about this amazing structure, which was here in Assisi at the time that Francesco and his devotees were attempting to make an impact on the corruption that had so infused the Catholic hierarchy at the time.

This is an electrifying environment, even though it is serene and noticeably quiet. There is a statue of Jesus on the cross, and I am to speak in a few moments beneath this ancient sculpture. As I wait in the wings, I feel a tingling unlike anything I have ever experienced before speaking.

Prior to my lecture, my children Serena, Sands, and Saje each personally give me a loving introduction. I then tell of my long history with St. Francis and feel as if I'm in a supercharged energy field. I can't shake the idea that he is right here with me.

As I prepare to conclude my two-hour videotaped presentation, I read from Nikos Kazantzakis's profoundly moving fictional story titled simply, *Saint Francis*. It tells of Francesco's transformation from a young soldier who had almost died in prison to a renunciate who gave away everything he possessed and dedicated his life to repair his church and live the message of Jesus uncompromisingly. The story is told through the eyes of Francesco's constant companion, Brother Leo.

I have read this particular novel five or six times, and it always stirs deep emotions within me. Now I elect to read a short excerpt in which Francesco is confronting the thing he fears the most, a leper, whom Jesus has instructed him to kiss on the mouth to eradicate his apprehension toward those so horrifically afflicted with leprosy.

As I read the story to the group, I am suddenly filled with emotion. I freeze onstage and am unable to continue speaking. I am sobbing uncontrollably. I have lost control of myself. I feel as if I have been taken over by another being. For the first time in over 40 years of public speaking, I feel as though I am not myself. I am not Wayne Dyer, giving a lecture that is being filmed to be part of a spiritual travelogue. I am merged with this being who has been in and out of my life, sometimes on the periphery and other times deep within my soul. We become one.

Tears are flowing down my face, and I feel Francesco as if he has merged with me. There are no words to describe this feeling. My hands are outstretched, and the audience stands in the church and simply holds out their arms back to me. They stay with me, and I feel their loving embrace even though there is no touching or even movement. There is no applause—the lecture is complete. I am at the same time both an emotional wreck as well as a supremely ecstatic piece of God.

People approach me as I walk out of the church and tell me they have never been in such a quickening space and had their breath taken away at the same time. I know something very dramatic and powerful has just transpired. I have experienced the merging of my inner self with a spirit who has long played a dominant role in my personal and spiritual development.

The group heads out to a restaurant, but I am unable to even think about eating. I return by cab to my hotel room, where I meditate for two hours. I have no appetite. I feel spent—as if I have somehow been through a powerful detoxification procedure. I am awake all night reliving what took place at the church and trying to figure out how I, as a seasoned professional speaker, could have "lost it" so unabashedly onstage.

I Can See Clearly Now

There is a clear sequencing of circumstances and events that led up to my experience at the Church of San Pietro in Assisi, when I felt the presence of St. Francis enter my body and render me speechless and immobile as well. Up until that summer-solstice day in 2011, I had written and spoken a great deal about the concept of oneness and the merging of souls as God-realization is achieved. In each of my books—beginning with *You'll See It When You Believe It,* written more than 20 years earlier, where I wrote an entire chapter on oneness —I was able to talk sensibly about these esoteric subjects. I can see clearly now that the many books that followed were attempts by me to further expand upon this idea that we are all connected, and that this idea of being fully merged with another spiritual counterpart is a genuine possibility.

But my clearest vision today as I look back is a view of myself at that altar in the amazing church where St. Francis once stood, in that magnificent city of Assisi. I was taken to a place where I could actually experience the difference between *writing* about oneness and *experiencing* it firsthand. It is like the difference between knowing about God via the writing of others, and knowing God by making conscious contact with God.

It was time for me to see the bigger picture of my life's journey from a young writer and speaker about psychological matters, to a supposed level of expertise on spiritual pursuits, to ultimately coming to know via my own personal experience with St. Francis. This was truly a Divine appointment arranged by whatever invisible forces handle such celestial matters.

It is akin to my absolute knowing today that my years spent in a series of foster homes and orphanages in the first decade of my life were offered to me as the only way I could actually come to *know* about the idea of self-reliance. I look upon those early years as the path that I was directed to traverse, the necessary beginning baby steps I needed to internalize in order to have self-reliance firmly implanted on my consciousness. My early writings on oneness and the interconnectedness of all souls on a spiritual level were my tentative steps toward the ultimate realization of being able to experience them firsthand.

St. Francis has been a prominent figure in the overall pattern of my life, from the time I was a young boy who was intrigued by the possibility of there being a secret garden, to the present day in which I have become a well-recognized spiritually influential teacher. In the eyes of the creator I had to have more than a cursory acquaintance with Francesco of Assisi—I had to not only come to know *about* him, I had to *become* him. That summer-solstice day, I knew beyond a shadow of a doubt that we had momentarily merged.

Everyone present in the abbey that day could feel Francis's presence as well. And when I saw photos of myself from a variety of different cameras at that moment, there were huge orbs visible. In fact, I included one of those photos filled with those mysterious orbs in an insert in *Wishes Fulfilled.*

As I was putting the finishing touches on that book, I received a letter from Brenda Babinski, who had been in the audience at a recent talk I gave in Canada. She wrote to tell me about a light that surrounded me onstage throughout my presentation:

> *Then something even stranger happened. Dr. Wayne, you were talking about Saint Francis and before my very eyes, you transformed. Your body was clad in a long robe and your features transformed so that you were Saint Francis of Assisi. It lasted for only a moment, but it was powerful, emotional, and very, very real.*

But then something even stranger happened. You began to talk about Lao-tzu, and you transformed into him! A long braid tailed down your back and I could see your face completely transform into Lao-tzu. Again, it only lasted for a moment, but the experience will last with me forever.

For the major part of my life, up until only recently, I would have assuredly rejected such a happening as not only impossible but delusional as well. But now I see with a much clearer vision. I was there in the abbey of San Pietro in Assisi once before when this saintly man came to me—I saw for a split second a vision of him imploring me to rise, and at that time I had a healing of my impaired knee that defied all medical guidance. Before that, Francesco entered my wife's heart and mine and touched our souls as we sat and meditated in the chapel where he lived and died. On that solstice day in 2011, I felt myself become one with this Divine being for a few precious moments, in front of the video camera and before 162 spiritual seekers.

Francesco experienced stigmata during the final two years of his life. His devotion to Christ consciousness was such that he became one with Jesus. I see clearly today that the real essence of living from a place of pure unconditional Divine love is in becoming one with our Source of being, thinking and acting in a steadfast manner as God. When one's being becomes saturated with pure love, as it was for me on my third miraculous visit to Assisi—giving a talk on the impact that this saint has had on me, relating the story of how Francesco discovered that Jesus had come to him in the form of a leper and how he had overcome his fear by kissing that leper on the mouth—in that moment, Divine love united me with Francesco and we became one.

I've always loved Mother Teresa's observation, as she looked into the eyes of those she literally pulled out of the gutter: "Each one of them is Jesus in disguise." I know we are all connected—all one.

Unconditional Divine love can become so empowering that it can give one the wounds of Christ; it can allow one to see the unfolding of God in everyone; and as I learned in those magical moments in Assisi that are recorded in a DVD program called *Experiencing the*

Miraculous, it can fuse together into oneness the souls of what only *appear* to be two separate beings.

Since that day in the Church of San Pietro with St. Francis, I have felt him with me at all times. I am humbled by the mere thought that I could have been blended as one with such a being, if only for a moment . . . but more likely for eternity.

58

I'm meeting with 350 people who have agreed to come with me on a cruise of the Mediterranean Sea, on board Celebrity Cruises' fabulous 17-story flagship, *Equinox.* I announce to the group that I've arranged to give five two-hour lectures while at sea, traveling between Rome, Santorini, Istanbul, Athens, Mykonos, and Naples. In addition, I plan to give a one-hour lecture at the site of the House of the Virgin Mary, in Ephesus, Turkey. The topic for this particularly special lecture will be, "In the Wake of Our Spiritual Ancestors," which is also the theme of this odyssey.

During the previous two weeks I gave two public lectures in Scotland and England, where I spent time preparing for the special date of September 30, 2012. This is when we'll gather at the stone house that is believed to be the one where the mother of Jesus was taken by St. John after the Crucifixion, and where she lived until her ascension. This home is now both a Catholic and a Muslim shrine, located on Mount Koressos in the vicinity of Ephesus, Turkey. My lecture will be given just outside the ancient stone house where hundreds, if not thousands, of people will be walking by. A film crew is to record this event, as they've been doing for all of the lectures and visits to these historical Mediterranean locations.

I have been thinking about the spiritual saint who lived not far from this site in Turkey: Mawlana Jalal al-Din Rumi. He was a poet, jurist, theologian, and most significantly, a Sufi mystic. And his life actually overlapped with St. Francis of Assisi by approximately 19 years (Rumi was born in 1207 and was 19 years of age when Francesco passed in 1226). Although he lived during the 13th century, in 2007 he was described as "the most popular poet in America."

I have been reading and quoting Rumi for almost 30 years now. He has become a very significant figure in my life, on a par with so many of the spiritual teachers whom I have written about here in these pages. In fact, I've been almost obsessed with the life of this man considered to be a saint in both the Muslim and Christian worlds—his importance is considered to transcend national and ethnic borders.

In the early 1980s, shortly after the revolution in Iran, I received a letter from a woman named Mariam who lived in Tehran. She had read in her native Farsi a recently published edition of *Your Erroneous Zones*, and she brought the works of Rumi into my awareness. She has since been in continuous communication with me, through letters from her home in Iran.

Almost three decades have passed since Mariam first connected with me after falling in love with the ideas presented in my earliest books. Although she lives in a country that seriously limits and discourages any contact with people from America, she has a profoundly abiding love for me and the works that I have produced over the past 30 or more years. Mariam had polio as a child and was unable to stand or walk from the age of two until six. In a dream a Divine spiritual female apparition beckoned her to rise and walk and she did so, first in the dream, and then in her physical awakened state as well.

She sends me the poetry of Rumi, and dreams of one day meeting up with the one she calls her "Shams-love." It seems that she has developed the same kind of relationship with me as Rumi had with the great spiritual teacher Shams of Tabriz, who was the inspiration for so much of Rumi's vast array of poetry. In 1244 at the age of 37, Rumi met his master Shams, and this meeting was said to change his life. The love that existed between them for the four years of their companionship was considered to be Divine. His love for Shams and his bereavement upon his master's death (some say brought about by Rumi's own son) inspired an avalanche of love poetry that's been translated into many languages and persists to this day.

Mariam's letters, gifts, and occasional phone calls over the decades all speak to a kind of holy love alliance between us that transcends the cultural and global divide that separates us. Her most fervent wish is that we could one day meet in person, although that has always appeared to be an impossibility because she is forbidden by the laws of her land to obtain a visa to visit North America.

On the morning of September 28, 2012, our group is getting ready for a tour of the enchanting ancient city of Istanbul, which I haven't seen since I lived in Karamursel in 1974, when I was forced to bribe my way out of Turkey due to the impending war with Greece over the erupting crisis on Cyprus. I am about to board my bus when a woman wearing a head covering steps in front of me with a handwritten sign that says: YOU'LL SEE IT WHEN YOU BELIEVE IT. She asks, "Do you know who I am?"

When I discover that it is Mariam, we are both overwhelmed by joy. It turns out that she was able to get a visa to come to Turkey and has waited all night to meet me at this crowded port teeming with thousands of visitors.

One person from our group was unable to come on the bus tour due to illness, so there is one empty seat. Mariam spends the entire day with me and my daughter Serena, and we share a tearful goodbye at the end of our visit to the incredible Blue Mosque.

I return to the ship and continue my preparations for my lecture at the House of the Virgin Mary in Ephesus. I have been totally immersed in the works of Rumi and Shams of Tabriz, and I pick out the poems and stories I wish to include at my presentation. I feel the presence of both Rumi and Shams, and of Mariam after seeing her for the very first time following so many years of communication, especially related to the teachings of these two spiritual ecumenical giants. These teachings go way beyond religion; they represent the very essence of Divine love, which is where I see myself now. A student and a teacher of a kind of love that never changes—never varies. It is the same love that is directed at all of humanity from God.

I arrive via this magnificent cruise ship—a literal floating city—at Ephesus, and again board a bus. Our group will spend a full day in this ancient city, which conceals the remains of a Neolithic settlement dating back to 6,000 B.C. It also contains the largest collection of Roman ruins east of the Mediterranean Sea. It is a fascinating place to see and to recall that only an estimated 15 percent has been excavated.

As I walk to my bus, once again I see Mariam. She has changed her plans to fly back to Tehran and has taken a flight, a train, and a bus to join up with me for this visit to Ephesus. Of course she also wants to attend my lecture on Rumi and Shams, since much of it was garnered from material she's sent to me for almost 30 years. I think about the time, trouble, and expense that Mariam has gone through and I look at her and see the pure joy that she feels at finally fulfilling her lifelong dream to meet with me in person.

I am in a state of shock and excitement. Having Mariam accompany me and my daughter through the excavated city of Ephesus still feels almost dreamlike, and now to lecture on Rumi at the House of the Virgin Mary with her in attendance will be exciting and challenging as well. This woman has read all of Rumi's works, including the six-volume Masnavi, which is a spiritual writing that teaches Sufis how to reach their goal of being in true alignment with God.

We take a bus to the top of Nightingale Mountain, where the House of the Virgin Mary is located in a nature park. All 350 members of our group are seated in an area adjacent to the stone house, the foundation of which dates back to the first century A.D. Legend tells us that the Virgin Mary came with the apostle John to this home, where she lived until her death.

I introduce Mariam to the group, including the hundreds of visiting tourists who have stopped to listen to my talk and observe the video camera crew recording this event. I recite a series of Rumi and Shams poems and tell of the great love that existed between these venerable spirits. I relate the story of Mariam and myself, and all that it took for her to be next to me on this stage. I recall the story that Mariam told me of her years as a polio victim and how a blessed woman in her dream told her to rise up and walk, after over four years of being unable to even stand.

I recall the vision I had of St. Francis while in Assisi and how he appeared for a few seconds as an apparition and instructed me to rise and healed my ailing right knee, right on the spot. I look to my left and see the actual home where the Virgin Mary came, and I recall how Mary is mentioned not only in the poetic works of Rumi but in the Koran as well.

I complete a 70-minute videotaped presentation on "The Wake of Our Spiritual Ancestors," particularly Shams and Rumi, who spoke of a kind of healing love that goes beyond any religion. It is September 30, 2012, the 805th birthday of this man who has become such a Divine force in my life, largely because of the love that Mariam in Iran had for me, and continues to have right up until this day. We say a happy birthday to Rumi, and proceed to the house of the Virgin to light a candle and feel the energy of love that is enveloping everyone in attendance today.

I have spent a considerable amount of time in recent months in Assisi, Lourdes, Medugorje, and now Ephesus, all places of worship where the apparitions of the Mother of Jesus have been recorded and documented. I am speaking on the birthday of the man whose teachings on Divine love have inspired millions of people throughout the world, irrespective of their cultural or religious persuasions. I am with Mariam, who was healed from the devastating effects of polio as a young Muslim girl by a vision of a spiritual apparition. Everyone in attendance is touched by these and so many other ironies.

We board our buses after a deeply portentous experience in the House of the Virgin. We return to the port, and I am in the throes of the most tearful sobbing as Mariam tells me, "Now I will carry you with me into eternity." She gives me a slew of gifts for all of my children, and almost collapses in my arms as I hug her and say good-bye.

I Can See Clearly Now

You who seek God, apart, apart
The thing you seek, thou art, thou art.
If you want to seek the Beloved's face.
Polish the mirror, gaze into that space.

These words were written by Rumi as a tribute for his master guru Shams of Tabriz. As I look back at the very impactful day at Ephesus I believe that these words, which I read just prior to giving my lecture at the House of the Virgin Mary, are symbolic of the place where I have been guided to—not just on this Mediterranean cruise and my meeting with Mariam, but for my entire life as well. It is all about recognizing that God is not something that lives apart from us. If we polish the mirror and gaze into that space, what we will discover is that God resides in that which is reflected back.

On the 805th anniversary of the birth of Rumi, when I made my presentation at that sacred spot, I had been doing almost nothing else the previous three weeks other than immersing myself in the life and teachings of both Mawlana Jalal al-Din Rumi and Shams of Tabriz. They both were visitors into my heart and soul, much like Ellis, Maslow, St. Francis, Lao-tzu, and others had been at earlier times in my life.

To have Mariam, who had first introduced Rumi and Shams to me almost 30 years earlier, show up so completely unexpectedly and stand beside me while I spoke and recited Rumi's poetry was to me a Divine appointment. This felt particularly significant since this took place at the last earthly residence of the Mother of Jesus, who Mariam suspects may have been instrumental in her healing from the polio that she experienced until she was six.

I can see clearly today that all of these "coincidences" that coalesced on Rumi's birthday in Ephesus let me *know* the meaning of the words attributed to him as tribute to his master, whom he loved so adoringly and unconditionally. For Rumi, love is the urge to rejoin Spirit, the divinity, and the goal toward which all things move. The illusion is that we are apart from this Divine Source of ours. All of our efforts at love, according to Rumi, are to come closer and closer to that which is our original nature. This was the essential lesson of both St. Francis and Lao-tzu: To merge into oneness with God. To abandon the demands of the ego, and to live from a place of Divine love, a love that never changes, never varies, is steadfast, never slipping—as is the love of Jesus, Buddha, and all Divine spiritual masters.

I can see clearly now that I was being directed to go even beyond knowing that we are all pieces of God, and to experience the inner radiance that comes to us when we finally know this at an experiential level. I attained a new level of insight from all that I was reading in the weeks leading up to meeting Mariam and delivering my talk on the works of this great Sufi master who transcended all religious and cultural identities. This essential message was, and is, that all matter in the universe obeys the law of Divine love, which is a movement to evolve and seek unity with the divinity from which it has emerged.

These poetic lines express Rumi's teaching, and my calling to Divine love:

I roamed the lands of Christendom from end to end
Searching all over, but He was not on the Cross.

I went into the temples where the Indians worship idols
And the Magians chant prayers to fire—I found no trace of Him.

Riding at full speed, I looked all over the Kaaba
But He was not at that sanctuary for young and old.

Then I gazed right into my own heart:
There, I saw Him . . . He was there and nowhere else.

The "Him" that Rumi saw was his own highest self—God within. But beyond this recognition of our own holy presence is the willingness to be an instrument of this love and to radiate it outward to all of God's creations. I am challenged to love all as Rumi was challenged by Shams to love beyond any conditions or restrictions. To love as Mariam has loved me and my teachings for three decades without ever having seen me with her eyes. These are the words she wrote to me after our visits in Turkey:

I have not stopped crying about my leaving you yet, on the way coming back home, at work, day and night. Tears flowing down my eyes wherever I go, whatever I do. There is no one, even you, who can understand how I feel after having come back—only me, God, and Molanaye Rumi. . . . You thank me, but I am the one who should thank you to call me on the stage to have the honor to stand beside you and talk about Molanaye Rumi . . .

Mordeh bodam zeneh zendeh shodam
(I was dead I became alive)
Geryeh bodam khandeh shodam
(I was tears I became laughter)
Dowlateh eshgh amado man dowlateh payandeh shodam
(The kingdom of love came and I became the eternal kingdom)
Molanaye Rumi

Wayne, I feel that Rumi is between us, I mean not in between, but inside you and me and makes us to feel closer than any time else. This is not an accident. Love is our destiny.

As I look back at the astonishing events that transpired on that day, I recall how over three decades, Mariam has loved me—through the births of many of my children, through the deaths of her own parents, through the healing of her own infirmities, through political extremism, through wars and enforced separations, she never wavered. She has been a messenger of God, bringing Rumi and Shams of Tabriz to me, and allowing my heart to open to a new kind of love. Not a human love, which changes and varies; not a spiritual love, which varies but never changes; but a Divine love, which never changes and never varies.

All of my endless hours of reading and preparation for that presentation at Ephesus, and still I had no idea that Mariam would just appear on a crowded pier as I boarded a bus. I had no idea as I engaged in my preparations and research that I would be at the House of the Virgin Mary. Nor did I realize that I'd be there on the birthday of the world's most beloved teacher of Divine love.

I sit here and write in a state of stupefaction at all that transpired on that day. All to teach me those words of Rumi:

Love has come and it is like blood in my veins and in my flesh.
It has annihilated me and filled me with the Beloved.
The Beloved has penetrated every cell of my body.
Of myself there remains only a name, everything else is Him.

This is what I can see clearly now. My name remains. Love is my essence. And it is my destiny to practice and teach Divine love.

AFTERWORD

Seeing Your Life More Clearly—Now!

There are so many benefits that can and will accrue for you if you are willing to examine your own personal story from the perspective of having an open mind, and with the intention of seeing all that has come your way with a clearer vision. In relating all of the circumstances that were major turning points in my life throughout the pages of this book, I discovered some truths I would like to share with you so that you too might enjoy the benefits of looking at your life, then and now, through unclouded lenses.

The one overriding insight I have is that we all live in a universe that has intelligence behind life—and that intelligence is innate in each creation. This universal mind is complete within each of us, and we have only to discover it for its power and perfection to be ours.

I urge you to apply an unobstructed view to everything that has ever happened to you, and everyone that has ever come into your life. You are a piece of the creative force that is the matrix of all matter.

The events or people that show up in your life are not because of happenstance and coincidence.

Armed with this awareness that "accidents" cannot occur in a universe that's being directed by a conscious intelligent mind, and that there is some sort of purpose associated with everything that arrives in your life because you are a part of this matrix of all matter, you can begin to do what I have been doing throughout the writing of this book. Begin to pay close attention and view every event and every circumstance—in particular, those that result in dramatic shifts—as guidance from this Divine organizing intelligence.

Throughout history there have been so many familiar names for this force that inspires human beings to choose to go in a direction that yields beauty, love, and truth. This invisible intelligence is eternally with you, and it offers something for you in every moment—in every encounter, every situation, and every circumstance. There is something right in front of you, staring you in the face, offering you a choice to grab ahold and get on board to travel in a new direction, or to ignore it and attribute it to nothing more than chance. As you adopt more of an *I can see clearly now* attitude, you will look very differently at every aspect of your life.

With the advantage of hindsight, I am able to see and write about these momentous shifts that were in the process of taking place. I had no idea how far-reaching they truly were. I can now see the entire tapestry of my life as a continuous design. I see that this invisible force was offering me free passes to move in the direction of my life's purpose. I urge you to look back on your own life with as much honesty and openness as you can muster and see how those strangers who "just showed up" or those significant events that transpired were offered to you to encourage you to align with your own life's purpose.

You always have the choice to *pay attention* and take an unfamiliar and perhaps risky path. Likewise, you can choose to *not pay attention* and stay with the version of your life implanted in you by familial and cultural influences dictating precisely what your limitations and aspirations ought to be. The real benefit of looking back at all of those significant events of your life and seeing how that invisible hand of God was there for you at the time is not to rehash your entire past looking for the hidden meanings, but to awaken you to becoming a more conscious person now, today, in the present moments of your life.

What I know for certain is that there are teachers and teachings everywhere. Every moment of our lives offers us the opportunity to pay close attention to see the person who approaches us not as a stranger, but as someone who showed up in the right place, at the right moment. To view an unfortunate happening not as "my bad luck," but to ask, "What might I learn from this right here, right now?" rather than going through a long period of suffering before seeing why you aligned with this seemingly regrettable circumstance.

As I look back over my life, it is not a far reach for me to conclude that there is some kind of a plan that is always at work, even if it is largely unknown as it unfolds. It is not a great stretch for me to conclude that this plan is being directed by the same force that keeps the planets aligned, opens the buds of all the flowers, and gives life to all manner of creation here and everywhere else in the universe as well. I now pay much closer attention to what shows up for me, and I'm willing to listen carefully to any inclination I might have and act accordingly, even if it leads me into unknown territory. I urge you to do the same.

Examine the major turning points in your life and look carefully at all of the so-called coincidences that had to arise in order for you to shift direction. At that moment you think of as a coincidence, you had a free will and you made a choice. At that same moment there was something much bigger than you, something you're always connected to, that was also at play. That "something" was setting up the details so that you could fulfill the purpose you signed up for when you made the leap from Spirit to form—from *nowhere,* to *now here.*

The teachers are always there. Your degree of readiness to pay attention and listen carefully to your highest self, and act on what your intuitive self tells you, enlivens your awareness of your teachers. Sharpen your insight and be willing to trust that what you are feeling inside is what you should be doing, regardless of what everything and everyone around you might be saying to the contrary. This is the advantage of adopting an *I can see clearly now* mentality.

There are many discoveries to be made when you open your mind to the possibility that there's Divine intelligence moving all of the pieces of your life around in harmony with your ability to have free will and make choices. You discover that in fact your life's dharma has been laid out, and within that same predetermined reality set, you are free to make choices. You will also discover that this Divine force, or the Tao, is really nothing more than pure unconditional love. One of my most respected teachers, Carl Jung, expressed the paradox this way: "In the same moment that you are a protagonist in your life making choices, you're also a spear carrier or extra in a much larger drama. You are doomed to make choices."

This love is boundless and infinite, and when you think and behave in ways that match this Divine love, that is when you are able to attract the guidance from this realm to assist you in steering your life in a God-realized way. It is in these moments of pure love that you are able to experience miraculous happenings. This is when the angels of the Divine realm of Spirit are able to be there for you and you become aware of their presence.

It is in these times of unqualified giving, or when your inner focus is exclusively on, *How may I reach out and serve?* rather than the selfish demands of the ego, saying, *What's in it for me?* that these guides of pure love recognize themselves in you and reach out to put you on your path toward reemerging with your original Source of being—with God and your appointed guides.

Throughout my life, it was when I suspended and tamed my ego that miracles occurred and I was invisibly urged to make a shift in my life's path. I urge you to look at the events of your own life, even way back when you were a child and right up to the present, and examine what was taking place within you that propelled you in a new direction. Then, and this is of the utmost urgency, *become aware of any of your own internal thoughts that are judgmental, critical, or condemnatory toward any of God's children, including yourself.* When you're able to shift your inner thoughts to unconditional love, even toward those who've been designated as your enemies, you will open yourself to the guidance that nudges you toward the path leading to your own self-actualization and God-realization. This is the advantage of seeing with clearer eyes—it can aid you now, in this present moment, in shifting away from a path that leads to self-sabotage.

As you change the way you look at things so as to stay in that place of Divine love, the things you look at begin to change as well. This is because at these highest vibrational frequencies of unconditional love, you are vibrating in unity with the Source of all, that which we have come to call God. As I've stated many times in the writing of this book, with God (with love) all things are possible, and that includes attracting angels of love to guide you right in the moment.

Seeing your own life more clearly involves being acutely aware of anything and everything that creates excitement within your being. If it excites you, the very presence of that inner excitement is all the evidence you need to remind you that you're aligned with your true essence. When you are following your bliss, you are most amenable to receiving guidance from the spiritual realm. This is called *synchronicity*—a state in which you almost feel as if you are in a collaborative arrangement with fate.

This has been the overriding story of my own life. When I listen carefully to those inner signals, they seem to say to me, *This is why you are here, now you are truly aligned with your highest self, there is nothing to fear, just do what your excitement tells you to do.* And that is precisely what I've done in recapitulating the seemingly disparate events that formed the entire tapestry of my life up until now.

For much of your life you've very likely been cautious about following your inner passion, because you've been programmed since childhood to follow someone else's idea of what you should be doing. Your family, your culture, your circle of friends, your immediate surroundings—all conspire to lay out the path of your life. When you've ignored that programming and followed what your inner excitement dictated, you probably thrived in a more satisfying way, even when criticized and judged as selfish.

As I look back at many of the decisions I made that took me down a very different path, it's clear that I was making those decisions exclusively on the basis of what felt right, what made me feel passionate and enthusiastic, even when the potential for failure and disappointment was a real possibility.

See your own life more clearly today—right here, right now in this moment—by refusing to ignore that which stirs passion and excitement within you. You came here with music to play, so when you begin to harmonize with what only you hear playing in your mind, listen carefully and stop yourself right in your tracks and be willing to take the first step in the direction of those synchronistic callings. This is your highest self calling! This is your reemergence with your Source of being.

It may not make any sense to anyone around you, and might even appear to be preposterous to you as well, but just know that in the end you will not be disappointed. In fact, whoever and whatever you need will eventually appear in their unforeseen Divine perfection. Even if nothing seems to be going right and it all looks like doom and gloom, stay with your excitement. Declare yourself to be in a state of faith and trust, meditate on your vision, and the support will ultimately be forthcoming. The reason that it serves your inner excitement is because in those moments, known only to you, you are in alignment with who you truly are.

During your life, just as in mine, there have been special teachers who have repeatedly made themselves known. I've detailed how St. Francis of Assisi, Lao-tzu, Jalal al-Din Rumi, Abraham Maslow, Dr. Mildred Peters, Albert Ellis, and many others have continually shown up and presented their offerings to me precisely when they have been most needed, and when it was clear that I was finally ready to accept and implement their Divinely inspired guidance.

If you are willing to review your past with loving awareness, you will recognize many teachers who have been there for you throughout your own life. Some of them you were willing to listen to at the time and act on what they offered you because of your readiness level, and other times your readiness level was at such a low level that you didn't even recognize the Divine timing of their arrival or re-appearance. Begin now to become aware of and welcome the assistance that continually makes itself available to you in daily life.

After spending the better part of this past year reviewing the many teachers and teachings that have influenced the general path that my life has taken, I can see clearly that I've been in some kind of invisible ascended-master training since my arrival here back in May of 1940. *And so have you.* We all originate from the same Source of Divine love. As we grow and mature, we are all given free choice to stay connected to this Source, or to **e**dge **G**od **o**ut and live by the demands and inclinations of our false self—the ego.

Ralph Waldo Emerson, another of those ascended masters who have been knocking on the door of my inner awareness since I was a teenager, and perhaps even before that, offers us this observation:

> *Within man is the soul of the whole; the wise silence,*
> *the universal beauty, to which every part and*
> *particle is equally related; the eternal One.*

Yes, he did say it is within us. That means *you* as well. This is your inheritance from your originating Source, and this "eternal One" is continuously sending emissaries. They are comprised exclusively of the wise silence, the universal beauty. It is your choice whether or not to follow their energetic promptings or to ignore them because of your unreadiness for such counsel.

These beings of light and love are all around you, and have been since your arrival into this physical presence that you identify with so strongly. They leave clues and omens, and sometimes their guidance is subtle and confusing—but they are there, and all you need do is begin to pay attention to your intuitive feelings and then act fearlessly on what they seem to be communicating to you. The more you trust in this intuition, the more you will see things in pure alignment with your own dharma.

Go with what you feel inside—your soul-beat activating your excitement—it's inviting you to the next step up the ladder of a life that leads to the light. As Rumi said: "The second you stepped into this world of existence a ladder was placed before you to help you escape it." (Translation by Andrew Harvey; I am grateful to him for granting me permission to reprint this quote.)

There are so many helping hands beckoning you to take hold and move up to escape the illusion of this world of existence. Ascended masters, angels of your higher self, well-intended teachers, family members, strangers, a host of events, and what seem like bizarre circumstances are all working earnestly to help you move up the ladder that's rooted in ordinary consciousness—and ascends to the celestial world of extraordinary living and higher awareness. Be willing to let yourself be persuaded to step fearlessly on the next rung, and the next, by paying close attention to your guides.

Our ultimate mission here in this physical incarnation on planet Earth is to reemerge with our Source, the one eternal One, to recognize ourselves as a being of love and light—a piece of God, if you will—and to practice thinking and acting in the same way that God does.

Every turning point or moment of insight that helped me climb up that ladder that was placed before me at my birth came about as a result of an inner intuitive knowing that I had to put less and less emphasis on my ego and its continual thoughts of *What's in it for me?* I learned that I wanted and needed to shift toward acting and thinking like God.

God, our Source, the great Tao, Divine mind, is all about serving, reaching out and taming the selfish demands of the ego that is always insisting on more stuff, more popularity, more approval, more recognition, more winning, and more ownership.

When I *shift to* contemplating what is the best way to reach as many people as possible with a message of hope, kindness, joy, and most of all, love—and *shift from* the material benefits—I feel excitement expanding within me. Then more synchronistic help seems to just turn up right on some invisible-to-me schedule.

Examine your own movement toward seeing more clearly, and when you are at what you know to be a crossroads, or where two roads are diverging in a wood, ask for assistance. Seek advice toward moving in the direction where ego is less and less a determining factor. Ask yourself how to fulfill your soul purpose by serving others first.

Critics may say that my life's work is about making money, and making a name for myself so that I might bask in the limelight of fame and popularity. I have spent thousands upon thousands of hours sitting alone at a desk, facing blank sheets of paper waiting to be filled with the ideas that are reverberating within me. I can say with all honesty that I've never engaged in this solitary activity of writing 41 books with the idea in my head that I was going to make money, or acquire fame for all of my efforts.

Every step up that ladder that Rumi speaks about has been taken because I've been guided and prodded by so many profound teachers and teachings that it was almost impossible for me not to put my foot on the next upward rung and pull the rest of my physical apparatus up toward more exalted and heightened awareness. It all happened because I was willing and ready to reach out and serve and to spend the time and energy all alone in a room far from all distractions, and put onto the pad of paper before me what was absolutely insisting upon being expressed by me for the betterment of others in some way that I needn't ever fully comprehend.

Whatever fame and wealth that arrived in my life isn't because I was chasing after it. All of the results are because I actively followed my excitement and trusted in guidance that surfaced along the way, and because *something* within me practically forced me to do this work. It's the same thing that has pushed me tonight to leave the comfort of my home and family and sit here writing.

As Dr. Redl used to tell us, self-actualizing people must be what they can be. They don't know how to suppress those inner burning desires that simply must be expressed. The external rewards are just bonuses that arrive when one *advances confidently in the direction of his own dreams, and endeavors to live the life which he has imagined,* to cite Henry David Thoreau. As you've read, he is one of those teachers who's shown up for me since I was a 15-year-old-boy awaiting punishment for my "civil disobedience" in high school.

Look back over your life at the key turning-point moments when you were involved in some kind of a peak experience and being pulled in a new direction. Think about your soul and what it truly means to be motivated by *your* inner thoughts, rather than using some artificial external barometer as your life's guide. Promotions are nice; salary increases are of course welcomed; a gold watch is a fine symbol of a long and devoted life; a grade on a transcript, a trophy, and so many more are all external indices. They do not soothe or satisfy your soul. Your soul is not finite—it has no form—no beginning or end. It needs to expand—to grow, to avoid being labeled or compartmentalized.

Every move I made in my life was in the direction of more freedom that gave me the ability to decide for myself where to be each day, what to wear, how to speak, how my writing would proceed. These were nudges from my soul—the inner invisible part of me that is infinite and therefore always seeking expansion.

Stay in touch with and honor the calling you feel deep within you. Ignoring that will leave you feeling like a prisoner in your own body and in your own private world. Your soul is miserable when it is confined, or labeled, or told what it can or cannot do. Its theme song shouts out, "Don't fence me in!"

As you begin to see more and more clearly not only how and why your life took all of its twists and turns but what direction it is going to take from here on in, you will see that your soul will not ever lead you astray. This is because this is truly who you are—not your accomplishments or possessions, but that inner sense of purpose that seeks out immensity and expansion.

Listen when it beckons you in a certain direction, or when it sends you a teacher, or sets up a synchronistic series of events. It all feels so mysteriously exciting when it occurs because your outer world is finally meshing with your soul's innate need to keep on expanding. It must and always will prod you this way because it is infinite, and therefore it must just keep growing. That which is infinite cannot be labeled or put into any kind of a box for safekeeping. To do so would deny its very nature and turn it into the opposite of infinite, which is finite.

As I review so many of the momentous shifts that took place in my life, I can see much more clearly now that much of what urged me onto higher rungs of the ladder, which Rumi described as my escape hatch from this material world, was the use of my own imagination. If I could get a clear picture of myself focused on a new endeavor within my imagination, and if I could train myself to act as if that inner picture were already a present fact, the rest of the work of having it all materialize seemed to be almost effortless.

When I was in the Navy, I declared to myself, *I am attending college.* Attempting to escape from a war zone in Turkey, I saw myself leaving the country way before the opportunity actually presented itself. Dealing with the resistance of my first publisher, I had a very different picture in my imagination from what the experts had in mind for me and my book. And so it has been for the greater percentage of my life.

Use your own imagination as an inner blueprint for what you absolutely intend to manifest. Then act *as if* that current dream is a present fact. This has been my secret tactic for manifesting the life I intended to live. I urge you to make full use of this procedure that is spelled out in detail in my book *Wishes Fulfilled.* Examine the relevant moments in your own life where you felt prompted to move in a particular direction, considering how much faith you were able to place in that magical creative place within you—your imagination. Everything that now exists in your life and in this entire physical world had to first be imagined. Thus if you can't imagine it and act as if it were already an accomplished fact, then you cannot possibly make it your reality.

I use the phrase *I am* as a declaration of fact, regardless of what anyone around me says, or even what my own eyes and ears tell me is true. *I am* is the name that God used to identify himself to Moses and to all future generations. I encourage you to use these two words to see first in your imagination what it is that you intend to see, manifest into your physical reality. I declare every day that *I am well, I am perfect health,*

I am content, I am love, I am God. I do not need to look at numbers on a medical report or hear anyone else's opinion about my health.

This great mystical power is available to you. Use the name of God as your affirmation for creating the life you desire, for becoming the person you intend to become. When you make an absolute declaration by placing your *I am* presence squarely in the center of your imagination, and refusing to entertain any other options, you achieve the results you thought you were only imagining. When you assume the feeling of your wish as already fulfilled, ultimately your wish is hardened into a physical reality.

Use this *I am* presence for all that you intend to manifest from this day forward. When you do so with integrity and an inner knowing that does not allow for skepticism or doubt, you will begin to see how you can take the reins of your life into your human hands. Reconnect yourself to your Source of being and live a Divinely inspired life as a co-creator with God.

I love this quotation by Oscar Wilde: "To become the spectator of one's own life . . . is to escape the suffering of life." It offers the key to the end of all suffering. All you have to do is to become a spectator of your own life.

I call this "cultivating the witness": The way out of any discomfort is simply to just begin noticing who's doing or not doing anything. If you are sad, all you have to do is notice who is experiencing the sadness. The one who notices is already free of the sadness. As you pay close attention you will notice that the sadness is not you; it is nothing more than a part of the nature of a human being. But you as the spectator are simply the indwelling being that is aware of all that you are noticing.

Daily I cultivate and invite the gentle loving witness to replace my being so identified with what I am observing. Who I am is an invisible formless piece of the great Divine mind, the Tao, God. When I observe all that I envision before me—not as that to which I am attached and connected, but rather as a caring, curious spectator—I eliminate my potential suffering. My attachment to the outcome dissolves. Any beliefs that I'm unworthy are eliminated, and I answer the question of *Who am I?* as Michael Singer did so lucidly in his stimulating book *The Untethered Soul*: "I am the one who sees. From back in here somewhere, I look out, and I am aware of the events, thoughts, and emotions that pass before me."

This is where you and I both live. This is precisely how you come to see your life more clearly than ever before. Just notice, and then notice who is noticing, and remind yourself that this is you, this is your true essence.

I have noticed throughout the writing of this book and reviewing so many of the salient factors that pushed me up to a higher rung on the ladder that the less I identified with what I wanted to accomplish, the freer I was to allow it to manifest. Just by sitting back and observing as an interested but unattached spectator, I was frequently able to go way beyond even what I was noticing. The less attached I felt to what I wanted to accomplish in my life, and the more I cultivated this idea of the witness, the more I was able to look at the next stage of my life with a new, less worrisome vision. I loved what was placed before me, but I had no attachment to the outcome.

As I come to the end of looking back at my life up until now, I'm grateful to have been able to see so much more clearly how and why so many of the events, circumstances, and teachers showed up to guide me on this path of self-discovery. All my life I wanted to feel the excitement of being a person who would and could make a difference in this world. There has been invisible guidance there for me each and every step of the way, just as there is for you as well.

In order to access that guidance, I encourage you to *make a commitment to be absolutely faithful to that which exists nowhere but within yourself.* This is the great secret for seeing ever more clearly and living your life from a place of passion and purpose.

— Love,
I AM Wayne

ABOUT THE AUTHOR

Dr. Wayne W. Dyer is an internationally renowned author and speaker in the field of self-development. He's the author of more than 40 books, has created many audio programs and videos, and has appeared on thousands of television and radio shows. His books *Manifest Your Destiny, Wisdom of the Ages, There's a Spiritual Solution to Every Problem,* and *The New York Times* bestsellers *10 Secrets for Success and Inner Peace, The Power of Intention, Inspiration, Change Your Thoughts—Change Your Life, Excuses Begone!* and *Wishes Fulfilled* have all been featured as National Public Television specials.

Wayne holds a doctorate in educational counseling from Wayne State University and was an associate professor at St. John's University in New York.

Website: www.DrWayneDyer.com

Hay House Titles of Related Interest

YOU CAN HEAL YOUR LIFE, the movie, starring Louise L. Hay & Friends
(available as a 1-DVD program and an expanded 2-DVD set)
Watch the trailer at: www.LouiseHayMovie.com

THE SHIFT, the movie,
starring Dr. Wayne W. Dyer
(available as a 1-DVD program and an expanded 2-DVD set)
Watch the trailer at: www.DyerMovie.com

THE BIOLOGY OF BELIEF: Unleashing the Power of Consciousness, Matter & Miracles, by Bruce H. Lipton, Ph.D.

DYING TO BE ME: My Journey from Cancer, to Near Death, to True Healing, by Anita Moorjani

FOR THE SENDER, Love Is (Not a Feeling), by Alex Woodard

LEFT TO TELL: Discovering God Amidst the Rwandan Holocaust, by Immaculée Ilibagiza, with Steve Erwin

NO STORM LASTS FOREVER: Transforming Suffering Into Insight, by Dr. Terry A. Gordon

THE PERFECT GENE DIET: Use Your Body's Own APO E Gene to Treat High Cholesterol, Weight Problems, Heart Disease, Alzheimer's . . . and More!, by Pamela McDonald, N.P.

YOU ARE THE PLACEBO: Making Your Mind Matter, by Dr. Joe Dispenza (available April 2014)

All of the above are available at your local bookstore,
or may be ordered by contacting Hay House (see next page).

We hope you enjoyed this Hay House book. If you'd like to receive our online catalog featuring additional information on Hay House books and products, or if you'd like to find out more about the Hay Foundation, please contact:

Hay House, Inc., P.O. Box 5100, Carlsbad, CA 92018-5100
(760) 431-7695 or (800) 654-5126
(760) 431-6948 (fax) or (800) 650-5115 (fax)
www.hayhouse.com® • www.hayfoundation.org

Published and distributed in Australia by: Hay House Australia Pty. Ltd., 18/36 Ralph St., Alexandria NSW 2015 • *Phone:* 612-9669-4299 • *Fax:* 612-9669-4144 www.hayhouse.com.au

Published and distributed in the United Kingdom by: Hay House UK, Ltd., Astley House, 33 Notting Hill Gate, London W11 3JQ • *Phone:* 44-20-3675-2450 *Fax:* 44-20-3675-2451 • www.hayhouse.co.uk

Published and distributed in the Republic of South Africa by: Hay House SA (Pty), Ltd., P.O. Box 990, Witkoppen 2068 • *Phone/Fax:* 27-11-467-8904 www.hayhouse.co.za

Published in India by: Hay House Publishers India, Muskaan Complex, Plot No. 3, B-2, Vasant Kunj, New Delhi 110 070 • *Phone:* 91-11-4176-1620 *Fax:* 91-11-4176-1630 • www.hayhouse.co.in

Distributed in Canada by: Raincoast Books, 2440 Viking Way, Richmond, B.C. V6V 1N2 • *Phone:* 1-800-663-5714 • *Fax:* 1-800-565-3770 www.raincoast.com